Helena Gomm

Inside Out

Teacher's
Book

MACMILLAN

Macmillan Education
Between Towns Road, Oxford OX4 3PP, UK
A division of Macmillan Publishers Limited
Companies and representatives throughout the world

ISBN 0 333 97580 4
ISBN 1 405 01436 9 (Level I)
ISBN 1 405 01438 5 (Level I Pack)

Text © Sue Kay and Vaughan Jones 2003
Text by Helena Gomm and Jon Hird
Design and illustration © Macmillan Publishers Limited 2003

First published 2003

All rights reserved; no part of this publication may be reproduced, stored in a retrieval system, transmitted in any form, or by any means, electronic, mechanical, photocopying, recording, or otherwise, without the prior written permission of the publishers.

> **Note to teachers**
> Photocopies may be made, for classroom use, of pages marked 'photocopiable' without the prior written permission of Macmillan Publishers Limited. However, please note that the copyright law, which does not normally permit multiple copying of published material, applies to the rest of this book.

Project management by Desmond O'Sullivan, ELT Publishing Services.
Edited by Celia Bingham.
Designed by Ann Samuel.
Cartoons on p10 by Ed McLachlan.
Cover design by Andrew Oliver.

The authors and publishers would like to thank the following for permission to reproduce their material:
John Kitching for 'I Love Geography', copyright © John Kitching 2002 from *The Works 2* edited by Brian Moses and Pie Corbett (Macmillan, 2002), reprinted by permission of the author. *She's Got You* Words and Music by Hank Cochran copyright © Sony/ATV Acuff Rose Music 1971, reprinted by permission of Sony/ATV Music Publishing.

Painting on page 7 *After Visiting David Hockney* © Gagosian Gallery, London.

Printed and bound in Spain by Edelvives SA

2007 2006 2005 2004 2003
10 9 8 7 6 5 4 3 2 1

Introduction

At the heart of 'Inside Out' is the belief that the most effective conditions for language learning come about when students engage in activities on a personal level rather than just 'going through the motions'. Engagement can be triggered by anything from understanding and smiling at a cartoon to talking at length to a partner about your last summer holiday.

Teaching strategies

All the strategies employed in *Inside Out* aim to promote learning by focusing on personal engagement, both intellectual and emotional. Students come to class with their own knowledge of the world, tastes, feelings and opinions. *Inside Out* tries to tap into this rich resource by focusing on topics that students can relate to. We believe our job as teachers is to concentrate on *how* they speak and write. This can be achieved when *what* they speak and write about is part of their life experience. It is much more difficult to achieve when the topic of the lesson is alien to students – something they have never considered before.

Organising learning around topics that encourage personal engagement also helps ensure that we never lose sight of meaning as the key ingredient in effective language learning. As Rod Ellis remarks: 'It is the need to get meanings across and the pleasure experienced when this is achieved that motivates second language acquisition.'

Accessible topics and tasks

Each unit is built around a set of two or three related topics. They provide an interesting and wide-ranging selection of subjects about which most students have something to say. (Website addresses are provided in many cases if you want further information about these subjects.) However, as Penny Ur explained many years ago: 'The crux is not *what* to talk about, but *why* you need to talk about it.' The tasks in *Inside Out* have been designed to set up opportunities for genuine communicative exchanges.

Grammar awareness / Grammar practice

The course covers the main grammar areas you would expect in an elementary course book.

We recognise that learning grammar is a messy, non-linear process – often a case of two steps forward, one step back. All the research suggests that a student's internal grammar is in a permanent state of flux. The constant restructuring necessary to incorporate new rules into the system can adversely affect language already 'learned'. A typical example is the student who learns *bought* as the past form of *buy*, but then starts to over-generalise the regular *-ed* inflection for past tense marking and uses the incorrect form *buyed* for a while. This characteristic of language learning is perfectly natural and mirrors the process children go through when mastering their native tongue.

We feel that the key to learning grammar then, is to provide students with as many opportunities as possible for meaningful practice. Practice makes perfect. It is only through frequent manipulation of form that students begin to increase the complexity of their output – use more grammar – and in doing so, improve their ability to communicate effectively.

To provide appropriate grammar study, *Inside Out* includes regular 'Close up' sections. These follow a three stage approach: language analysis; practice; personalisation.

1 Language analysis

The language analysis stage promotes 'noticing' of language features and usage. The language to be 'noticed' almost always comes out of a larger listening or reading text where it occurs naturally in a wider context. We do not believe that self-contained, pre-fabricated, random example sentences are a good starting point for analysis. At this point students are encouraged to articulate and organise what they know, and incorporate new information. At the elementary level it is inevitable that some of this discussion will take place in the students' native language. We think this is okay, as this stage is more a question of 'getting your mind around it' than 'getting your tongue around it'.

The language analysis stage will work both as individual study or as pair/groupwork. In general, we recommend pair/groupwork as this provides a forum for students to exchange and test out ideas before presenting them in the more intimidating arena of the whole class.

Unlike other books which use the 'guided discovery' approach to grammar, we have generally avoided gap fills and multiple choice questions. Research showed us that most students are unenthusiastic about using these techniques to study grammar. This may be because they associate them with testing rather than learning. Instead, we provide questions and discussion points where appropriate.

2 Practice

In the practice activities students manipulate or select structures, testing their theories. As they do this, they also become more comfortable with the grammar point. Integrated into the Student Book units are many pairwork activities based on the information gap principle. These are marked in the following way: **Pairwork: Student A & B**. The Pairwork: Student A and Pairwork: Student B sections are arranged separately at the back of the book: Student A (pages 86 to 93, identified by a red tag) and Student B (pages 98 to 105, identified by a blue tag).

The sentences in the practice stage are designed to be realistic and meaningful rather than relying on invented scenarios about imaginary people or places. In our study of form, we do not believe that it is necessary completely to abandon meaning. Many of the sentences can be applied to the student's own lives, and this facilitates the next stage.

3 Personalisation

The personalisation stage is not a conventional free practice, where students, for example, take part in a role play which 'requires' the target structure. As Michael Lewis has pointed out, very few situations in real life actually require a particular structure. Furthermore, when they are faced with a challenging situation without time to prepare, many students will, naturally, decide to rely on what they know, rather than what they studied half an hour ago. For these reasons, personalisation is based on actual examples of the target structure. Students apply these examples to their own lives, opinions and feelings. Very often the sentences or questions from the practice stage are recycled for the personalisation. For example:

- Re-write the sentences in 1 so that they are true for your partner.
- Work with a partner. Ask each other the questions you have written in 2.
- Replace the names in 3 with the names of people in the class.

All the Close up sections are supported by Language reference boxes, which give accurate, clear explanations backed up with examples. Language toolboxes provide additional information as necessary. Both the Language references and the Language toolboxes appear in the unit, right where they are needed, rather than being tucked away at the back of the book.

Contemporary lexis in context

The valuable work done over the years on various dictionary corpora has informed us that relatively few words – around 3,500 – account for over 80% of all English usage. In the recent *Macmillan English Dictionary* and *Macmillan Essential Dictionary* these most frequent and useful words are printed in red. They are given a 'star rating' of three, two and one stars – three stars showing the most common and basic words. One of our guiding principles has been to write materials that expose students to as many of these three star words as possible.

In *Inside Out* we also make sure that the lexis we focus on is always presented in context and is related to the themes and topics in the unit. Vocabulary is first of all highlighted in exercises which draw attention to it, then recycled in back-up exercises. The Workbook provides further recycling, as do the photocopiable tests in the Teacher's Book. The exercises encourage students to deal with lexis as part of a system, rather than as a list of discrete words. There are a variety of tasks which focus on collocation and typical usage. In addition, a comprehensive unit-by-unit wordlist, based on data from the *Macmillan Essential Dictionary*, is included in the Student Book as a valuable reference and learning tool.

Although there is a lot of work on lexis in *Inside Out*, we urge you to expose your students to as much English as possible from as wide a variety of sources as you can. There are lots of good, practical ideas and ready-made lessons on the Macmillan website for teachers – *www.onestopenglish.com*. The more English input they receive, the more likely this input will become intake and eventually output. In particular, we would encourage you to get your students reading graded readers. The benefits of extensive reading are well researched and documented. Get your students hooked on books!

Personalised speaking tasks

Inside Out is filled with speaking tasks. Their main purpose is to develop fluency. While they are not intended principally as grammar practice, they are linked to the topics, lexis and grammar in the unit so as to include opportunities for students to turn input into intake and then into output.

The tasks do not require complicated classroom configurations. They are easy to set up and enjoyable to use. Most of them encourage the students to talk about things that actually matter to them, rather than playing roles or exchanging invented information. Personalised, authentic tasks challenge and engage students, and this encourages linguistic 'risk taking': *Can I use this word here? Is this how this structure works?*

Research into second language acquisition suggests that when students take risks they are experimenting, testing theories about how the language works and restructuring their internal language system accordingly. This is an essential part of language learning.

Anecdotes

There are also extended speaking tasks, where students tackle a longer piece of discourse. We have called these 'Anecdotes'. They are based on personal issues, for example, memories, stories, people you know. When you learn a musical instrument, you cannot spend all your time playing scales and exercises: you also need to learn whole pieces in order to see how music is organised. Anecdotes give students a chance to get to grips with how discourse is organised. We have found the following strategies helpful in getting our students to tell their Anecdotes.

1 Choose global topics that everybody can relate to

One of the main objectives of an Anecdote is to encourage students to experiment with, and hopefully grow more competent at, using language at the more demanding end of their range. It therefore seems only fair to ask them to talk about subjects they know something about. With familiar subject matter students can concentrate on *how* they are speaking as well as *what* they are speaking about. The ten Anecdote topics in *Inside Out Elementary* have been carefully selected to appeal to the widest range of students whilst at the same time, fitting in with the context of the unit.

2 Allow sufficient preparation time

Students need time to assemble their thoughts and think about the language they will need. The Anecdotes are set up through evocative questions. Students read or listen to a planned series of questions and choose what specifically they will talk about; shyer students can avoid matters they feel are too personal. This student preparation is a key stage and should not be rushed. Research, by Peter Skehan and Pauline Foster among others, has shown that learners who plan for tasks attempt more ambitious and complex language, hesitate less and make fewer basic errors.

The simplest way to prepare students for an Anecdote is to ask them to read the list of questions in the book and decide which they want to talk about. This could be done during class time or as homework preparation for the following lesson. The questions have check boxes so that students can tick the ones they are interested in. Ask them to think about the language they will need. Sentence beginnings are provided in the Student's Book to give the students some extra help. Encourage them to use dictionaries and make notes – but not to write out what they will actually say. Finally, put them into pairs to exchange Anecdotes.

A variation is to ask the students to read the questions in the book while, at the same time, listening to you read them aloud. The Anecdote questions have been recorded so you could play the Class Cassettes or CDs instead. Then ask them to prepare in detail for the task, as above.

Alternatively, ask the students to close their books – and then to close their eyes. Ask them to listen to the questions as you read them aloud or play the recording, and think about what they evoke. Some classes will find this a more involving process. It also allows you to adapt the questions to your class: adding new ones or missing out ones you think inappropriate. After the reading, give them enough time to finalise their preparation before starting the speaking task.

3 Monitor students and give feedback

It is important for students to feel that their efforts are being monitored by the teacher. Realistically, it is probably only possible for a teacher to monitor and give feedback to one or two pairs of students during each Anecdote activity. It is therefore vital that the teacher adopts a strict rota system and makes sure that everyone in the class is monitored over the course of a term. Constructive feedback helps students improve their delivery.

4 Provide a 'model anecdote'

It is always useful for the students to hear a model Anecdote at some stage during the Anecdote activity. The most obvious model is you, the teacher. Alternatively you might ask a teaching colleague or friend to talk to the students. In several cases there is a model Anecdote on the Class Cassettes/CDs accompanying *Inside Out Elementary* which you can use.

5 Repeat the same anecdote with a new partner at regular intervals

Consider going back to Anecdotes and repeating them in later classes. Let the students know that you are going to do this. This will reassure them that you are doing it on purpose, but more importantly, it will mean that they will be more motivated to dedicate some time and thought to preparation. When you repeat the task, mix the class so that each student works with a new partner, i.e. one who has not previously heard the Anecdote.

In our experience, most students are happy to listen to their partner's Anecdotes. If, however, any of your students are reluctant listeners you might think about giving them some sort of 'listening task'. Here are three examples:

- Ask the listener to tick the prompt questions that the 'Anecdote teller' answers while telling the Anecdote.
- Ask the listener to time the 'Anecdote teller'. In *Teaching*

Collocations (page 91) Michael Lewis suggests reducing the time allowed to deliver the Anecdote each time it is repeated. For example, in the first instance the student has five minutes; for the second telling they have four minutes; and the third three minutes.

- Ask the listener to take brief notes about the Anecdote and write them up as a summary for homework. Then give the summary to the 'Anecdote teller' to check.

The pedagogic value of getting students to retell Anecdotes – repeat a 'big chunk' of spoken discourse – cannot be overstated. Repeating complex tasks reflects real interactions. We all have our set pieces: jokes, stories, etc. And we tend to refine and improve them as we retell them. Many students will appreciate the opportunity to do the same thing in their second language. Research by Martin Bygate among others has shown that given this opportunity students become more adventurous and at the same time more precise in the language they use.

You can also use the Anecdotes to test oral proficiency and thereby add a speaking component to accompany the tests in the Teacher's Book.

Realistic reading

In theory, no matter how difficult a text may be, the task that accompanies it can be designed to be within the competence of the student, i.e. 'grade the task not the text'. However, conversations with students and teachers and many years in the classroom have convinced us that this is an insight of only limited value. However easy the task, students are quickly disillusioned by an incomprehensible text.

At the other extreme, many of the texts that have appeared in ELT coursebooks in the past have obviously been written merely in order to include examples of a given grammatical structure. Texts like this are often boring to read and unconvincing as discourse.

The solution adopted in *Inside Out* has been to base all reading texts on authentic modern sources, including magazines, novels, newspapers, websites and personal communications. In *Inside Out Elementary*, the source texts have been adapted and graded so as to make them challenging without being impossible. The texts have been selected not only for their language content but also for their interest and their appropriacy to the students who will use this course.

Varied listening work

The listenings include texts specially written for language learning. There are dialogues, conversations, monologues and classic pop songs. There is a variety of English accents – British, American, Welsh, Scots, North Country – and some examples of non-native speakers. The tasks are designed to develop real life listening skills.

Pronunciation improvement

Work on particular areas of sound, stress and intonation is integrated into units as appropriate.

Motivating writing practice

The coursebook contains six structured writing tasks which offer the students opportunities to get to grips with a variety of formats: narrative, descriptive, biography, formal letters, postcards and application forms.

This is backed up by a self-contained writing course which runs through the Workbook.

Components

Inside Out Elementary includes a Student's Book, a Teacher's Book, a Workbook (including a CD) with or without key, Class Cassettes and CDs and a photocopiable Resource Pack. There is also a Resource Site on the internet at *www.insideout.net*.

Student's Book

The Student's Book covers about 90 hours of classroom teaching. It is made up of sixteen main units (1–4, 6–9, 11–14 and 16–19) and four review units (5, 10, 15 and 20). There is also a Zero unit introducing classroom language. The units (apart from Unit 0) are all four pages long but do not follow a rigid template: the flow of each one comes from the texts, tasks and language points in it.

The Pairwork: Student A and Pairwork: Student B activities are at the back of the book along with Additional material.

The book includes all the tapescripts, plus a list of verb structures, a glossary of grammatical terminology, sections on classroom language and on numbers, a guide to the phonemic alphabet, a list of irregular verbs and a comprehensive unit-by-unit wordlist.

Class Cassettes (2) and CDs (2)

These have all the listening materials from the Student's Book.

Workbook and CD

The Workbook provides revision of all the main points in the Student's Book, plus extra listening practice, pronunciation work and a complete self-contained writing course. There are with or without key versions.

Teacher's Book

In this book you'll find step-by-step notes and answers for every exercise. These notes include closed-book activities to warm the class up before beginning a new set of work. The tapescripts are included in the body of the teacher's notes for easy reference.

For every one of the main units there is a one-page photocopiable test, for use as soon as you finish the unit or a couple of weeks later. There are longer mid-course and end-of-course tests which go with the four review units (5, 10, 15 and 20).

At the beginning of the book there is a Zero unit. This consists of two parts.

- The first part is a quiz about the Student's Book to help familiarise students with it: how language is described, the kinds of activities they will do, how the list of contents works, what they can find at the back of the book.
- The second part is a Student profile. It aims to discover something about each student's language learning history and reasons for studying English, for example, for an exam, for academic studies, for work reasons, out of personal interest, etc. (Where your students share the same language you might like to translate the profile for them.) Students can fill the form out individually or by interviewing each other in pairs. The Student profile is similar to needs analysis, which has been used in business English for many years. But it is not only business students who have reasons for learning. General English students also have needs and wants. Knowing about them will help you to plan lessons, to use the Student's Book more appropriately and to get to know your students better.

Resource Pack

The Resource Pack contains photocopiable worksheets designed to supplement or extend the Student's Book. The worksheets are based on the themes and grammar points in the book and are linked to the book unit by unit. They were written for this project by a range of different ELT teachers. They are very varied, but one thing they have in common is that they provide practical, useful classroom practice. There are full teaching notes for every worksheet.

Resource Site and e-lessons at *www.insideout.net*

The *Inside Out* website is a constantly updated resource designed to supplement the Student's Book with a guide to useful websites and a topical weekly e-lesson which you can receive free of charge by subscribing online at *www.insideout.net*.

Over to you

If you have any comments about *Inside Out*, you can contact us via the *Inside Out* website at *www.insideout.net*. Your opinions will help to shape our future publishing. We look forward to hearing from you.

Zero unit answers

(Page numbers refer to the Student's Book.)

1   a) Twenty.
     b) They are review units (pp 22, 42, 62, 82).

2   a) Unit 3 *Days* (p 14)
     b) Unit 12 *Reality* (p 51)
     c) Unit 16 *dotcom* (p 68)
     d) Unit 18 *Justice* (p 77)

3   a) English; that
     b) shop
     c) help you

4   Past simple (p 40).

5   a) Unit 6 *Food* (p 29)
     b) Unit 8 *Sea* (p 36)
     c) Unit 17 *Drive* (p 72)

Join us online at www.insideout.net

The *Inside Out* website is a huge teacher resource designed to supplement and enrich your teaching with a wealth of fresh, topical, up-to-the-minute material. And it's all FREE!

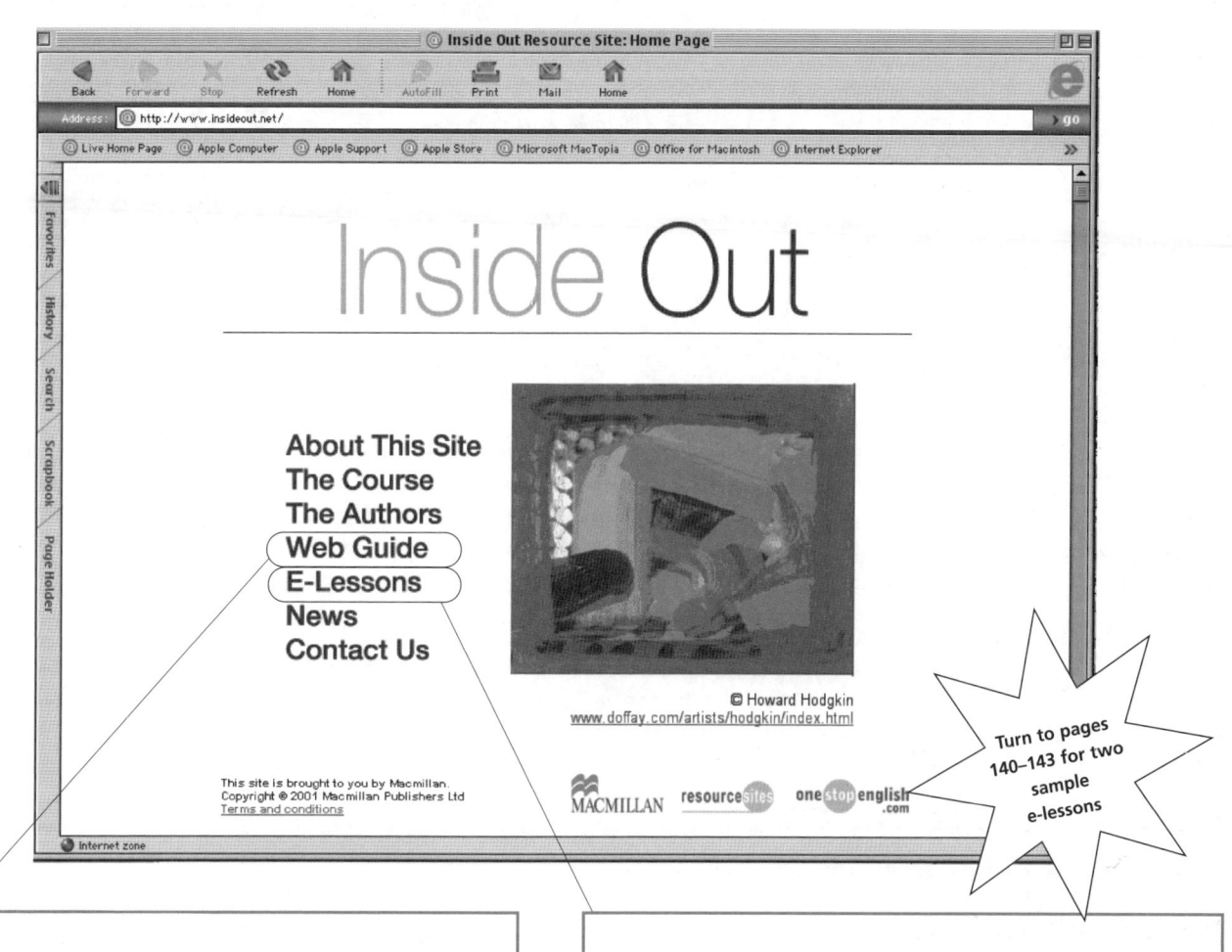

Turn to pages 140–143 for two sample e-lessons

Click on **Web Guide** to add an extra dimension to your teaching.

For every unit in the Student's Book there are direct links to a variety of carefully-selected websites. They provide you with a truly limitless supply of extra supplementary material.

You'll never be stuck for ideas again!

Click on **E-lessons** to receive a free weekly lesson from the *Inside Out* team.

Once you've registered, *English Inside Out* arrives in your email inbox every week. Up-to-date and topical, the E-lessons cover a wide range of topics, including famous people, current events and events in history.

A great start to the week!

(Don't forget to check in the E-lesson Archive for any E-lessons you might have missed.)

Feedback from teachers on the *Inside Out* website.

* 'I'm really satisfied with the service you provide. Every week I receive enjoyable activities to do with my students. Congratulations!'

* 'Your site has proved to be of great use in my classes, and my students really enjoy using the material I take to class. Thank you for helping us teachers with so many attractive ideas.'

* 'Thanks again for the materials! You saved me a lot of time this week!'

* 'I'm astonished by the website and happy to have chosen *Inside Out*.'

* 'The book is very interesting, and the topics are up-to-date. I find the E-lessons fascinating.'

* 'All your free lessons are much appreciated and heavily utilised by the staff of this centre in our general English classes.'

Find out more at: *www.insideout.net*

Units & topics	Speaking & writing	Reading & listening texts	Grammar, Lexis & Pronunciation
0 Classroom page 4	Activities to introduce classroom language. Includes classroom vocabulary, teacher's instructions, ways of asking for repetition and spelling etc.		
1 You Introductions Favourites page 6	Exchanging personal information Talking about favourites	A man joining a sports club Two women talking about a man UK travel: useful numbers *She's Got You*	**G** Possessive adjectives. *be*. Questions & short answers **L** Telephone numbers. Days. Months. Colours **P** Sounds of the alphabet
2 People Family Friends Jobs page 10	Talking about family Talking about people you know **Anecdote**: one of your relatives	*Meet the Taits* Two women talking about a family photograph Two women talking about their relatives	**G** Present simple: auxiliary verbs. Possessive *'s* **L** Family. Jobs. Nationalities **P** Word stress
3 Days Habits Likes & dislikes page 14	Talking about a perfect day Talking about habits & routines Talking about likes & dislikes	Eight people talking about free time *On a perfect day in New York* *Little and large* Talking about two people's likes & dislikes	**G** Adverbs of frequency. *like* + *-ing*. Object pronouns **L** Daily activities. Prepositions of time: *in, on, at*. *make/do*. Leisure activities **P** 3rd person endings: /s/, /z/, /ɪz/
4 Living Houses Homes page 18	Talking about houses & furniture Talking about where you want to live **Anecdote**: your home Writing a postcard	*Beckingham or Buckingham?* *Your house in the stars* *The best in the world*	**G** *there is / there are*. *some/any* **L** Rooms & furniture. Prepositions of place. Positive & negative adjectives
5 Review 1 page 22	Activities to review all the main language points in Units 1–4. Includes a letter from a homestay family to a foreign student and a sketch entitled *Why do you want to work here?*		
6 Food Eating Diets page 26	Talking about food Talking about food combining Talking about famous singers' backstage demands	*Eat well, enjoy your food and keep slim* Two people talking about food combining Conversation in a delicatessen	**G** Nouns: countable & uncountable. Quantity: *How much / How many?* **L** Food & drink. Containers. *would like* **P** Vowel sounds
7 Work Personality Jobs page 30	Talking about your personality Talking about qualities needed for different jobs **Anecdote**: a good job Writing a formal letter	Personality exercise *From mountains to modelling* Interview with two celebrities	**G** Modals: *can, can't, have to, don't have to* **L** Describing character. Jobs **P** Word stress
8 Sea Water sports Holidays page 34	Talking about water sports Writing a simple narrative **Anecdote**: your last summer holiday	Three people talking about water sports *It's always summer on the inside* *Shark attack!* A woman talking about her last holiday	**G** Past simple: regular & irregular affirmative forms. *ago* **L** Water sports. Time expressions: *on, in, at, last*. Time linkers **P** *-ed* endings
9 Solo Feelings Experiences page 38	Talking about feelings Talking about things you do alone Talking about Hollywood stars Writing a biography	*Going it alone* Interview about Debra Veal *I want to be alone*	**G** Past simple: regular & irregular negative & question forms **L** Feelings. Adjective + particle collocations **P** Past simple vowel sounds
10 Review 2 page 42	Activities to review all the main language points in Units 6–9. Includes a reading about a famous politician, an **Anecdote** about a delicious meal, and a board game entitled *Let's talk about …*		

Units & topics	Speaking & writing	Reading & listening texts	Grammar, Lexis & Pronunciation
11 *Looks* Description Clothes page 46	Talking about similarities between family members Talking about who you look like Talking about what people wear	A man talking about his clothes *Image – Quiz of the month* TV presenter describing people arriving at the Oscars	**G** Present continuous **L** Physical description. *look like*. Clothes **P** Numbers *13/30, 14/40*, etc.
12 *Reality* Dreams Television page 50	Talking about dreams & reality Talking about television Writing an online application to appear on *Big Brother* Talking about reality TV Talking about hopes & desires for the future	*Glenna's dream book* A woman telling the 2nd part of Glenna's story Interview between TV presenter & winner of *Big Brother* *I Have A Dream*	**G** Future forms: *want to, would like to, hope to, going to* **L** TV programmes. Collocations **P** Vowel sounds /iː/, /ɪ/, /aɪ/, /eɪ/
13 *Things* Possessions Shopping page 54	Talking about lost property **Anecdote**: the last time you went shopping Talking about your city Talking about valuable things	*Lost property* A woman phoning a lost property office *savekaryn.com* *Happy Birthday, Mr President*	**G** Comparative & superlative adjectives. Comparison structures **L** Describing objects. Money. Big numbers **P** Schwa /ə/
14 *Energy* Health The body Character page 58	Talking about daily activities Talking about health & exercise Talking about character Talking about advice for everyday problems	*Joaquín Cortés: body and soul* *How do other people really see you?* Two people talking about doing exercise	**G** Problems & advice: *too, enough, should* **L** Frequency expressions. *How often …?* Parts of the body. Collocations. Describing character **P** /ʌ/ sound
15 *Review 3* page 62	Activities to review all the main language points in Units 11–14. Includes an interview with a famous athlete, an **Anecdote** about a good-looking person, and a sketch entitled *I haven't got anything to wear*.		
16 *dotcom* Computers School friends page 66	Talking about websites Talking about old friends Talking about things you have done **Anecdote**: an old school friend	A son helping his mother to send an email *Where are they now?* *Darren & Geoff* Conversation between two old school friends	**G** Present perfect + *ever*. Past participles **L** *to*-infinitive. Computer terms. Phrasal verbs
17 *Drive* Journeys Traffic page 70	Talking about drives to work Talking about problems on the road Game: *On the way home*	*Driving to work* Six people talk about what drives them mad on the road Directions from A to B	**G** Question forms: *How* + adjective/adverb; *What* + noun **L** Prepositions of movement. Traffic situations. Directions **P** Ordinal numbers: *1st, 2nd …*
18 *Justice* Revenge Story-telling page 74	Talking about revenge Talking about stories Writing a story	*Revenge is sweet & Dinner by post* *Usher's revenge* A modern fairy tale	**G** Punctuation. Past continuous **L** Time adverbials. Adverbs of manner
19 *Extreme* Nature Weather Predictions page 78	Talking about nature Talking about hotels & buildings Talking about the weather **Anecdote**: your favourite time of year	*I love Geography* *The coolest hotel in the world* *The North Pole in winter* London winter weather forecast A woman talks about her favourite time of the year	**G** Passives **L** Geographical features. Weather. *will/might* **P** Word & sentence stress
20 *Review 4* page 82	Activities to review all the main language points in Units 16–19. Includes a funny story, an **Anecdote** about a journey you did when you were younger, and a board game entitled *The Revision Game*.		

Pairwork: Student A page 86 • *Additional material* page 94 • *Pairwork: Student B* page 98 • *Word list* page 106 • *Verb structures* page 114 • *Adjectives* page 115 • *Grammar glossary* page 116 • *Classroom language* page 116 • *Numbers* page 116 • *Phonetic symbols* page 116 • *Irregular verbs* page 117 • *Tapescripts* page 118

0 Zero unit

Book quiz

Look through your book and find the answers to these questions.

1 a) How many units are there in the book?
   _____

   b) Why are Units 5, 10, 15 and 20 different?
   _____

2 Look at the list of contents. In which unit can you:

   a) read about a perfect day in New York?
   _____

   b) talk about reality TV?
   _____

   c) listen to a conversation between two old school friends?
   _____

   d) write a story?
   _____

3 Look at the back of the book.

   a) Complete these sentences from the *Classroom language* section on page 116:

      What's this in _____ ?

      Can you repeat _____ ?

   b) Which word illustrates /ʃ/ in the table of phonetic symbols on page 116?
   _____

   c) Complete this question from the beginning of tapescript 05?

      Good afternoon. Can I _____ ?

4 Which grammar structure is dealt with in the Language reference section in Unit 9 *Solo*?
   _____

5 Look at the list of contents. Decide which units you think these pictures are in and then check in the unit.

   a) _____

   b) _____

   c) _____

Student profile

- **Name**
  _____

- **Have you studied English in the past?**

  No ☐   Yes ☐ → When and where? _____

- **Have you got any English language qualifications?**

  No ☐   Yes ☐ → What are they and when did you take them? _____
  _____

- **Do you use English outside the class?**

  No ☐   Yes ☐ → When do you use English and where? _____
  _____

- **Are you studying English, or in English, outside this class?**

  No ☐   Yes ☐ → Please give details _____
  _____

- **Do you speak any other languages?**

  No ☐   Yes ☐ → Which ones? _____
  _____

- **Why are you studying English?**

  I need it for work.

  No ☐   Yes ☐ → What do you do? _____
  _____

  I need it to study.

  No ☐   Yes ☐ → What are you studying? _____
  _____

  Where? _____

  I'm going to take an examination.

  No ☐   Yes ☐ → What examination are you going to take? _____
  _____

  When? _____

  I'm doing it for personal interest.

  No ☐   Yes ☐ → What do you like doing in your free time? _____
  _____

© Sue Kay & Vaughan Jones, 2003. Published by Macmillan Publishers Limited. This sheet may be photocopied and used within the class.

0 Classroom Teacher's notes

Lexis: the classroom (p 4)

1 Pairwork. Students work together to identify the objects in the picture and match them with a word from the box. Allow them to ask for help and to compare answers with other pairs, but do not check answers at this stage. Students may ask why some words have the definite article (*the*) and some the indefinite article (*a/an*). Point out that we tend to use *the* when there is only one of something (eg: *the teacher*) and *a/an* when the thing is just one example of others that may be present (eg: *a window, a student*).

2 **01 SB p 118**
Play the recording for students to listen and check their answers to Exercise 1. Then play it again for them to repeat the words.

01
a) a picture
b) a window
c) the board
d) a word
e) a definition
f) a sentence
g) a question
h) an answer
i) the teacher
j) a map
k) the door
l) the cassette player
m) a student
n) a chair
o) a piece of paper
p) a dictionary
q) a pen
r) a desk
s) a book
t) a bag

3 **02 SB p 118**
Play the recording and ask students to point to the things mentioned in their own classroom. If space and constraints on noise level permit, you could have this as a race with the first student to touch the thing mentioned winning a point.

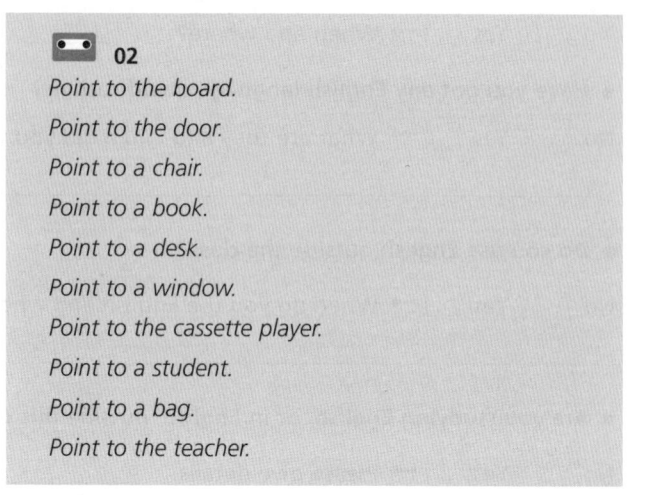

02
Point to the board.
Point to the door.
Point to a chair.
Point to a book.
Point to a desk.
Point to a window.
Point to the cassette player.
Point to a student.
Point to a bag.
Point to the teacher.

4 Pairwork. Draw students' attention to the Language toolbox and explain that these small sections occur in the margin throughout the book and are there to help them with specific language points. This one explains the difference between *this* and *that*. Make sure that students understand that it is a question of the distance between the object and the speaker. Go through the examples with the class.

Students then take turns to point to things around their classroom and ask their partner *What's this in English?* or *What's that in English?* Go round, checking that they are forming the questions correctly. Remind students that we tend to use *the* when there is only one of something and *a/an* when the thing is just one example of others that may be present.

5 This could be set for homework, if you wish.

Lexis: teacher language (p 5)

This section teaches some of the language you will be using throughout the book. If you teach these expressions now, you will be able to use English to give instructions throughout the course, thus exposing the students to more language use.

1 Pairwork. Students choose words from the box to complete the instructions. Allow them to compare with other pairs, but do not check answers at this stage.

a) Work
b) Look
c) Listen
d) Write
e) Read
f) Use

2 📼 **03 SB p 118**

Play the recording for students to listen and check their answers to Exercise 1.

> 📼 **03**
> a) *Work with a partner.*
> b) *Look at the board.*
> c) *Listen to the conversation.*
> d) *Write the answers on a piece of paper.*
> e) *Read the text.*
> f) *Use your dictionary.*

3 Pairwork. Students make more teacher instructions by replacing the underlined words in Exercise 1 with words from the box. Check answers with the class.

> a) Work in groups of three.
> b) Look at the photograph.
> c) Listen to the song.
> d) Write your name.
> e) Read the article.
> f) Use a piece of paper.

Lexis: student language (p 5)

As with the teacher language above, the more your students get used to using English in the classroom, the more familiar they will become with the language and the more confident they will be in speaking English to other students.

1 📼 **04 SB p 5**

Play the recording and ask students to read the conversation as they listen to it. They then decide on the correct order of the pictures. Check answers with the class.

> 1 b 2 a 3 c

2 Groupwork. Students work in groups of three and practise saying the conversation. Finally, they each take a role in the conversation and act it out. In monolingual classes, students can substitute *compañero* for an appropriate word in their language.

1 You Overview

The topic of this unit is personal information, particularly people's names and telephone numbers. The grammar focus is on the present simple tense, questions and short answers.

Students start by listening to Mike who is applying to join a sports club. The receptionist asks him questions to elicit personal information for an application form. This provides practice in the use of the pronouns *you* and *your* and leads into practice of direct questions and questions about a third person, using *he* and *his*. Students practise asking questions to elicit personal details about each other and classmates.

The focus then changes to the pronunciation of letters of the alphabet and numbers. Students categorise the letters of the alphabet according to vowel sounds, and listen and distinguish between different readings of the vowels *A E I O U*. Students then listen to speakers spelling out their names and choose the correct name. They then practise conversations in which one person asks another for clarification of the spelling of a name. Finally, they practise the pronunciation of telephone numbers. They dictate names and telephone numbers to each other.

Next, students match category words with objects in the context of Enrique Iglesias' favourite things. They add further words to the categories and talk about their own favourite things.

Students then take a closer look at the form of questions and short answers, both affirmative and negative, using the verbs *be*, *do* and *have*. They complete questions and interview each other using these questions.

Finally, students match words and pictures and listen to the song *She's Got You* by Patsy Cline. They answer questions on the lyrics of the song and then talk about particular objects that have memories for them.

Section	Aims	What the students are doing
Introduction page 6	*Listening skills*: listening for specific information	Listening to a man being asked about personal details and completing the questions. Asking questions to find out personal information.
Name and number page 7	*Pronunciation*: letters of the alphabet and numbers	Categorising letters of the the alphabet according to vowel sounds. **Pairwork: Student A & B**
	Listening skills: listening for specific information	Writing down abbreviations and matching them to names. Checking the correct spelling of names. Dictating and writing down telephone numbers.
Favourites page 8	*Lexis*: category words	Matching items to the correct categories. Asking questions about favourite things.
Close up pages 8–9	*Grammar*: questions and short answers	Practising questions and short answers with *be*, *do* and *have*. Completing questions to ask about feelings, likes and possessions.
She's Got You page 9	*Listening skills*: listening for detail	Matching words and pictures. Listening to a song and answering questions on the lyrics. Talking about objects that remind students of people, things or events.

More information about topics in this unit

Favourites, Lexis 1 *www.enriqueiglesias.com*
She's Got You, 2 *www.patsycline.com*

1 You Teacher's notes

Books closed. Whole class. The focus of this first unit is on personal information, so, particularly if the students are new to you, you might like to take the opportunity to share some of your personal information with them. This could be done by putting some numbers, dates or names on the board which are significant in your life and have the students ask you about their significance.

Listening (1) (p 6)

1 Focus attention on Mike's *Personal details* form and give students time to read it. Tell them that in the photograph Lina (who works for Sportica Health Club) is asking Mike some questions. Establish the difference between *you* and *your* (*you* is the subject, *your* is possessive) and elicit a couple of sentences using each word. In pairs, students decide how to complete the questions. Do not check answers at this stage.

2 05 SB p 118

Play the recording for students to check their answers.

a) your
b) your
c) you
d) your
e) you
f) you
g) you
h) you

05

(L = Lina; M = Mike)

L: Good afternoon. Can I help you?
M: Yes, I'd like to join the club, please.
L: Certainly. I just need to ask you a few questions. What's your first name?
M: Mike.
L: And what's your surname?
M: Turnbull.
L: How do you spell that, please?
M: T-U-R-N-B-U-double L.
L: Okay. Now, your address, where do you live?
M: 23 Trinity Road, London SW18.
L: Lovely. And what's your telephone number?
M: 09732 176 double 7 3.
L: Sorry, can you repeat that?
M: Yes – 09732 176 double 7 3.
L: Okay. How old are you?
M: I'm 27.
L: 27. And what do you do?
M: I'm an engineer. I work for a mobile phone company.
L: Oh, very nice. And are you married?
M: No, I'm not. I'm single.
L: Okay. Last question. What are you interested in: gym, aerobics, swimming, yoga, tennis, squash, boxing or tai chi?
M: Um, gym, squash and tai chi. And maybe tennis.
L: Lovely.

Elicit what other questions Lina asked Mike (she asked him to spell his surname and to repeat his telephone number). Draw students' attention to the Language toolbox and go through the language for asking for spellings and asking someone to repeat something. Point out that when a word contains the same letter twice in succession, we say *double L*, *double T*, etc, and we also use *double* in numbers where one digit is repeated. Also draw students' attention to the pronunciation of *0*. Mike pronounces this *oh*, though we can also say *zero*. In telephone numbers *oh* is probably more common in British English. In American English it is *zero*.

3 06 SB p 118

Students listen to the questions again and repeat each one after the recording.

06

a) What's your first name?
b) What's your surname?
c) Where do you live?
d) What's your telephone number?
e) How old are you?
f) What do you do?
g) Are you married?
h) What are you interested in?

4 If space permits, get students to walk round the class to find out the information about their classmates. Otherwise students can work in pairs to ask and answer the questions in Exercise 1. Encourage them to ask their partners to spell any difficult words and to repeat anything they don't hear.

Listening (2) (p 6)

1 Draw students' attention to the photo and to Kate, who is next to Lina. Refer back to the Language toolbox and elicit that the possessive form of *he* is *his*. Establish that the female forms are *she* and *her*. Students complete Kate's questions with *he* or *his*. Do not check answers at this stage.

2 🔲 **07 SB p 118**

Play the recording for students to check their answers. See if they can tell you the order in which Kate asks the questions without listening for a second time. Then play the recording again for them to check.

a) his
b) he
c) his
d) he
e) he
f) he

1 a 2 e 3 d 4 b 5 f 6 c

🔲 **07**

(K = Kate; L = Lina)
K: Ooh, he's nice!
L: Hm, he's okay.
K: What's his name?
L: Mike.
K: Ooh, I like the name Mike. What does he do?
L: He's an engineer.
K: Ooh, really? How old is he?
L: Kate!
K: What?
L: He's 27.
K: Where does he live?
L: In Trinity Road.
K: Is he …
L: What?
K: Is he married?
L: Yes.
K: Oh.
L: Actually, he isn't married. He's single.
K: What's his telephone number?
L: Kate!

3 Students work in pairs to ask and answer questions using the questions in Exercise 1 and *he/his* and *she/her*. Go through the examples with the class and then monitor to make sure that they are using the pronouns correctly. Again, encourage students to ask for spellings or repetition where appropriate.

Name & number (p 7)

This section is concerned with letters and numbers and gives students plenty of practice in spelling out names and giving telephone numbers. To combine the two (and exploit the fact that your students probably bring their mobile phones to class) you could write some names in code, using the numbers assigned to the different letters on a mobile phone keypad. For example, Mike would be 6453 and Lina would be 5462. Students can then make up their own coded names and test each other. This way they are practising saying both letters and numbers.

Alphabet (p 7)

1 🔲 **08 SB p 118**

Ask students to say the letters *A, E, I, O* and *U* aloud. You might like to point out that these letters are called *vowels* and the other letters of the alphabet are called *consonants*. (*Y* is also sometimes regarded as a vowel.) Draw attention to the chart and elicit the pronunciation of the words *face, green, ten, eye, nose, blue* and *start*. Point out that each of the letters of the alphabet contains the vowel sound represented in one of these words. Students add the vowels to the appropriate sound groups. Play the recording for them to check their answers, then encourage them to say each group of letters aloud.

You might like also to draw students' attention to the phonemic symbols at the top of each column in the chart and also the full list of symbols on page 116. It is very useful for students to learn phonemic symbols as they can then check the pronunciation of new words in a dictionary.

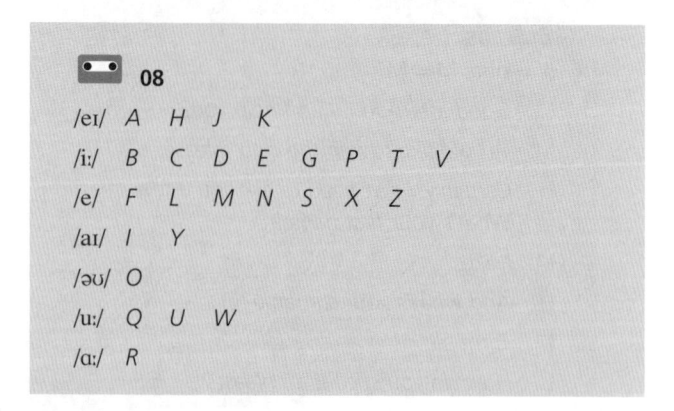

/eɪ/ **face**	/iː/ **green**	/e/ **ten**	/aɪ/ **eye**
A H J K	B C D E G P T V	F L M N S X Z	I Y

/əʊ/ **nose**	/uː/ **blue**	/ɑː/ **start**
O	Q U W	R

🔲 **08**

/eɪ/ A H J K
/iː/ B C D E G P T V
/e/ F L M N S X Z
/aɪ/ I Y
/əʊ/ O
/uː/ Q U W
/ɑː/ R

2 🔲 **09 SB p 118**

Before you play the recording, ask selected students to read out the five options. To make this more fun, ask the rest of the class to stand up if they think a student has read the group of letters correctly, and to remain seated if they think a mistake has been made.

Play the recording and elicit the order in which the groups of letters were read.

```
1 c   2 e   3 b   4 a   5 d
```

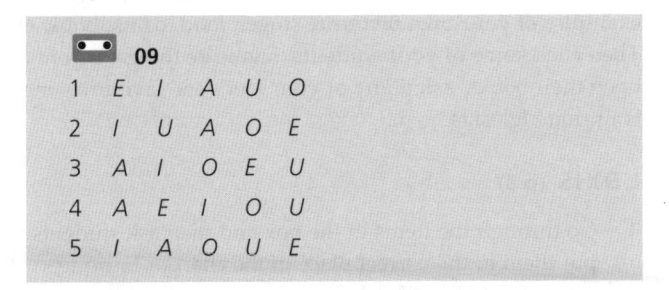

🔊 09

```
1   E  I  A  U  O
2   I  U  A  O  E
3   A  I  O  E  U
4   A  E  I  O  U
5   I  A  O  U  E
```

3 **Pairwork: Student A & B** Students turn to their respective pages and follow the instructions. This exercise is an information gap activity based on an optician's eyechart. If students enjoy doing this, they might like to make up their own pairs of charts for other students to try.

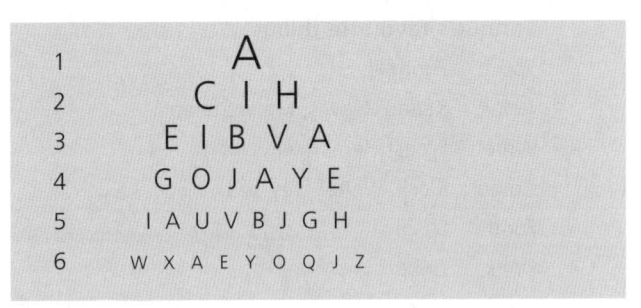

```
1              A
2           C  I  H
3        E  I  B  V  A
4        G  O  J  A  Y  E
5        I  A  U  V  B  J  G  H
6     W  X  A  E  Y  O  Q  J  Z
```

4 🔊 **10 SB p 118**

Establish that an abbreviation is a short way of expressing a word or phrase, using only a few letters. Give an example, such as PTO (please turn over) or UK (United Kingdom) and elicit a few examples from the class, but not too many to avoid pre-empting the exercise. Play the recording for students to write down the abbreviations they hear. Then check answers before they start the matching part of the exercise.

1   UFO: Unidentified Flying Object
2   CNN: Cable News Network
3   BBC: British Broadcasting Corporation
4   CIA: Central Intelligence Agency
5   VIP: Very Important Person
6   IOC: International Olympic Committee
7   UN: United Nations
8   IBM: International Business Machines

🔊 10

1   UFO
2   CNN
3   BBC
4   CIA
5   VIP
6   IOC
7   UN
8   IBM

5 Students could discuss these questions in small groups and then report back to the class. You could have a competition to see which group can think of the most abbreviations in English.

Spelling (p 7)

1 🔊 **11 SB p 118**

You might like to point out that several English names can be spelled in different ways and ask students if it is the same in their language. There are ten examples in Exercises 1 and 2. Sometimes the difference in spelling indicates the sex of the person. For example, Frances is a girl's name, but Francis is a boy's name. Other examples of this include Lindsey/Lindsay and Leslie/Lesley, although with these two the distinction is becoming blurred and you can encounter both men and women with both spellings.

Play the recording for students to underline the correct spelling of each name. Allow students to compare their answers in pairs before checking with the class.

a) Stewart
b) Claire
c) Graeme
d) Kathryn

🔊 11

(L = Lina; S = Stewart; C = Claire; G = Graeme; K = Kathryn)

a)
L: What's your name?
S: Stewart.
L: Is that S T U A R T?
S: No, it's S T E W A R T.
L: Okay, thanks.

b)
L: What's your name?
C: Claire.
L: Is that C L A R E?
C: No, it's C L A I R E.
L: Okay, thanks.

c)
L: What's your name?
G: Graeme.
L: Is that G R A H A M?
G: No, it's G R A E M E.
L: Okay, thanks.

d)
L: What's your name?
K: Kathryn.
L: Is that K A T H R Y N?
K: Yes, it is.
L: Oh ... great. Er ... Thanks.

2 🔊 **12 SB p 7**

Play the recording for students to listen and repeat the names.

3 Pairwork. Students use the names in Exercise 2 to substitute in the conversation from Exercise 1. You might like to demonstrate a conversation with one student as an example. Draw attention to the word *it's* (= *it is*) and refer students to the chart in the Language toolbox for the present tense of the verb *be*. Make sure students swap roles each time so they both get the chance to ask the questions and to spell the names.

Telephone numbers (p 7)

1 🔊 **13 SB p 119**

Remind students that they heard Mike giving Lina his telephone number in the last section. Draw their attention to the *UK travel – useful numbers* box and ask students to practise saying the numbers in pairs (the Language toolbox will help them). Encourage them to do this out loud so that they get a feel for the way the words sound and remind them of the use of *double* for repeated numbers and the pronunciation of *O*. Play the recording for them to check their answers.

> Heathrow flights: oh eight seven oh, oh double oh, oh one two three. (0870 000 0123)
>
> UK train times: oh eight four five, seven four eight, four nine five oh. (0845 748 4950)
>
> National Express buses: oh eight seven oh, five eight oh, eight oh eight oh. (0870 580 8080)
>
> Hertz Car Rental: oh two oh, double eight nine seven, two oh seven two. (020 8897 2072)
>
> British Tourist Authority: oh two oh, double eight four six, nine oh double oh. (020 8846 9000)

> 🔊 **13**
>
> *Here are some useful numbers for travellers in the UK.*
>
> *For flight information to and from Heathrow airport dial oh eight seven oh, oh double oh, oh one two three.*
>
> *For UK train times dial oh eight four five, seven four eight, four nine five oh.*
>
> *For National Express bus and coach information ring oh eight seven oh, five eight oh, eight oh eight oh.*
>
> *Hertz Car Rental is oh two oh, double eight nine seven, two oh seven two.*
>
> *And the British Tourist Authority can help you with other information. Dial oh two oh, double eight four six, nine oh double oh.*

2 Pairwork. Students work in pairs to dictate names and telephone numbers to each other. Go round checking that they are saying the letters and numbers correctly.

Favourites (p 8)

Books closed. Establish the meaning of *favourite*, giving some examples of your own favourite singer, food, drink, book, etc. Then elicit some of your students' favourite things. Before they open their books, ask if any of your students' favourite singer is Enrique Iglesias.

Lexis (p 8)

1 Go through the items in the box and then ask students to put them in the correct place in the chart of Enrique's favourite things. Check answers and find out if anyone agrees with Enrique.

Note: If your students would like more information on this popular Spanish singer, they can log on to his official website: *www.enriqueiglesias.com*

> **Enrique's favourite things**
> Sport: Football
> Actor: Keanu Reeves, Meryl Streep
> Writer: Ernest Hemingway
> Colour: Black, white, grey, red
> Food: Sushi
> Drink: Coke
> Car: Jeep
> Day: Friday
> Month: May
> City: Madrid, Miami, Mexico City

2 Pairwork. Students may find it useful to write out the ten headings (Sport, Actor, Writer, etc.) down the side of a piece of paper and add the items next to the appropriate headings. Draw students' attention to the section on *Colours* and *Days of the week* on page 106. For *Months of the year* and *Sports* refer students to page 107.

> Sport: golf, skiing, tennis, basketball
> Actor: Robert de Niro, Julia Roberts
> Writer: Agatha Christie, Gabriel García Márquez
> Colour: blue, yellow, green
> Food: pasta, hamburgers
> Drink: coffee, tea, water
> Car: BMW, Fiat, Toyota
> Day: Thursday, Monday, Wednesday, Tuesday, Sunday, Saturday
> Month: January, April, June, September, December, November, July, February, October, August, March
> City: London, Paris

3 Students underline their favourite item for each category if it is already in the chart. If not, they should add it.

4 Demonstrate the example dialogue with a couple of students. Then, if space permits, allow students to mingle around the room asking and answering questions. When students encounter someone with the same favourite as themselves, they should ask about another category to see if they agree on that as well. At the end, find out which pair of students agreed on the most favourites.

Close up (p 8)

Questions & short answers

1 Pairwork. Go through the first three items with the class and establish that the verb in a short answer matches that used in the question. Three verbs are used in this exercise: *be*, *do* and *have*. Remind students of the present simple affirmative of the verb *be* which they saw in the Language toolbox on page 7 and refer them to the Language reference section on page 9 and Verb structures on page 114 for more information and practice in the present simple. If students are unsure, go through these carefully with the class first. Establish that the second column in the table here is the negative form. Students then complete the columns. Check answers with the class.

You might like to point out that in an affirmative short answer we don't contract *I am* to *I'm*, but we do in a negative short answer.

> a) Yes, I am. No, I'm not.
> b) Yes, I do. No, I don't.
> c) Yes, I have. No, I haven't.
> d) Yes, I am. No, I'm not.
> e) Yes, I do. No, I don't.
> f) Yes, I have. No, I haven't.
> g) Yes, I do. No, I don't.

2 14 SB p 119

Play the recording for students to listen and check. Play it again for them to repeat the sentences. They then work in pairs to ask and answer the questions about themselves.

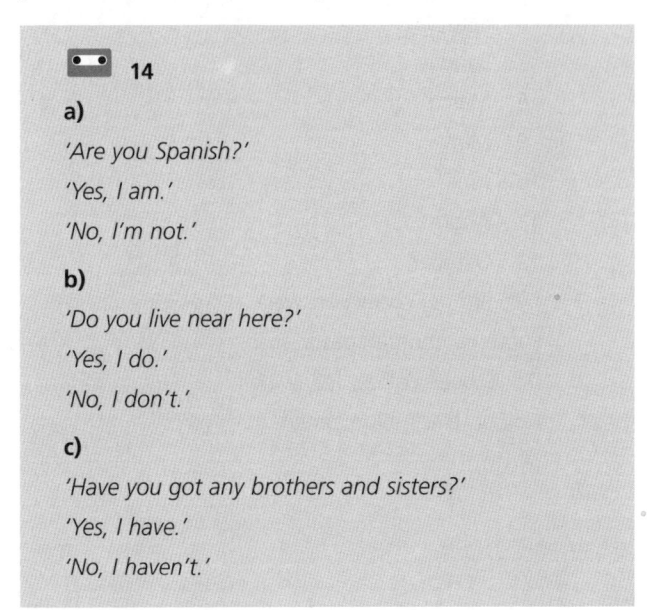

> 14
> a)
> 'Are you Spanish?'
> 'Yes, I am.'
> 'No, I'm not.'
> b)
> 'Do you live near here?'
> 'Yes, I do.'
> 'No, I don't.'
> c)
> 'Have you got any brothers and sisters?'
> 'Yes, I have.'
> 'No, I haven't.'
> d)
> 'Are you married?'
> 'Yes, I am.'
> 'No, I'm not.'
> e)
> 'Do you like Italian food?'
> 'Yes, I do.'
> 'No, I don't.'
> f)
> 'Have you got a motorbike?'
> 'Yes, I have.'
> 'No, I haven't.'
> g)
> 'Do you like watching television?'
> 'Yes, I do.'
> 'No, I don't.'

3 Pairwork. Students choose from the words given and/or add their own ideas to make three questions for each item. Go round checking that they have added appropriate items. Each student in the pair should make their own copy of the questions they decide on.

4 Students change partners and interview their new partners using the questions they chose in Exercise 3. Encourage them to report back to the class on any interesting answers they received.

She's Got You (p 9)

1 Allow students to work in pairs to match the pictures with the words in the box. They should then discuss the question and report back to the class on their ideas.

> a) a picture
> b) a pen
> c) records
> d) a bicycle
> e) a memory
> f) a class ring
> g) a penknife
> h) golf clubs

2 15 SB p 119

Focus attention on the picture and read the questions with the class before you play the recording. Students discuss their answers to the questions in pairs. They should first try to answer them without referring to the tapescript, but allow them to look at it if they need to. Check answers with the class. If the students like the song, play it again for them to listen for pleasure, or sing along to.

Note: American country singer Patsy Cline recorded several hits from 1957 to 1962. For more information about Patsy Cline, log on to her official web site: *www.patsycline.com*

> a) The singer has got: the picture, the records, the memory and the class ring.
> b) The other woman has got the man.
> c) The singer feels sad.

🔊 15

She's Got You

I've got your picture
That you gave to me,
And it's signed with love
Just like it used to be.

The only thing different,
The only thing new:
I've got your picture,
She's got you.

I've got the records
That we used to share.
And they still sound the same
As when you were here.

The only thing different,
The only thing new:
I've got the records,
She's got you.

I've got your memory,
Or has it got me?
I really don't know.
But I know
It won't let me be.

I've got your class ring
That proved you cared.
And it still looks the same
As when you gave it, dear.

The only thing different,
The only thing new:
I've got these little things,
She's got you.

3 Go through the instructions and the examples with the class. Students then work individually to complete the sentence in three ways that are true for them. Then put students into pairs to discuss their sentences. Encourage them to report back to the class on any interesting sentences their parnter wrote.

Test

Scoring: one point per correct answer unless otherwise indicated.

1
1 your
2 she
3 their
4 his

2
1 is your
2 are you
3 Are you
4 do you live
5 do you live
6 Have you got
7 do you do?
8 Do you like

3 (½ point per correct answer)
1 Are, am
2 Do, don't
3 Do, do
4 Have, haven't
5 Is, isn't
6 Does, does

4
1 01852 621669
2 oh double seven five, four oh nine double five double eight

5 1 a   2 k   3 e   4 g   5 f   6 s   7 i   8 w

6 (½ point per correct answer)
1 M<u>on</u>day
2 T<u>ues</u>day
3 W<u>ednes</u>day
4 Th<u>urs</u>day
5 F<u>ri</u>day
6 S<u>a</u>turday
7 S<u>un</u>day
8 March
9 May
10 June
11 August
12 October

7 (½ point per correct answer)
Food: hamburger, pasta, sushi
Drink: beer, coffee, tea, water
Colour: black, blue, green, grey, yellow

20 UNIT 1 *You*   Visit *www.insideout.net*

1 You Test

Name: _____   Total: _____ /40

1 Possessive pronouns & adjectives *4 points*
Choose the correct alternative.
1. What's **you / your** favourite colour?
2. Does **she / her** like dancing?
3. Where is **they / their** house?
4. What's **he / his** email address?

2 Questions *8 points*
Write the questions.
1. 'What _____ name?' 'Silvia Gomez.'
2. 'How old _____ ?' 'I'm twenty-two.'
3. '_____ married?' 'No, I'm single.'
4. 'Where _____ ?' 'I live in Madrid.'
5. 'Who _____ with?' 'I live with my mum.'
6. '_____ any brothers or sisters?' 'Yes, a brother.'
7. 'What _____ ?' 'I'm a student.'
8. '_____ studying?' 'Yes, I like it very much.'

3 Questions & short answers *6 points*
Complete the questions and answers with the correct form of *be*, *do* or *have*.

For example: '*Are* you tired?' 'Yes, I *am*.'
1. '_____ you hungry?' 'Yes, I _____ .'
2. '_____ you live near here?' 'No, I _____ .'
3. '_____ you like skiing?' 'Yes, I _____ .'
4. '_____ they got a car?' 'No, they _____ .'
5. '_____ he nervous?' 'No, he _____ .'
6. '_____ she speak Russian?' 'Yes, she _____ .'

4 Vocabulary – telephone numbers *2 points*
Write the first telephone number in figures and write the second in words.
1. oh one eight five two, six two one double six nine
   _____
2. 0775 4095588
   _____

5 Pronunciation – sounds of the alphabet *8 points*
Add each letter (*a, e, f, g, i, k, q, s*) to the group with the same sound.

/eɪ/ *face*: (1) ____ h, j, (2) ____
/i/ *green*: b, c, d, (3) ____, (4) ____, p, t, v
/e/ *ten*: (5) ____, l, m, n, (6) ____, x, z
/aɪ/ *eye*: (7) ____, y
/əʊ/ *nose*: o
/u/ *blue*: (8) u, ____
/ɑ/ *start*: r

6 Vocabulary – days & months *6 points*
Add the missing letters to the days and complete the missing months.

1. M __ __ day   5. F __ __ day
2. T __ __ __ day   6. S __ __ __ __ day
3. W __ __ __ __ __ day   7. S __ __ day
4. T __ __ __ __ __ day

*   *   *

January	July
February	11 A_____
8 M_____	September
April	12 O_____
9 M_____	November
10 J_____	December

7 Vocabulary – food, drink & colour *6 points*
Put the words in the box into the correct categories.

beer black blue coffee green grey hamburger
pasta sushi tea water yellow

Food	Drink	Colour
1 _____	4 _____	8 _____
2 _____	5 _____	9 _____
3 _____	6 _____	10 _____
	7 _____	11 _____
		12 _____

2 People Overview

In this unit, the focus moves away from the individual to people in general and family members in particular. More grammar work is done on the present simple and vocabulary for families, jobs, countries, nationalities and languages is introduced.

Students begin by reading a description of two families and naming the people in a photo. They then read short texts and identify the person being described, write their own short texts and talk about members of their own families.

In the next section, several words for jobs are introduced and students use the present simple to make sentences about what people do and where they work. They then change the sentences so that they are true for their own family members.

Some grammar work on the present simple follows, with particular focus on *Yes/No* questions and short answers.

Next, students listen to Beth talking about a couple of family photos. They identify the photos and make further sentences describing the people Beth talks about. They then study Beth's family tree and say who each person is in relation to Beth. This leads into students drawing their own family trees and explaining them to a partner. Following on from this, they are introduced to their first Anecdote, a feature which occurs throughout the book and which provides guided extensive speaking practice.

The final section of this unit widens the theme of describing people to include countries, nationalities and languages. Students learn some useful vocabulary and use it to describe people they know or know of who come from different countries.

Section	Aims	What the students are doing
Introduction page 10	*Lexis*: family words	Matching names from a text to people in a photograph.
	Reading skills: reading for specific information	Identifying family relationships.
		Writing short descriptions of family relationships.
		Comparing information about two families and completing a table. **Pairwork: Student A & B**
		Talking about students' own families.
What do you do? page 11	*Lexis*: jobs	Matching pictures and jobs.
		Completing present simple sentences about jobs with *a/an* and *in/for*.
		Changing the sentences to make them true for students' own relatives.
Close up pages 11–12	*Grammar*: present simple	Completing a conversation.
		Completing questions and short answers with auxiliary verbs.
Family pages 12–13	*Listening skills*: listening for gist	Matching family pictures with what a speaker says.
		Making sentences about two people.
		Using the possessive *-'s* to talk about family relationships.
	Conversation skills: fluency work	Anecdote: talking about a relative.
International relations page 13	*Pronunciation*: word stress	Completing a table with country, nationality and language words.
	Lexis: words for countries, nationalities and languages	Talking about people students know from other countries.

2 People Teacher's notes

Books closed. Whole class. Students are usually interested in their teachers' home lives, so it may be worthwhile to bring in some family photos of your own and to be prepared to talk about members of your own family and answer questions. Encourage students to bring in their own family photos so that they can do the same. Invite volunteers to show their photos to the class and explain who each of the people in the photos is. This will have the effect of preteaching a lot of the family vocabulary in this lesson.

Lexis: family words (p 10)

1 Focus students' attention on the photo and read the text aloud to them. Then give them time to read the text again silently to themselves and to match the names to the people in the photograph. Allow students to compare answers in pairs before checking with the whole class. Draw their attention to the Language toolbox which gives information about the verb *have got* and plurals of words for family members.

a)	Kylie
b)	Kevin
c)	Lisa
d)	Claire
e)	Scott
f)	Michael
g)	Dawn
h)	Becky

2 Pairwork. Students work together to read the short texts and identify the people. Allow them to compare their answers with other pairs before checking with the class. Draw students' attention to the section on *Family words* on page 107.

1	Kevin
2	Becky
3	Charlie
4	Michael and Scott
5	Willie and Dawn

3 Students work individually to write their descriptions. They then swap with a partner and try to identify the correct person.

4 **Pairwork: Student A & B** Students turn to their respective pages and follow the instructions. Encourage students to do the exercise by asking questions, not by showing each other their information. If necessary, get them to sit with their back to each other. When they have finished, they should see if they agree on the five differences between the Tait families. Then check answers with the class.

Student A
a) ✘ 23 Dover Street
b) ✔
c) ✘ A green Renault Clio
d) ✘ W303 XBL
e) ✘ 01792 800 761
f) ✔
g) ✔
h) ✘ Cider (an alcoholic drink made from apples)

Student B
a) ✘ 24 Dover Street
b) ✔
c) ✘ A blue Renault Clio
d) ✘ W302 XBL
e) ✘ 01792 880 761
f) ✔
g) ✔
h) ✘ Beer

5 Pairwork. This should be done orally, but you may like to give students a minute or two to prepare. When they have finished, you could ask students to report back to the class on their partner's families.

What do you do? (p 11)

Books closed. Whole class. The focus of the next section is jobs and you might like to preteach some vocabulary by playing *What's my job?* Begin by miming a job to the class and getting them to guess what you are. A student who guesses correctly then chooses a job and mimes it for the rest of the class to guess, and so on.

Lexis: jobs (p 11)

1 Pairwork. Students look at the pictures and match the objects with the jobs in the box. You may like to use the box to point out or elicit the rule for the use of *a* and *an*: we use *a* with nouns that begin with a consonant and *an* with those that begin with a vowel. They will need to know this for the next exercise. Allow students to compare answers with other pairs before checking with the class.

> a) a secretary
> b) a student
> c) a DJ
> d) a mechanic
> e) a nurse
> f) an engineer

2 Go through the Language toolbox with the class before they do this exercise to make sure they are all clear about the formation of the present simple. Point out the use of the third person 's'. Look at the example with the whole class before they work individually to complete the sentences. Do not check answers at this stage.

3 🔊 **16 SB p 119**
Play the recording for students to check their answers. They may ask for clarification of when we use *in* and when we use *for*. Generally speaking, we use *in* when we are talking about an actual place or building and *for* when we are talking about an organisation or a person. However, distinctions are sometimes blurred. For example, in sentence b) here, *He works in a big construction company* would not sound odd.

> a) a, in
> b) an, for
> c) a, in
> d) a, in
> e) a, for

> 🔊 **16**
> a) My mother is a nurse. She works in a hospital.
> b) My father is an engineer. He works for a big construction company.
> c) My cousin is a DJ. He works in a night club.
> d) My friend is a secretary. She works in an office.
> e) My uncle is a mechanic. He works for his father.

4 Students should work individually to make the sentences in Exercise 2 true for members of their own family. Be prepared to help with any difficult vocabulary. They should then compare their sentences with a partner. If anyone has a family member with an unusual job, this could be reported back to the class.

Close up (p 11)

Refer students to the Language reference section on page 12 and Verb structures on page 114 if they need more help with the formation and use of the present simple.

Present simple (p 11)

1 🔊 **17 SB p 119**
You might like to go through the Language reference section on page 12 with the class before they work on this exercise. Allow students to work in pairs and to discuss their answers before you play the recording for them to check.

> 1 Is
> 2 isn't
> 3 Has
> 4 hasn't
> 5 does
> 6 Does
> 7 doesn't
> 8 Is

> 🔊 **17**
> (B = Beth; A = Angie)
> B: This is me with my brother.
> A: Oh, he's nice. Is he married?
> B: No, he isn't. He's single.
> A: Has he got a girlfriend?
> B: No, he hasn't.
> A: Oh. What does he do?
> B: He's a doctor.
> A: Oh. Does he live near here?
> B: No, he doesn't. He lives in Australia, actually.
> A: Oh. Is this your father?
> B: No, that's my boyfriend.
> A: Oh, sorry.

2 Elicit answers from the class.

> Beth's brother, Beth and Beth's boyfriend.

3 To make this more interactive, when checking answers, allocate one student to read out a question and two others to read out the affirmative and negative answers. Alternatively, wait until you play the recording in the next exercise to check answers.

> a) Are; Yes, I am. No, I'm not.
> b) Have; Yes, I have. No, I haven't.
> c) Do; Yes, I do. No, I don't.
> d) Is; Yes, he is. No, he isn't.
> e) Has; Yes, he has. No, he hasn't.
> f) Does; Yes, she does. No, she doesn't.
> g) Do; Yes, I do. No, I don't.
> h) Does; Yes, she does. No, she doesn't.

4 🔊 **18 SB p 119**
Play the recording. Students then work in pairs to ask and answer the questions. Make sure they keep changing roles so they both have the chance to ask and answer.

📼 18

a)
'Are you a student at university?'
'Yes, I am.'
'No, I'm not.'

b)
'Have you got a part-time job?'
'Yes, I have.'
'No, I haven't.'

c)
'Do you work in an office?'
'Yes, I do.'
'No, I don't.'

d)
'Is your grandfather retired?'
'Yes, he is.'
'No, he isn't.'

e)
'Has your father got an interesting job?'
'Yes, he has.'
'No, he hasn't.'

f)
'Does your mother speak English?'
'Yes, she does.'
'No, she doesn't.'

g)
'Do you play the piano?'
'Yes, I do.'
'No, I don't.'

h)
'Does your grandmother live near you?'
'Yes, she does.'
'No, she doesn't.'

Optional activity

Ask students to work with a partner and do the following task.

1. On a piece of paper, write down the name of a) a relative, b) a friend and c) a neighbour.

2. Ask your partner *Yes/No* questions about each person on their piece of paper. Find out at least five pieces of information about each person.

   For example: *Is he/she married? Has he/she got any children? Does he/she live near here? Does he/she work for a company? Does he/she speak English?* etc.

Family (p 12)

If you didn't have your students bring in family photos earlier in this unit, it might be a good idea to do it now. Students can then use them to talk about their own family members, and therefore personalise the language they are learning.

Listening (p 12)

1 📼 **19 SB p 119**

You may like to remind students of the possessive pronouns in the Language toolbox on page 6 as possessive pronouns are used a lot when talking about family members.

Focus attention on the four pictures and play the recording. Elicit from the class which pictures Beth is talking about.

> b and c

📼 **19**
(B = Beth; A = Angie)

B: This is Amy. She's my sister.
A: Oh – older sister or younger sister?
B: Older!
A: Oh! Where does she live?
B: In the city centre. She lives with her husband and her baby boy.
A: Ah. What's her baby's name?
B: Brad. He's lovely.
A: Oh. So, is Amy a housewife?
B: No, she's a teacher. She works in a school in the city centre. She's a French teacher.
A: Oh.
B: And this is Robert. He's my favourite cousin.
A: Wow, he's nice.
B: I know. He lives in San Francisco.
A: Oh no, why?
B: He's an actor. Well, he's an actor and a waiter. He works in an Italian restaurant. But he's a very good actor.
A: Is he married?
B: No, no, he isn't married but he's got lovely friends.
A: How often do you see him?
B: I see him every year.

2 Students make sentences about Amy and Robert using the words in the box. Play the recording again for them to check their sentences. Then check answers with the class.

> *Suggested answers*
>
> Amy:
> She lives in the city centre.
> She's got a baby boy.
> Her baby boy is lovely.
> She's a teacher.
> She works in a school.

People UNIT 2 25

> Robert:
> He lives in San Francisco.
> He's an actor and a waiter.
> He works in an Italian restaurant.
> Beth sees him every year. / He sees Beth every year.

Possessive -'s (p 12)

It is a good idea to establish right from the start that there are two kinds of -'s: the possessive -'s which denotes that something belongs to someone – *Beth's cousin, Amy's baby*, etc. and the abbreviation for *is* and *has* – *he's nice, she's got two brothers*, etc. You may also like to warn students that the possessive pronoun *its* (as in *The dog likes its dinner*) has no apostrophe and that even native speakers sometimes confuse this with *it's* (= it is).

1 Pairwork. Students study Beth's family tree and make sentences describing each person's relationship to Beth. Go through the examples with the class first. For extra practice of numbers, ask students to say how old each of the family members is.

> Terry is Beth's grandfather.
> June is Beth's grandmother.
> Roger is Beth's father.
> Pat is Beth's mother.
> Annie is Beth's aunt.
> Phil is Beth's uncle.
> Colin is Beth's brother-in-law.
> Amy is Beth's sister.
> Adrian is Beth's brother.
> Robert is Beth's cousin.
> Helen is Beth's cousin.
> Brad is Beth's nephew.

2 Students might like to draw their family trees for homework and bring them to class to discuss with a partner. They could add photos or drawings to make them more interesting. Go through the question words in the box with the class and elicit some example questions using these words to make sure everyone is clear about how to form the questions they will need.

Optional activity

Use the family trees that the students have drawn to do this activity, called *How many different relatives are you?* Students look at their own family tree and make sentences as follows:
I'm Rosa's daughter.
I'm Pablo's granddaughter.
I'm Maria's sister-in-law.
etc.

They get a point for every different relation word they can use about themselves. Some students can get upwards of ten true sentences. You can feed in new vocabulary if the students are interested, eg: *great-nephew, stepdaughter*, etc.

Anecdote (p 13) ✓

See the Introduction on page 4 for more ideas on how to set up, monitor and repeat Anecdotes.

1 📼 20 SB p 119

Pairwork. Give students plenty of time to decide who they are going to talk about and to read and listen to the questions. Play the recording several times, if necessary.

> 📼 20
> Think about one of your relatives.
> Is it a man or a woman?
> What's his or her name?
> What relation is he or she to you?
> Where does he or she live?
> What does he or she do?
> Is he or she married?
> Has he or she got children?
> What do you do and what do you talk about when you see him or her?

2 Give students time to prepare what they are going to say. They can use the sentence beginnings to help them, but discourage them from writing down whole sentences and simply reading them out.

3 Students should maintain eye contact with their partners as much as possible as they talk about their relatives so that they are not tempted to read from a script.

International relations (p 13)

An extra element to describe people is added here with vocabulary to talk about countries, nationalities and languages. If you have a large map of the world, you could use it to locate all the countries mentioned in this section and any others that are relevant to your students. When teaching new country names, it is a good idea to elicit or teach the appropriate nationality and language words at the same time.

Word stress (p 13)

1 Pairwork. Focus attention on the table. If your students' country or countries are not represented here, you could ask them to add them. Students copy and complete the table. When they are underlining the stressed syllables, encourage them to say the words out loud so that they get a feel for what sounds right. Do not check answers at this stage.

2 📼 21 SB p 119

Play the recording for students to listen and check their answers. Then play it again for them to repeat. Encourage them to add as many countries as possible to the table. They might like to make a large poster for the classroom wall to which they can add new countries, nationalities and languages as they learn them. Draw their attention to the section on *Countries* and *Languages* on page 107, and *Nationalities* on page 108.

Country	Nationality	Language
'I come from ...'	'I am ...'	'I speak ...'
Argentina	Argentinian	Spanish
Brazil	(1) Brazilian	Portuguese
France	French	(2) French
(3) Germany	German	German
Italy	Italian	(4) Italian
Japan	(5) Japanese	Japanese
(6) Poland	Polish	Polish
Spain	(7) Spanish	Spanish
the United Kingdom	British	(8) English
(9) the United States of America	American	English

🎧 21

Argentina, Argentinian, Spanish
Brazil, Brazilian, Portuguese
France, French, French
Germany, German, German
Italy, Italian, Italian
Japan, Japanese, Japanese
Poland, Polish, Polish
Spain, Spanish, Spanish
the United Kingdom, British, English
the United States of America, American, English

3 Go through the instructions and the examples with the whole class. Students then work individually to write down the names and then in pairs to talk about the people they have chosen. Go round making sure that students are using the present simple and the country and nationality words correctly.

Test

Scoring: one point per correct answer unless otherwise indicated.

1
1. I work in a sports shop.
2. My best friend works in Paris.
3. Are you a student?
4. Have you got a job?
5. Do you work in an office?
6. Is your job interesting?
7. What does your girlfriend do?
8. Where does your boyfriend work?

2 (1 point per correct verb)
1. Do, do
2. Are, 'm not
3. Does, doesn't

3
1. mother
2. brother
3. daughter
4. uncle
5. nephew
6. cousin

4
1. people
2. children
3. men
4. women

5
1. Brazilian
2. German
3. Italy
4. Japanese
5. Poland
6. Spanish
7. British
8. American

6
1. doctor
2. engineer
3. secretary
4. mechanic
5. nurse
6. student

7
1. Juan's
2. Peter's

2 People Test

Name: _____   Total: _____ /40

1 Present simple 8 points
Correct the mistake in each sentence.

1 I works in a sports shop.
2 My best friend work in Paris.
3 Do you be a student?
4 Do you have got a job?
5 Are you work in an office?
6 Does your job interesting?
7 What do your girlfriend do?
8 Where does your boyfriend works?

2 Short answers 6 points
Complete both the questions and answers with the correct auxiliary verbs.

1 '_____ you play the piano?'
   'Yes, I _____ .'
2 '_____ you French?'
   'No, I _____ .'
3 '_____ your boyfriend live near you?'
   'No, he _____ .'

3 Vocabulary – family 6 points
Complete the table.

Male	Female
father	1 _____
2 _____	sister
son	3 _____
4 _____	aunt
5 _____	niece
cousin	6 _____

4 Vocabulary – irregular plurals 4 points
Write the plural of each word.

1 person _____
2 child _____
3 man _____
4 woman _____

5 Vocabulary & pronunciation – nationalities & word stress 8 points
Complete the table and underline the stressed syllable in the countries and nationalities you write.

Country	Nationality
Bra<u>zil</u>	1 _____
<u>Ger</u>many	2 _____
3 _____	I<u>tal</u>ian
Ja<u>pan</u>	4 _____
5 _____	<u>Pol</u>ish
Spain	6 _____
the U<u>nit</u>ed <u>King</u>dom	7 _____
the U<u>nit</u>ed States	8 _____

6 Vocabulary – jobs 6 points
Add the missing vowels (a, e, i, o, u) to complete the jobs.

1 d __ ct __ r
2 __ ng __ n __ __ r
3 s __ cr __ t __ ry
4 m __ ch __ n __ c
5 n __ rs __
6 st __ d __ nt

7 Possessive -'s 2 points
Complete the second sentence so the meaning is the same as the first.

1 Silvia is married to Juan.
   Silvia is _____ wife.
2 Peter has got a very big house.
   _____ house is very big.

3 Days Overview

This unit is about daily activities, the frequency with which people do things and likes and dislikes. The grammar focus is on adverbs of frequency, time expressions, the use of pronouns and constructions using *like* and *dislike*.

Students begin by studying everyday activities: listening to some people talking about what they do to relax and talking about a perfect day. This leads into some pronunciation work on third person singular verb endings.

Students then use adverbs of frequency to talk about how often they do things. They use time expressions in conjunction with adverbs of frequency to say when and how often they do certain things.

Next, they study the daily routines of two very different people: a sumo wrestler and a model. First, they predict which sentences describe which person and then they go on to talk about their own daily routines. This leads into some work on the use of the verbs *make* and *do* to talk about common activities.

In the next section, students put verbs of liking on a scale from strong liking to strong disliking. They read about two people's likes and dislikes and use the information to predict what other things they like and dislike. They then look at the structure of sentences talking about likes and dislikes and study the rules for the spelling of *-ing* forms.

Section	Aims	What the students are doing
Introduction pages 14–15	*Lexis*: daily activities	Completing a table with verbs to make ten daily activities.
		Listening to people describing what they do to relax.
	Reading skills: reading for specific information	Reading an article about Suzanne Vega's perfect day.
		Talking about students' own perfect day.
	Pronunciation: /s/, /z/ and /ɪz/ endings	Examining the different ways of pronouncing words ending in *s*.
Close up page 15	*Grammar*: adverbs of frequency; time expressions	Talking about how often students do everyday activities. **Pairwork: Student A & B**
		Using time expressions to say when students do things.
		Writing sentences about things students do.
A day in the life of … page 16	*Reading skills*: reading for specific information	Reading sentences and predicting which of two people they refer to.
		Reading an article about two very different people.
	Lexis: *make* and *do*	Completing diagrams with *make* or *do* to form common expressions.
		Talking about who does certain things in their homes.
Love it. Hate it. page 17	*Listening skills*: listening for gist	Completing a table to show degrees of liking.
		Reading a short text about the likes and dislikes of Jack and Layla.
		Predicting more of Jack and Layla's likes and dislikes, then listening to them talking.
Close up page 17	*Grammar*: verbs expressing likes and dislikes; object pronouns	Matching questions and answers.
		Studying the spelling of *-ing* forms.
		Completing sentences to guess partner's likes and dislikes. **Pairwork: Student A & B**

More information about topics in this unit

Introduction, Reading 1 *www.suzannevega.com*
A day in the life of …, Reading 2 *www.sumo.or.jp*

3 Days Teacher's notes

Books closed. Whole class. Tell students that you are going to mime some of the things that you do every day. Ask them to work in groups and to write down in English what they think you did. Mime a few daily activities such as putting on your clothes, brushing your teeth, driving to work, etc. At the end, see which group got the most activities correct. If students enjoy the game, invite a member of the winning group to mime some more activities for the class.

Lexis: daily activities (p 14)

1 Pairwork. Students decide which verb goes with which column. Encourage them to try saying the activities aloud so that they get a feel for what sounds right. When they have finished, allow them to compare their results with other pairs, but do not check answers at this stage. Draw students' attention to the sections on *Some expressions with 'do', 'go', 'have'* and *'make'* on page 108.

2 22 SB p 120

Go through the instructions with the students first. Perhaps elicit a few ideas from them for ways to relax. Play the recording and then check answers to Exercise 1.

> a) do
> b) go
> c) have
> d) listen to
> e) watch

> 22
> *We asked people in the street: 'What do you do when you want to relax?' Here are some of the answers.*
> 1 'I have a cup of tea and watch television. I watch films and sport.'
> 2 'I listen to the radio and do the washing up.'
> 3 'I have a nice long bath.'
> 4 'I go to the park with my son.'
> 5 'I listen to music and do yoga.'
> 6 'I go for a walk and listen to the birds singing.'
> 7 'I go swimming and then I have lunch with friends.'
> 8 'I do the ironing or I watch a video.'

3 Play the recording again and then ask students to add one more activity to each of the columns. In pairs, they then discuss which of the activities they do.

> *Possible answers*
> do yoga
> go swimming
> have a bath
> listen to music
> watch a video

Reading (p 14)

1 Pairwork. First, focus attention on the photograph and find out if any of the students are familiar with Suzanne Vega's music. Students then work in pairs to match the verbs and phrases. Allow them to compare answers with another pair before checking with the class.

Note: Suzanne Vega grew up in New York and was influenced by the music of Leonard Cohen and Lou Reed. She made her debut album in 1985. The Suzanne Vega website is: *www.suzannevega.com*

> 1 get up late
> 2 go for a drink
> 3 watch the people walk by
> 4 have breakfast
> 5 go out with my friends
> 6 read the newspaper
> 7 go sailing

2 Pairwork. Students work together to complete the tasks. Find out what the students think about Suzanne Vega's day. Would they like to have a lifestyle like this? Give them plenty of time to discuss their own perfect days. Ask them to report back to the class on their partner's perfect day.

> a)
> a 2 and 3 b 7 c 1 d 4 e 5 f 6
> b)
> 1 c 2 f 3 d 4 b 5 a 6 e

3rd person endings: /s/, /z/ and /ɪz/ (p 15)

1 23 SB p 15

Play the recording for students to listen and repeat. Then ask them to put the verbs in the correct columns. Encourage them to say the words aloud as they do this so that they get a feel for what sounds right. Do not check answers at this stage.

30 UNIT 3 *Days* Visit *www.insideout.net*

2 🎧 **24 SB p 120**

Play the recording for students to listen, check their answers and repeat the verbs. Then check answers with the class.

> 🎧 **24**
> Ending with /s/: *acts, laughs, takes*
> Ending with /z/: *needs, pays, wins*
> Ending with /ɪz/: *finishes, relaxes, teaches*

3 🎧 **25 SB p 120**

Allow students to work in pairs to complete the chants. Then play the recording for them to listen, check and repeat the answers.

1	laughs
2	takes
3	pays
4	wins
5	teaches
6	finishes

> 🎧 **25**
> (W = Woman; M = Man)
> W: *I cry, he laughs.*
> M: *I give, she takes.*
> W: *I think, he acts.*
> M & W: *We're different.*
> M: *I want, she needs.*
> W: *I spend, he pays.*
> M: *I lose, she wins.*
> M & W: *We're different.*
> M: *I learn, she teaches.*
> W: *I work, he relaxes.*
> M: *I start, she finishes.*
> M & W: *We're married!*

Close up (p 15)

Adverbs of frequency

1 Pairwork. Explain that adverbs of frequency tell us how often something happens. Focus attention on the chart, or the section on *Adverbs of frequency* on page 108, which shows these adverbs on a scale from 0% to 100%. Remind the students of Suzanne Vega's perfect day, which they read earlier and look at the example with the whole class. Students then ask and answer questions to find out how they compare to Suzanne Vega. When they have finished, encourage them to ask other questions and to answer them with the adverbs of frequency.

2 **Pairwork: Student A & B** Students turn to their respective pages and follow the instructions. This information gap exercise provides more opportunities for practising adverbs of frequency. To prevent students from simply looking at each other's charts, you could ask them to move their chairs so that they are sitting back to back as they ask and answer the questions. When they have completed their charts, they can compare them to check that they have understood correctly.

3 Draw students' attention to the Language toolbox which gives examples of when we use *in*, *on* and *at*. They should then be able to complete the sentences. Check answers with the class, and elicit a few examples.

a)	on
b)	in
c)	at
d)	on
e)	on
f)	in

4 Students work individually to write their sentences. They then compare them with a partner. Go round, making sure they are using the adverbs of frequency correctly. Refer them to the Language reference section at the bottom of the page if they need more help.

A day in the life of ... (p 16)

Whole class. Focus attention on the two photographs, then ask students to close their books. Elicit suggestions for the things that these two people might do every day and write them on the board. Getting students to predict what they are going to read is a good way of activating vocabulary and encouraging interest. They will want to know if they predicted correctly.

Reading (p 16)

1 Allow students to work in pairs to decide which person each sentence describes. When they have finished, read out each one (omitting the pronoun) and ask students to stand up if they thought it described the man and to remain seated if they thought it described the woman. Do not confirm or deny answers at this stage.

2 Students read the article and find out if they predicted correctly in Exercise 1.

a)	She
b)	He
c)	He
d)	She
e)	He
f)	He
g)	He
h)	He
i)	She
j)	She

Note: If students would like to know more about Sumo wrestling, they could log on to *www.sumo.or.jp* where they can find a beginner's guide to sumo wrestling and some information on individual sumo wrestlers including Musashimaru.

3 Pairwork. Go through the example and the instructions with the class to make sure everyone knows what to do. Students then ask and answer about the sentences in Exercise 1 and write true sentences about their partners. In a class feedback session, encourage students to read out their sentences.

Lexis: *make & do* (p 16)

1 Students complete the diagrams. When checking answers, ask students to read out the complete expressions so that they get used to hearing the words used together.

> A   do
> B   make

2 Allow students plenty of time to write their sentences and then compare them with a partner. Pairs can then join other pairs to form small groups and compare again.

Love it. Hate it. (p 17)

Listening

1 Establish that the key is a scale of 'liking' with the strongest expression for liking at the far left and the strongest expression for disliking at the far right. Give students a few minutes to decide which words go with which diagrams. Check answers with the class and elicit a few examples. Say, for example, *homework* and elicit (probably) *I hate it* from a student. Then try with *ice-cream, chocolate, school, sport, TV,* etc.

> a) I love it
> b) I really like it
> c) I like it
> d) I don't mind it
> e) I don't like it
> f) I hate it

2 Ask a couple of students to read out the texts about Jack and Layla. Elicit which one students think they are similar to. See how many Jacks and how many Laylas there are in the class. If the result is roughly half and half, you might like to pair each 'Jack' with a 'Layla' for the next exercise.

3 26 SB p 120
Pairwork. Based on the texts they have read, students discuss and decide which activities they think Jack likes and which ones Layla likes. When they have made their decisions, play the recording for them to check their ideas.

> Jack: playing football, swimming, jogging, going to the gym
> Layla: shopping, clubbing, eating out in restaurants, going to rock concerts

 26
Jack loves water, really likes being outside, really likes sport, hates towns and cities and doesn't like loud music. He loves playing football, swimming, jogging and going to the gym. But he doesn't like shopping, clubbing, eating out in restaurants or going to rock concerts. ... Oh, and he really likes Layla.

Layla loves spending money, doesn't like being outside, hates doing housework but doesn't mind cooking, likes dancing but hates sport. She loves shopping, clubbing, eating out in restaurants and going to rock concerts. But she doesn't like playing football, swimming, jogging or going to the gym. ... And Jack? She really likes him.

Close up (p 17)

Likes & dislikes

1 Point out the use of the pronouns *them, me, it, him* and *her* in the answers in this exercise. Also draw students' attention to the Language toolbox where they can see subject and object pronouns laid out in a table. You may like to go through the Language reference box at the bottom of the page with the class too at this stage.

Students then match the questions with the correct answers. Check answers with the class.

> a 3   b 4   c 1   d 5   e 2

2 Give students time to alter the answers so that they are true for them. They then compare them with a partner. Encourage them to do this by taking turns to ask a question and supply the answer.

3 Pairwork. First, draw students' attention to the examples in the table and make sure everyone knows the difference between a vowel (*a, e, i, o, u*) and a consonant (the other letters of the alphabet). Students then work in pairs to complete the table. Check answers with the class.

> *Verbs ending in -e*
> dance → dancing
> write → writing
> phone → phoning
>
> *Verbs ending in 1 vowel + 1 consonant*
> swim → swimming
> shop → shopping
> jog → jogging

32 UNIT 3 *Days*   Visit *www.insideout.net*

Other verbs
read → reading
cook → cooking
draw → drawing

4 **Pairwork: Student A & B** Students turn to their respective pages and follow the instructions. Make sure they each fill in all their predictions about their partners before they start asking and answering questions to find out the truth.

Test

Scoring: one point per correct answer unless otherwise indicated.

1 1 reads
   2 listen to
   3 watches
   4 have

2 1 laughs or takes
   2 laughs or takes
   3 needs or wins
   4 needs or wins
   5 relaxes or teaches
   6 relaxes or teaches

3 1 in
   2 on
   3 at
   4 at
   5 in
   6 at
   7 in
   8 on

4 1 usually
   2 sometimes
   3 hardly ever
   4 never

5 1 I am never late for work.
   2 She usually goes to the gym on Fridays.
   3 Is he always happy?
   4 Do they often go to bed late?

6 1 do
   2 do
   3 make
   4 do
   5 make
   6 make

7 2 a 3 d 4 f 5 b

8 1 dancing
   2 shopping
   3 cooking
   4 swimming

3 Days Test

Name: _____   Total: _____ /40

1 Vocabulary – daily activities *4 points*
Complete the sentences with the verbs in the box.

watches   listen to   reads   have

1 He _____ the newspaper every day.
2 I _____ the radio in the morning.
3 She _____ television every evening.
4 We _____ lunch at one o'clock.

2 Pronunciation – 3rd person endings *6 points*
Complete the table with the verbs in the box.

needs   laughs   relaxes   takes   teaches   wins

Ending with /s/	Ending with /z/	Ending with /ɪz/
acts	pays	finishes
1 _____	3 _____	5 _____
2 _____	4 _____	6 _____

3 Vocabulary – prepositions of time *8 points*
Add the correct preposition: *in*, *on* or *at*.

1 _____ the morning
2 _____ Tuesday
3 _____ night
4 _____ the weekend
5 _____ April
6 _____ five o'clock
7 _____ summer
8 _____ 15th May

4 Adverbs of frequency (1) *4 points*
Write the adverbs in the correct positions.

hardly ever   usually   never   sometimes

100% ——————————————— 0%
always   1 ____   often   2 ____   3 ____   4 ____

5 Adverbs of frequency (2) *4 points*
Put the adverb into the correct place in the sentence.

1 I am late for work. (never)
2 She goes to the gym on Fridays. (usually)
3 Is he happy? (always)
4 Do they go to bed late? (often)

6 Vocabulary – *make* & *do* *6 points*
Complete the expressions with *make* or *do*.

1 _____ your homework
2 _____ the washing up
3 _____ a decision
4 _____ the shopping
5 _____ a phone call
6 _____ a lot of noise

7 Likes & dislikes (1) *4 points*
Match the symbol with the verb.

1 ♥☺   a) really like
2 👍☺   b) don't like
3 ☺   c) love
4 😐   d) like
5 ☹   e) hate
6 ☹👎   f) don't mind

1 c   2 ___   3 ___   4 ___   5 ___   6 e

8 Likes & dislikes (2) *4 points*
Complete the sentences by putting the verb into the correct form.

1 I love _____ . (dance)
2 I don't mind _____ . (shop)
3 I hate _____ . (cook)
4 I like _____ . (swim)

4 Living Overview

This unit is about places – the homes in which people live and the locations in which they would like to live. The grammar focus is on prepositions and the use of *there is / there are*.

Students start by studying two 'palaces'; one is a real royal palace and the other the home of celebrity couple David and Victoria Beckham. They look at the kinds of things that can be found at such houses and then examine the contents of rooms in more familiar homes. This leads into work on prepositions and students discuss the exact location of items in their own homes.

They then do some grammar work on questions and answers using *there is* and *there are*.

The focus then widens to the location of people's homes and students read a horoscope page which links people's star signs with the places in which they like to live. There is more practice of prepositions, and students discuss whether the horoscopes are accurate for them and their attitudes to horoscopes in general. At the end of this section, there is an Anecdote – an opportunity for extended speaking, in which students tell each other about their homes.

In the final section, the focus on location is extended to a discussion of the best places in the world. Students match description to photos and decide if they agree that these really are the best in the world. Finally, they rewrite a postcard with positive or negative comments.

Section	Aims	What the students are doing
Introduction pages 18–19	*Reading skills*: reading for gist; reading for detail	Matching two texts about 'palaces' to photographs.
		Answering questions on the texts.
		Predicting further information about the two places. **Pairwork: Student A & B**
	Lexis: rooms	Identifying objects in a living room. Discussing what things you find in other rooms in a house.
	Lexis: prepositions (1)	Rearranging words to make sentences.
		Completing sentences with numbers and explaining the exact location of things in their homes.
Close up pages 19–20	*Grammar*: there is / there are	Completing questions and writing answers with *there is / there are*.
		Asking questions to find similarities between pictures of different living rooms. **Pairwork: Student A & B**
Where do you want to live? pages 20–21	*Lexis*: prepositions (2)	Reading and completing horoscopes linked to locations.
		Discussing the text and attitudes to horoscopes.
	Conversation skills: fluency work	Anecdote: talking about students' homes.
The best in the world page 21	*Reading skills*: reading for gist	Matching short descriptions to photos.
		Talking about the best places in students' countries.
	Writing: a postcard	Rewriting a postcard to make it either positive or negative in tone. **Pairwork: Student A & B**

More information about topics in this unit

Introduction, Reading 3 www.royal.gov.uk   www.beckham-magazine.com.
The best in the world, Reading 2 www.whc.unesco.org   www.travelchinaguide.com
www.tanzania-web.com

4 Living Teacher's notes

Books closed. Whole class. Write the word *palace* on the board and ask students what kind of person lives in a palace. Ask them to say what they think a palace is like and put any ideas they come up with on the board. Then tell them that they are going to look at two palaces in England.

Reading (p 18)

1   Focus students' attention on the photographs. Ask them which one they think is a real royal palace. Elicit any information about it that they know. If anyone has actually visited Buckingham Palace (parts of it are open to the public for a limited period each summer), encourage them to tell the class about the experience.

Ask students who they think lives in the other 'palace'.

> Buckingham Palace

2   Read the two texts aloud, ignoring the gaps, or give students time to read them silently to themselves. They match the texts to the photos and complete the gaps. If the students are interested in David and Victoria Beckham, you might like to brainstorm any other information they know about them (eg: their children are called Brooklyn and Romeo). Use the photo at the left to explain the meaning of *throne*. Check that students understand the word *press* (newspapers).

> A: Buckingham
> B: Beckingham

3   Allow students to work in pairs to read the texts again and decide if the statements are true or false. Check answers with the class. If you like, you could ask students to correct the false statements.

> a) False.
> b) False.
> c) True.
> d) True.
> e) False.

4   Pairwork. Students read the sentences and decide which place they describe. You may need to help with difficult vocabulary. When they have finished, allow them to compare their answers with other pairs, but do not confirm or deny any answers at this stage.

> a) Beckingham Palace.
> b) Beckingham Palace.
> c) Buckingham Palace.
> d) Beckingham Palace.
> e) Buckingham Palace.
> f) Beckingham Palace.
> g) Buckingham Palace.
> h) Buckingham Palace.

5   **Pairwork: Student A & B**   Students turn to their respective pages and read the rest of the two articles. They then use the information they have read to check their answers to Exercise 4. Encourage them to do this by telling each other what they have read. Students could then go on to talk about the house of a celebrity from their country.

Note: For more information on Buckingham Palace and other royal residencies in Britain, log on to *www.royal.gov.uk* For fans of the English footballer David Beckham, log on to his official website: *www.beckham-magazine.com* for latest news, information, interviews, photos and downloads.

6   Students could discuss this question in small groups and then report back to the class.

Lexis: rooms (p 19)

1   Focus attention on the photograph and ask what kind of room this is (a living room). Students then read the words in the box and decide which of the things they can see in the photo. You may need to help with difficult vocabulary, but encourage students to help each other with words that they already know. Check answers with the class.

> armchair, rug, coffee table, cushions, lamp, picture(s), plant(s), radiator, sofa

2   Pairwork. Students work together to decide which rooms the other things in the box in Exercise 1 are usually found in. Allow them to compare their results with other pairs, but do not check answers at this stage. (Note that it is not possible to be dogmatic about which room each thing is found in. For example, pictures and shelves are often found in kitchens, and cupboards are often found in bedrooms and bathrooms.)

3   **27 SB p 120**
Play the recording for students to check their answers to Exercise 2. Then play it again for them to repeat the words. Remind students about the section on *Rooms* on page 109.

> **Possible answers**
> a) a kitchen: blinds, cooker, cupboard, dishwasher, fridge, radiator, sink, washing machine
> b) a bedroom: bed, curtains, carpet or rug, cushions, lamp, mirror, picture, radiator, shelf/shelves, wardrobe
> c) a bathroom: bath, mirror, radiator, shower, washbasin

> **27**
> a) In a kitchen: blinds, cooker, cupboard, dishwasher, fridge, radiator, sink, washing machine
> b) In a bedroom: bed, curtains, carpet or rug, cushions, lamp, mirror, picture, radiator, shelf/shelves, wardrobe
> c) In a bathroom: bath, mirror, radiator, shower, washbasin

Lexis: prepositions (1) (p 19)

Books closed. Whole class. Write the prepositions *on, above, in, next to* and *under* on the board. Check that the students understand them by asking them to say where various things in the classroom are, using the prepositions. Then make several false statements about things in the classroom, such as *The board is next to the door* and invite students to correct you. Draw students' attention to the section on *Prepositions of place* on page 109.

1 Pairwork. Students read the sentence beginnings and endings and match them up according to what they can see in the photo. Check answers with the class and draw their attention to the use of *there is a/an* for single objects and *there are* for plural objects. They will do more work on this later.

> a) ... on the armchair.
> b) ... in the corner.
> c) ... on the floor.
> d) ... under the coffee table.
> e) ... on the sofa.
> f) ... above the sofa.
> g) ... next to the sofa.

2 Give students time to think about their own homes and to work individually to complete the sentences. They then compare with a partner.

3 Pairwork. Students explain the location of the things in their homes. Go round making sure they are using *there is / there are* and the prepositions correctly.

Close up (p 19)

there is / there are

1 Pairwork. There is more information on the use of *there is* and *there are* in the Language reference section on page 20. You may like to go through this with the class before they start this exercise.

Students work together to complete the questions and write two possible answers. Do not check answers at this stage.

2 **28 SB p 120**

Play the recording for students to check their answers to Exercise 1. Then play it again for them to repeat the questions and answers. They then ask and answer in pairs, giving true answers.

> a) Is; Yes, there is. No, there isn't.
> b) Are; Yes, there are. No, there aren't.
> c) Are; Yes, there are. No, there aren't.
> d) Is; Yes, there is. No, there isn't.
> e) Is; a; Yes, there is. No, there isn't.
> f) Are; any; Yes, there are. No, there aren't.

> **28**
> a)
> 'Is there a fireplace in your living room?'
> 'Yes, there is.'
> 'No, there isn't.'
> b)
> 'Are there any posters on your bedroom walls?'
> 'Yes, there are.'
> 'No, there aren't.'
> c)
> 'Are there any plants in your kitchen?'
> 'Yes, there are.'
> 'No, there aren't.'
> d)
> 'Is there a carpet on your bathroom floor?'
> 'Yes, there is.'
> 'No, there isn't.'
> e)
> 'Is there a park near your home?'
> 'Yes, there is.'
> 'No, there isn't.'
> f)
> 'Are there any good shops near your home?'
> 'Yes, there are.'
> 'No, there aren't.'

Optional activity

Ask students to complete the following texts using their own ideas. They should then compare their texts with a partner.

A
In the bedroom of my dreams, ...
There's a ...
There's a ...
And there's a ...

B
In the house of my dreams, ...
There are some ...
There are some ...
And there are some ...

C
In the city of my dreams, ...
There aren't any ...
There aren't any ...
And there aren't any ...

3 **Pairwork: Student A & B** Students turn to their respective pages and follow the instructions. This is an information gap activity in which the students have different pictures of rooms. Make sure that they don't show each other their pictures. They have to find the similarities by asking questions about the things in the pictures. When they have found six similarities, they look at the pictures together to find more. They then discuss the questions. Encourage them to report back to the class on their discussion.

> a) Similarities: armchair, coffee table, cushion, fireplace, lamp, picture, plant, rug, sofa

Follow-up activity

Find magazine pictures of rooms, especially kitchens, bathrooms and bedrooms, and bring them to class. Repeat the information gap activity to give students practice using different vocabulary.

Where do you want to live? (p 20)

Lexis: prepositions (2)

1 Focus students' attention on the article. Read the introduction (the first column) with the class and then give them time to decide individually on their answers to the questions. They should compare answers with a partner.

2 Pairwork. Students work together to complete the horoscopes with appropriate prepositions. If they are having trouble, remind them of the work on prepositions that they did on page 19. You could also point out that a lot of the prepositions they will need are used in the questions. When they have finished, they look at their own particular horoscopes and decide if the description is accurate. Encourage them to report back to the class. Remind students about the section on *Prepositions of place* on page 109.

1	in
2	in
3	in
4	on
5	by / near
6	in
7	near
8	in
9	in
10	in
11	in
12	by / near
13	by / next to / near
14	in
15	in
16	on
17	in
18	by / next to
19	in
20	on
21	in
22	near / next to

3 Groupwork. In small groups, students discuss the questions and report back to the class. You may want to appoint a secretary in each group to make notes of the discussion for reporting back.

Anecdote (p 21)

See the Introduction on page 4 for more ideas on how to set up, monitor and repeat Anecdotes.

1 29 SB p 120
Go through the instructions with the class and get them thinking about their own homes. Then play the recording for them to listen to and read the statements and questions. Pause the recording after each one and allow plenty of time for them to think about their answers.

> **29**
> *Think about your home.*
>
> *You are walking to your home. Are you in the city or the country?*
>
> *You are in front of your home. Is it a house or a flat? Is it old or modern?*
>
> *What colour is the front door? Is there a number on it? What is the number?*
>
> *You open the door and go inside. What can you see?*
>
> *You go into the kitchen. Is it light or dark? What is there in the kitchen?*
>
> *You go into the living room. Is it big or small? What furniture is there?*

> *Now you go into your bedroom. Is it tidy? What furniture is there?*
>
> *You open the window and look out. What can you see from your window?*

2 Tell students that they are going to tell a partner about their home and they should take a few minutes to think about what they are going to say and how to say it. Remind them that the questions in Exercise 1 are there to help them.

3 Pairwork. Students tell each other about their homes.

The best in the world (p 21)

Books closed. Whole class. Write the words *The best in the world* on the board. Then invite one student to choose a category such as *football team, pop singer, tennis player*, etc. and another to say who or what is the best in the world in that category.

Reading (p 21)

1 Pairwork. Focus attention on the photos and go through the words in the box. You may need to explain *ruin* (the parts of a building that remain after it has been severely damaged by a natural disaster, war or years of neglect). Elicit the best description for each of the photos.

> a) The best ruin
> b) The best palace
> c) The best mountain

2 Give students time to read the descriptions and match them to the photos. They should compare their answers in pairs or small groups before you check with the class. Find out if they agree with the selection or if they think some other ruin, palace or mountain is the best in the world.

Note: For more information on Baalbek, log on to: *www.whc.unesco.org* and click on *World Heritage*.
For more information on the Forbidden City log on to: *www.travelchinaguide.com*
And for information on Kilimanjaro log on to: *www.tanzania-web.com*

> 1 c   2 a   3 b

3 Pairwork. Students talk about the best places in their countries. With multinational groups, it would be a good idea to have students of different nationalities working together. Encourage them to report back to the class.

Writing (p 21)

Pairwork: Student A & B Students turn to their respective pages and follow the instructions. Each has a postcard which they have to rewrite, changing it from positive to negative, or vice versa. Check answers with the class.

Test

Scoring: one point per correct answer unless otherwise indicated.

1
1 are there
2 There are
3 Are there
4 there is
5 Is there
6 there isn't

2 1 any   2 some   3 any   4 any

3 (½ point per correct answer)
1 bedroom
2 bathroom
3 kitchen
4 kitchen
5 kitchen
6 bathroom
7 bedroom
8 kitchen

4
1 curtains
2 carpet
3 cupboard
4 fireplace
5 shelves
6 sofa

5
1 on
2 in
3 next to
4 on
5 on
6 under

6
1 on
2 in
3 by / next to / near
4 in / near
5 in / near
6 on
7 near
8 by / next to / near

7
1 unfriendly
2 dirty
3 dry
4 wonderful
5 expensive
6 happy

4 Living Test

Name: _____   Total: _____ /40

---

1 there is / there are *6 points*

Complete the dialogue with the correct form of *there is* or *there are*.

A: How many students (1) _____ in your class?

B: (2) _____ fifteen of us, I think.

A: (3) _____ any students from Japan?

B: Yes, (4) _____ one from Japan. His name is Hiro.

A: (5) _____ a computer in the classroom?

B: No, (6) _____ .

2 some & any *4 points*

Complete the dialogue with *some* or *any*.

A: I'm having a coffee. Is there (1) _____ milk?

B: Yes, I think there is (2) _____ in the fridge.

A: And is there (3) _____ sugar?

B: No, there isn't (4) _____ . Sorry.

3 Vocabulary – rooms & furniture (1) *4 points*

In which room do you see these items? Write *bedroom*, *bathroom* or *kitchen*.

1 bed _____
2 bath _____
3 cooker _____
4 dishwasher _____
5 fridge _____
6 shower _____
7 wardrobe _____
8 washing machine _____

4 Vocabulary – rooms & furniture (2) *6 points*

Add the missing vowels (*a, e, i, o, u*) to complete these words.

1 c _ rt _ _ ns
2 c _ rp _ t
3 c _ pb _ _ rd
4 f _ r _ pl _ c _
5 sh _ lv _ s
6 s _ f _

5 Vocabulary – prepositions of place (1) *6 points*

Choose the correct preposition.

In my bedroom, there is …

1 a large rug **on / in** the floor.
2 a television **on / in** the corner.
3 a small table **above / next to** the bed.
4 a lamp **on / in** the table.
5 a mirror **on / in** the wall.
6 a lot of old toys **above / under** the bed.

6 Vocabulary – prepositions of place (2) *8 points*

Complete the sentences with the correct preposition. Choose from *in*, *on*, *by*, *next to* or *near*.

I want to live …

1 _____ an island.
2 _____ a big house.
3 _____ the sea.
4 _____ the city.
5 _____ the mountains.
6 _____ the top floor of a block of flats.
7 _____ some shops.
8 _____ a lake.

7 Vocabulary – positive & negative adjectives *6 points*

Complete the table with the opposite adjectives.

Positive adjective	Negative adjective
warm	cold
friendly	1 _____
clean	2 _____
3 _____	wet
4 _____	awful
cheap	5 _____
6 _____	miserable

5 Review 1 Teacher's notes

Destinations (p 22)

there is / there are

1 🎧 30 SB p 120

Focus attention on the photos and give students a minute or two to look at them and absorb the content. Then play the recording. Ask which hotel the people are talking about. If necessary, play the recording again. Elicit which details they heard helped them decide.

> They are talking about picture a.

> 🎧 30
> (R = Receptionist; C = Client)
>
> R: Good afternoon. Palm Beach Hotel.
> C: Hello. I'd like to book a room, with a beautiful view.
> R: All our rooms have beautiful views, madam. The hotel is on the beach. There are palm trees and wonderful beaches and little fishing boats ...
> C: Oh, oh, that's nice, but ...
> R: There's the sun and the sea ...
> C: Oh good, good. But are there any shops near the hotel?
> R: There aren't any clouds in the clear blue sky ...
> C: Um, are there any restaurants or clubs?
> R: Restaurants or clubs? Er ... no, madam, there aren't. At the Palm Beach Hotel there are palm trees and wonderful beaches and little fishing ...
> C: Okay, thank you. Goodbye.

2 Pairwork. Students work together to write similar conversations about one of the other hotels in the photos. Go round, making sure they are using the phrases in the box correctly.

3 Pairwork. Students describe the location of their favourite hotels to each other. If they have no experience of hotels, they could describe their ideal hotel or holiday destination.

Word stress (p 22)

1 Remind students that they have met all these words before in Units 1 to 4. You might like to ask them to try to remember the context in which they met each one. When they are deciding which column to put them in, encourage them to say the words aloud so that they get a feel for what sounds right. Allow them to compare answers with a partner, but do not check answers at this stage.

2 🎧 31 SB p 120

Play the recording for students to check their answers. Then play it again for them to repeat the words.

> A ■ ▪   B ■ ▪ ▪   C ▪ ■ ▪
> <u>cho</u>colate   <u>in</u>teresting   de<u>ci</u>sion
> <u>dif</u>ferent   <u>mi</u>serable   de<u>li</u>cious
> <u>eve</u>ning   <u>res</u>taurant   me<u>cha</u>nic
> <u>lis</u>tening   <u>sec</u>retary   re<u>cep</u>tion
> <u>Wed</u>nesday   <u>ve</u>getable   re<u>la</u>tion

> 🎧 31
> A: chocolate, different, evening, listening, Wednesday
> B: interesting, miserable, restaurant, secretary, vegetable
> C: decision, delicious, mechanic, reception, relation

in, on, at & adverbs of frequency (p 22)

1 Remind students of the work they did on prepositions of time and adverbs of frequency in Unit 3. Give them a few minutes to complete the sentences and compare with a partner before checking answers with the class.

> a) in
> b) at
> c) on
> d) at
> e) on
> f) in
> g) in

2 Students work individually to add the adverbs of frequency to the sentences, making them true for themselves. They then compare with a partner.

Pronouns, possessive adjectives & like + -ing (p 23)

1 Students complete the table. Allow them to compare answers with a partner before checking with the class. You might like to refresh their memories about how these pronouns are used by eliciting some example sentences containing them (see Unit 1). This will give students some preparation for the next exercise.

> Object pronouns: me, you, him, her, it, us, them
> Possessive adjectives: my, your, his, her, its, our, their

2 Go through the instructions with the class, then ask them to complete the letter with the appropriate pronouns. You could allow them to do this in pairs, if you wish.

Explain that a homestay family (or a host family) is a family that provides accommodation and meals in their home for students who are studying outside their own country.

Check answers with the class. Rather than just calling out the numbers and getting one-word answers from the students, encourage them to read the whole sentence, including the answer, so they get to hear the preposition in context.

> 1 your
> 2 your
> 3 our
> 4 My
> 5 my
> 6 his
> 7 it
> 8 him
> 9 her
> 10 her
> 11 them
> 12 you

3 This exercise could be set for homework. Remind students that they can use the letter in Exercise 2 as a model but they should insert details of their own families.

Collocation (p 23)

You may like to explain the word *collocation* to the class. In English some words frequently appear in combination with other words. These are known as collocations. So, for example, we always say ***make*** *a phone call*, not ***do*** *a phone call*.

1 When checking answers, make sure students say the whole collocation so that they get used to hearing these words in combination.

> make: international phone calls; difficult decisions; dinner for the family
> do: the washing up; the ironing
> go: swimming; sailing; for a drink after class
> have: breakfast in bed; a nap after lunch

2 Pairwork. This exercise allows students to use the collocations in context. This should make it easier to remember them. Make sure students take turns to ask and answer the questions. Remind them that they can use adverbs of frequency in their answers.

The interview (p 24)

1 📼 32 SB p 120

Go through the instructions carefully and give students a few minutes to look closely at the picture and absorb the details before you play the recording. Elicit what kind of room this is (*an office*). Students listen and put a tick in the box next to each object if its location is described accurately, and a cross if it is wrong. Allow them to compare answers in pairs before checking with the class.

> a) ✘ b) ✔ c) ✔ d) ✘ e) ✘ f) ✔

> 📼 32
> a) There's a clock next to the radiator.
> b) There's a mirror on the wall above the bookcase.
> c) There are some photos on the bookcase.
> d) There's a lamp in the corner.
> e) There are some flowers under the desk.
> f) There's a rug on the floor.

2 Pairwork. Students work together to complete the tasks. Give them plenty of time for this. Allow them to compare their answers with other pairs before checking with the class.

> a)
> a) There's a clock next to the window.
> d) There's a lamp on the desk.
> e) There are some flowers on the desk.
>
> b)
> 1 There's a plant in the corner.
> 2 There are some pictures on the wall.
> 3 There's a radiator under the window.
> 4 There's a telephone on the desk.
> 5 There's a calculator on the desk.
> 6 There are some pens on the desk.

3 Pairwork. Allow pairs to compare their questions with other pairs, but do not check answers at this stage.

4 📼 33 SB p 120

Play the recording for students to check their answers to Exercise 3.

> **📼 33**
> a) *What's your name?*
> b) *Have you got any children?*
> c) *Do you like watching football?*
> d) *Where do you live?*
> e) *Are you married?*
> f) *Why do you want to work here?*

5 Pairwork. Go through the instructions and then allow students a few minutes to work together to decide on the best order for the questions. In a class feedback session, find out how many pairs agreed on the same order.

6 📼 **34 SB p 25**

Play the recording and ask students to make a note of the order in which the questions are asked. They should then compare with the order they decided on in Exercise 5. Elicit what the confusion is between Mr Fenn and Mrs Kane, playing the recording again if necessary.

> Question order in the sketch:
> a) What's your name?
> d) Where do you live?
> c) Do you like watching football?
> e) Are you married?
> b) Have you got any children?
> f) Why do you want to work here?
>
> Mr Fenn thinks Mrs Kane is there for an interview.

7 Pairwork. Go through the instructions with the class and tell them that the script for the sketch is on page 25. Allow plenty of time for rehearsal and for the performances. If students enjoy drama and would like to perform the sketch with costumes and props, allow time in a subsequent lesson for them to do this.

Test

Scoring: one point per correct answer unless otherwise indicated.

1
1. your
2. him
3. her
4. its
5. us
6. their

2 (½ point per correct answer)
1. Are, 'm not
2. Have, have
3. Do, do
4. Has, hasn't
5. Is, is
6. Does, doesn't
7. Does, does
8. Do, do

3 (2 points per correct answer)
1. What's your name?
2. Where do you live?
3. What do you do?
4. Are you married?
5. What's your wife's name?
6. What does she / your wife do?
7. Have you got any children?
8. What are your hobbies?

4
1. I often watch television in the evening.
2. I usually read the newspaper every day.
3. I always go to the gym twice a week.
4. I am never bored.

5
1. Is there
2. there are
3. is there
4. there isn't

6
1. some
2. any
3. any
4. some

7
1. read
2. make
3. listen to
4. go
5. make
6. have
7. do
8. have

Visit www.insideout.net   Review 1 UNIT 5 43

8 1 French
   2 Japanese
   3 Argentinian
   4 British
   5 Italian
   6 Polish

9 1 on
   2 in
   3 in
   4 at
   5 at
   6 in
   7 at
   8 on

10 1 in
   2 on
   3 in
   4 in
   5 on
   6 in

11 (½ point per correct answer)

1 to 5: black, blue, grey, red, yellow

6 to 10: aunt, brother, cousin, daughter, nephew

11 to 15: engineer, mechanic, nurse, secretary, student

16 to 20: cupboard, dishwasher, fridge, shelves, wardrobe

5 Review 1 Test

Name: _____ Total: _____ /80

1 Personal pronouns & possessive adjectives 6 points
Complete the table.

Subject pronoun	Object pronoun	Possessive adjective
I	me	my
you	you	1 _____
he	2 _____	his
she	her	3 _____
it	it	4 _____
we	5 _____	our
they	them	6 _____

2 Questions & short answers 8 points
Complete the questions and short answers with the correct form of *be*, *have* or *do*.

1 '_____ you married?'
   'No, I _____ .'

2 '_____ you got a boyfriend?'
   'Yes, I _____ .'

3 '_____ you live with your boyfriend?'
   'Yes, I _____ .'

4 '_____ your boyfriend got a job?'
   'No, he _____ .'

5 '_____ he a student?'
   'Yes, he _____ .'

6 '_____ he study at university?'
   'No, he _____ .'

7 '_____ he study at an English School?'
   'Yes, he _____ .'

8 '_____ you speak English at home?'
   'Yes, we _____ .'

3 Questions 16 points
Read the answers and write the questions.

1 What _____ ?
   My name's Sven.

2 Where _____ ?
   I live in Stockholm in Sweden.

3 _____ ?
   I'm a doctor.

4 _____ ?
   Yes, I am. I'm married to a Swedish woman.

5 _____ ?
   My wife's name is Ulrika.

6 _____ ?
   She's an accountant.

7 _____ ?
   Yes, we've got two boys and a girl.

8 _____ ?
   My hobbies are going to the gym and tennis.

4 Adverbs of frequency 4 points
Reorder the words to make complete sentences.

1 often / I / in the evening / television / watch
   _____
   _____ .

2 read / I / the newspaper / usually / every day
   _____
   _____ .

3 twice a week / go / I / always / to the gym
   _____
   _____ .

4 never / bored / am / I
   _____
   _____ .

© Sue Kay & Vaughan Jones, 2003. Published by Macmillan Publishers Limited. This sheet may be photocopied and used within the class.

Photocopiable 45

5 there is / there are 4 points

Complete the sentences with the correct form of *there is* or *there are*.

1 _____ a café near here?
2 Yes, _____ two on this road.
3 And _____ a supermarket near here?
4 No, _____, I'm afraid.

6 some & any 4 points

Complete the dialogue with *some* or *any*.

A: We need (1) _____ milk, but I haven't got (2) _____ money. Have you?
B: No, I haven't got (3) _____ . Sorry.
A: Oh, I remember – there's (4) _____ on the table.

7 Verb collocations 8 points

Complete the sentences with the correct verb.

do go have have listen to make make read

1 I _____ the newspaper every day.
2 I need to _____ an important decision today.
3 I _____ the radio when I drive to work.
4 My wife and I _____ for a walk every Sunday.
5 I need to _____ a phone call.
6 I love to _____ breakfast in bed at the weekend.
7 I always _____ the washing up in our house.
8 We usually _____ lunch at one o'clock.

8 Countries & nationalities 6 points

Complete the sentences with the correct nationality.

1 I come from France. I'm _____ .
2 I was born in Japan. I'm _____ .
3 He's from Argentina. He's _____ .
4 I was born in the United Kingdom. I'm _____ .
5 They're from Rome, in Italy. They're _____ .
6 She's from Poland. She's _____ .

9 Prepositions of time 8 points

Add the correct preposition: *in*, *at* or *on*.

1 _____ Friday
2 _____ winter
3 _____ August
4 _____ 6.30
5 _____ the weekend
6 _____ 2004
7 _____ Christmas
8 _____ 21st September

10 Prepositions of place 6 points

Choose the correct preposition.

1 They live **at / in** a big house.
2 There's a lovely picture **in / on** the wall.
3 We love to walk **in / on** the mountains.
4 They live **at / in** the city centre.
5 Put the flowers **on / to** the table.
6 The bed is **at / in** the corner of the room.

11 Vocabulary – colours, family, jobs & things at home 10 points

Complete the table with the items in the box.

aunt black blue brother cousin cupboard daughter dishwasher engineer fridge grey mechanic nephew nurse red secretary shelves student wardrobe yellow

colours	family
1 _____	6 _____
2 _____	7 _____
3 _____	8 _____
4 _____	9 _____
5 _____	10 _____

jobs	things at home
11 _____	16 _____
12 _____	17 _____
13 _____	18 _____
14 _____	19 _____
15 _____	20 _____

6 Food Overview

In this unit, the topic of food is used to introduce the concept of countable and uncountable nouns and the structures associated with them.

Students begin by matching food items to food groups, thus learning some useful food-related vocabulary and preparing for the reading text in the second section, which is about combination diets. They also do some pronunciation practice and identify differences in vowel sounds.

The text on combination diets in the second section provides an opportunity for students to use the food vocabulary they have learned and leads into work on countable and uncountable nouns. They begin by identifying nouns as either countable or uncountable and then ask and answer questions about them.

The next section gives some entertaining information about the dressing room demands made by three famous singers. It gives an opportunity for students to look at vocabulary for different types of container and leads into work on talking about quantities in relation to countable and uncountable nouns.

In the final section, students complete a dialogue in a shop with *would* and practise using *would* to make requests and to offer choices.

Section	Aims	What the students are doing
Introduction page 26	*Lexis*: food	Matching pictures with words for food items and putting them in food categories.
		Talking about the food items students eat and how often they eat them.
	Pronunciation: vowel sounds	Identifying words with a different vowel sound from others in a list.
Food combining page 27	*Reading skills*: reading for specific information	Reading an article about a special diet and identifying the rules.
	Listening skills: listening to check	Listening to two people discussing the diet.
Close up page 27	*Grammar*: countable and uncountable nouns	Completing a table with food items according to whether they are countable or uncountable.
		Completing questions about food items.
	Conversation skills: fluency work	Asking and answering questions about food.
Divas page 28	*Lexis*: containers	Completing a table of the dressing room demands of famous singers.
		Talking about the demands the singers make.
		Matching containers with appropriate food items.
Close up pages 28–29	*Grammar*: quantity	Studying the use of *much, many, a lot*, etc. to talk about quantity.
		Asking and answering questions about the contents of students' fridges.
		Asking and answering questions about things you do in a normal day. **Pairwork: Student A & B**
Choices page 29	*Lexis*: would like	Reading and listening to a conversation in a shop.
		Completing the conversation with *would like*.
		Matching requests with situations.
	Writing: a conversation	Writing a conversation for a chosen situation.

> **More information about topics in this unit**
>
> **Divas, Lexis: containers 2** *www.monarc.com/mariahcarey*
> *www.p-diddy.com*   *www.jenniferlopez.com*

6 Food Teacher's notes

Books closed. Whole class. To activate the students' knowledge of food vocabulary, you could start by playing *Every day for lunch I have ...* . You start by naming a food item, such as *Every day for lunch I have pasta*. A student then has to repeat your sentence and add a food item of their own, eg: *Every day for lunch I have pasta and salad*. The next student adds a third food item, and so on. If students do not have enough vocabulary to do this, you could brainstorm some food items to begin with. When you have finished the unit, you could play the game again to see how many of the food items they have encountered during the unit the students can remember.

Lexis: food (p 26)

1   Pairwork. Students look at the pictures, match each one with a list and choose a title for each list. They should find it relatively easy to match up fruit and vegetables. Check that they understand the meaning of carbohydrates and proteins, perhaps by asking them to suggest another item for each of these lists. You may like to draw students' attention to the section on *Fruit* on page 109 and the section on *Vegetables* on page 110.

> a) List 3: Fruit
> b) List 4: Carbohydrates
> c) List 2: Vegetables
> d) List 1: Proteins

2   Pairwork. Students add the words in the box to the lists in Exercise 1. When you have checked answers, if you have not already asked students to suggest one more item of their own for each list, you could do so now.

> 1 Proteins: meat, chicken, eggs, seafood, cheese, fish
> 2 Vegetables: carrots, beans, peppers, a cauliflower, garlic, onions, mushrooms, olive oil, tomatoes
> 3 Fruit: apples, bananas, oranges, a melon, a lemon, strawberries, grapes, pears
> 4 Carbohydrates: bread, cereals, potatoes, rice, pasta, cakes

(Technically tomatoes are fruit, but most people regard them as vegetables. Olives are also sometimes thought of as fruit.) Point out to students that the plural of *fish* is *fish*.

3   Students work individually to choose the items from the lists that they often, sometimes and never or hardly ever eat. When they have compared answers with a partner, find out how much consensus there is in the class.

Vowel sounds (p 26)

1   Encourage students to read all the words aloud so that they get a feel for what sounds right and can more easily identify the words with the different vowel sounds. They can check their answers by listening to the recording in the next exercise.

2   35 SB p 26
Play the recording for students to check their answers. Then play it again for them to repeat the words.

> a) bread
> b) cereal
> c) potato
> d) pear
> e) onion
> f) garlic

Food combining (p 27)

Books closed. Small groups. Tell the class that in the next section they will read a text about a diet in which you have to eat certain foods in combination and avoid other combinations. For a bit of fun, ask them to think up a menu with the most disgusting combinations of food they can think of, eg: chocolate-covered fish and chips in a curry sauce. They should think of a starter, a main course and a dessert. The class can then vote on the most revolting menu.

Reading & listening (p 27)

1   Give students plenty of time to read the article. Give help with difficult vocabulary, such as *calories*, *digest*, *clinical research*. When they have finished reading, ask them to complete the sentences and check answers with the class.

> a) carbohydrates
> b) proteins
> c) fruit
> d) vegetables or salads

2   Pairwork. Remind students of the food categories they studied at the beginning of the unit. If they have difficulty, go through the food items in *a–e* individually and elicit which food category each should go in (note that chips are made of potatoes but go in the carbohydrate category rather than vegetables). They should then be able to make their decision about which meal is best according to the article. They can check their answers in the next exercise.

3 🔊 **36 SB p 120**

Play the recording for students to listen and check their answers to Exercise 2. Then elicit suggestions as to what the 'seafood diet' is.

> d) Fish and vegetables
> The seafood diet is 'when you see food, you eat it'.

> 🔊 **36**
> (A = Alan; K = Kathryn)
>
> A: I want to lose weight but I love my food. How do you stay so slim?
> K: I follow the food combining rules.
> A: Food combining? What's that?
> K: Well, for example, I never eat protein and carbohydrates together.
> A: What? Do you mean you never eat steak and chips?
> K: No, because steak is protein and chips are carbohydrates.
> A: Oh. What about fish and rice. That's healthy.
> K: No, fish is protein and rice is carbohydrate. Fish and vegetables is okay.
> A: Well, how about my favourite meal – spaghetti bolognese with fruit salad for dessert.
> K: No, sorry. There's meat in bolognese and spaghetti is carbohydrate. And you can't eat fruit as a dessert.
> A: Oh dear. I don't like this. My favourite diet is the seafood diet.
> K: Oh, what's that?
> A: When you see food, you eat it.
> K & A: Ha ha ha.

Follow-up activity

Pairwork. Students use the food combining rules to complete the following task.

a) Write one menu for a healthy day.

b) Write one menu for an unhealthy day.

c) Exchange your menus with another pair and decide which menu is healthy and which is unhealthy.

d) Decide which menu you like best. What do you think about the food-combining diet?

4 **Pairwork: Additional material** Ask students to turn to page 94 and follow the instructions. When they have compared information with a partner, they could report back to the class and find out how much agreement there is over the various categories.

Close up (p 27)

Nouns: countable/uncountable

1 Pairwork. Students look back at the photos on page 26 and complete the table. Draw their attention to the different categories of noun and demonstrate that you can count items such as melons, peppers, etc. but that you can't count liquids, such as olive oil, or foods, such as rice and pasta, which are regarded as a whole rather than as individual grains or pieces. Point out the use of *some* rather than *a* or *an* with uncountable nouns. Check answers with the class. Note: Although *onion* is countable, *garlic* is uncountable. Point out that *fish* can be both countable and uncountable. There is more information on countable and uncountable nouns in the Language reference section on page 29.

> *Example answers*
>
> There's a melon.
> There's a lemon.
> There's a red pepper.
> There are two bananas.
> There are three tomatoes.
> There are four pears.
> There's some bread.
> There's some rice.
> There's some cheese.

2 Pairwork. Students work together to complete the questions and write two possible answers for each one. Go through the examples first with the class. Check answers with the class.

3 🔊 **37 SB p 121**

Play the recording for students to listen, check and repeat. Students then work in pairs to ask and answer the questions in Exercise 2 with reference to the photos on page 26. Make sure they take turns to ask and answer the questions. They can then make up further questions of their own about the photos.

> a) Are; Yes, there are. No, there aren't.
> b) Is; Yes, there is. No, there isn't.
> c) Is; Yes, there is. No, there isn't.
> d) Is; Yes, there is. No, there isn't
> e) Are; Yes, there are. No, there aren't.
> f) Is; Yes, there is. No, there isn't.

37

a)
'Are there any mushrooms in picture C?'
'Yes, there are.'
'No, there aren't.'

b)
'Is there any cheese in picture A?'
'Yes, there is.'
'No, there isn't.'

c)
'Is there a cauliflower in picture C?'
'Yes, there is.'
'No, there isn't.'

d)
'Is there any pasta in picture B?'
'Yes, there is.'
'No, there isn't.'

e)
'Are there any bananas in picture A?'
'Yes, there are.'
'No, there aren't.'

f)
'Is there any bread in picture D?'
'Yes, there is.'
'No, there isn't.'

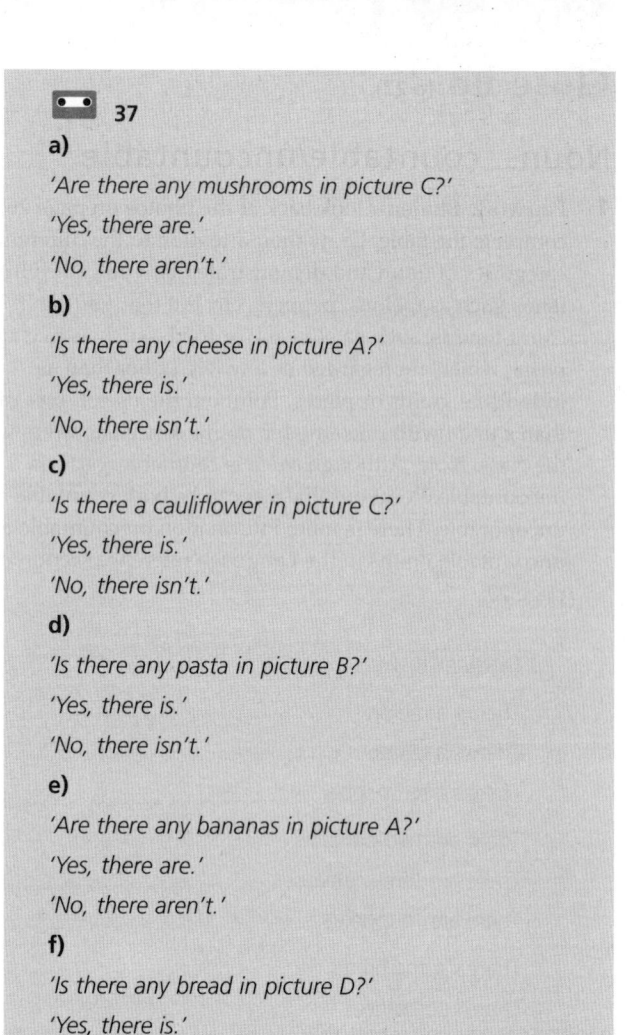

Divas (p 28)

You may like to explain to the class that the use of the word *diva* in English traditionally refers to a famous singer (usually a female opera singer, eg: Maria Callas). The word is used here to include pop singers, including a man. Divas have a reputation for being temperamental and for making outrageous demands.

Lexis: containers (p 28)

1 Focus attention on the singers in the photos. Find out if the students have heard their music and whether or not they like it. Go through the instructions with the class and the words for containers in the box. Then put students in pairs to complete the lists and match each list to one of the singers. Go round offering help and encouragement, but do not check answers at this stage. Draw students' attention to the section on *Containers* on page 109.

2 38 SB p 121
Play the recording for students to listen and check their answers to Exercise 1. Point out the use of *bar* with soap (*bar* can also be used for chocolate). You may also like to point out that different countries may package things differently, so whereas *cartons* of fruit juice are normal in the UK, elsewhere *bottles* may be more appropriate. Finally, have a class vote on which singer they think makes the strangest demands.

Note: If students are interested, they can find more information on Mariah Carey, P Diddy and Jennifer Lopez on the following websites: *www.monarc.com/mariahcarey* *www.p-diddy.com* and *www.jenniferlopez.com*

A (Jennifer Lopez)
a vase of
a bottle of
a packet of

B (P Diddy)
4 cartons of
12 bottles of
2 bottles of
2 bottles of
20 bars of

C (Mariah Carey)
2 bottles of
a bowl of
12 bottles of

38

Okay, let's see now. What do we need for P Diddy's dressing room? Ummm ... Four cartons of fruit juice, twelve bottles of mineral water ... Okay. Two bottles of Cristal champagne and two bottles of white wine ... Right. Twenty bars of soap and ninety-six hand towels ... Yep, all there ...

Now how about Jennifer Lopez? Er ... A white room with white furniture ... Yeah, that's okay. Some white candles, a vase of white flowers and a bottle of Evian water ... No problem. Some vanilla ice-cream and a packet of chocolate biscuits ... Yep, fine.

And last but not least, Mariah Carey ... Pink toilet paper ... Okay. Two bottles of Cristal champagne, a bowl of fresh fruit and twelve bottles of Poland spring water .... 'Poland' spring water?! All right ... Some little trees with lights on? And what's this ... kittens and puppies to play with!!! ... Whatever next!

3 Pairwork. Students discuss the items and assign containers to them. Allow them to compare answers with another pair before you check answers with the class.

a) a can of
b) a box of
c) a tub of
d) a packet of
e) a jar of
f) a tin of

4 Groupwork. In small groups, students make their lists of dressing room demands. Go round offering help and encouragement. You might want to put the following on the board to give them some ideas:

- Your favourite cold drink. (How many bottles or cans?)
- Your favourite snacks. (How many packets?)
- Your favourite flavour of ice-cream. (How many tubs?)
- Your favourite fruit. (How much fruit? What kind?)
- Your favourite decoration. (Furniture, plants, flowers?)
- Your favourite entertainment. (Videos, DVDs, computer games ...)
- Towels. (How many? What colour?)

In a class feedback session, decide which group made the most outrageous demands.

Close up (p 28)

Quantity

1 Establish that *much* is used in questions about uncountable nouns and *many* in questions about countable nouns. Refer students to the Language reference section on page 29 for more information on talking about quantity.

> You use *many* with countable nouns.
> You use *much* with uncountable nouns.

2 Pairwork. Draw attention to the symbols at the top of the table and establish that ●●●●●● means a big quantity, ●●● means only a small quantity and ○ means none at all. Elicit from the students that milk and cheese are uncountable and tomatoes and peppers are countable. Go through the examples, pointing out that we use *a lot* for affirmative statements about a large quantity for both countable and uncountable nouns and *not much/not many* for negative statements about a small quantity. If we have none at all of the item in question, we use *not any* for both countable and uncountable nouns.

Students then work together to complete the table. Allow them to compare their results with other pairs before checking answers with the class.

> a) much; a lot; much; any
> b) many; a lot; many; any
> c) much; a lot; much; any
> d) many; a lot; many; any

3 39 SB p 121

Play the recording once for students to check their answers again. Then play it a second time for them to repeat. Then students work in pairs to ask and answer questions about the contents of their fridges, adding three more questions of their own.

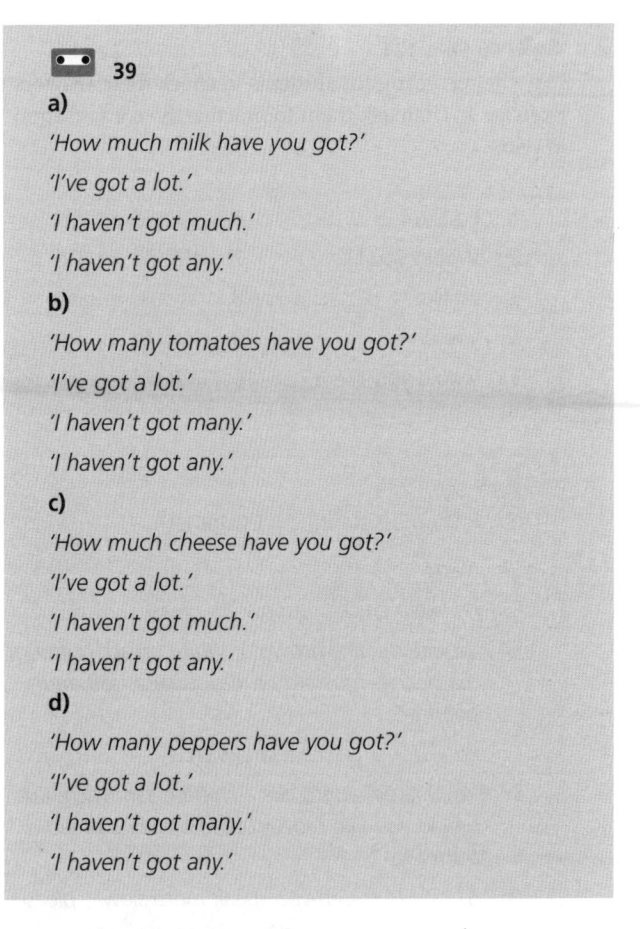

39

a)
'How much milk have you got?'
'I've got a lot.'
'I haven't got much.'
'I haven't got any.'

b)
'How many tomatoes have you got?'
'I've got a lot.'
'I haven't got many.'
'I haven't got any.'

c)
'How much cheese have you got?'
'I've got a lot.'
'I haven't got much.'
'I haven't got any.'

d)
'How many peppers have you got?'
'I've got a lot.'
'I haven't got many.'
'I haven't got any.'

4 **Pairwork: Student A & B** Students turn to their respective pages and follow the instructions. This activity gives more practice in asking and answering questions with *much* and *many*.

> Student A: all answers are *much*.
> Student B: all answers are *many*.

Choices (p 29)

This next section is about the use of *would* for making requests and asking about people's requirements. You might like to introduce the structure by telling the class something that you would like, eg: *I'd like a new sports car*. Encourage a student to say something that they would like, eg: *I'd like a holiday*. Follow this up with a question, such as *Would you like a holiday abroad or in your own country?* Then encourage other students to make statements and ask follow-up questions about them.

Lexis: *would like* (p 29)

1 Focus attention on the illustration and elicit that the conversation takes place in a café or sandwich shop. In pairs, students try to complete the gaps in the conversation using the words in the box. Draw their attention to the examples (1 and 2) which demonstrate the use of *would* for making requests (*I would like/I'd like*) and asking about what someone wants (*Would you like*). Point out that each space in the conversation requires three words. Allow pairs to compare their results with other pairs, but do not check answers at this stage.

2 ▭ **40 SB p 121**

Play the recording for students to check their answers to Exercise 1. Then ask them to practise the conversation in pairs.

1	I'd like	6	Would you like
2	Would you like	7	Would you like
3	I'd like	8	Would you like
4	you'd like	9	Would you like
5	would you like	10	Would you like

▭ **40**

(SA = Shop assistant; C = Customer)

SA: *Next!*
C: *I'd like a chicken sandwich, please.*
SA: *Would you like brown or white bread, butter or margarine, mustard or mayonnaise, salt and pepper?*
C: *I'd like ... a chicken sandwich.*
SA: *Yes, I know you'd like a chicken sandwich. But would you like brown bread or white bread, butter ...*
C: *STOP, STOP. Can you speak more slowly, please?*
SA: *Would you like white or brown bread?*
C: *Er ... brown bread, please.*
SA: *Would you like butter or margarine?*
C: *Butter.*
SA: *Would you like mustard or mayonnaise?*
C: *Mayonnaise.*
SA: *Would you like salt and pepper?*
C: *No, thank you.*
SA: *Would you like anything to drink?*
C: *Anything to drink? What is 'anything to drink'?*
SA: *Coke, orange juice, water ...*
C: *Ah, drink, drink – coke, orange juice, water. Yes, yes, I understand. No.*
SA: *That's two dollars. ... Next!*

3 Pairwork. Students work together to match the choices in column A with the situations in which those choices might be offered in column B. Check answers with the class.

a) 2 b) 5 c) 4 d) 3 e) 1

4 Pairwork. Students choose one of the situations in Exercise 3 and write a conversation, using the one in Exercise 1 as a model. Remind them to use the choices in column A in Exercise 3. Give them plenty of time to prepare their conversations and to perform them for the rest of the class.

Test

Scoring: one point per correct answer unless otherwise indicated.

1 (½ point per correct answer)
1 to 3: *lemon, melon, pear*
4 to 6: *mushroom, onion, pepper*
7 to 9: *cheese, eggs, seafood*
10 to 12: *cereals, pasta, rice*

2 1 c 2 e 3 a 4 b 5 f 6 d

3
1 beans
2 milk
3 chocolate
4 ice-cream
5 chocolates
6 fruit
7 coffee
8 flowers

4 (½ point per correct answer)
1 U 2 C 3 U 4 C 5 U 6 U

5
1 many
2 many / a lot
3 much
4 any
5 many / a lot
6 a lot
7 much
8 much

6 (1 point for each sentence; 1 point for each match)
1 We'd like a bottle of water, please.
2 I'd like a coffee, please.
3 I'd like to book a room.
4 Would you like a single or a double?
5 Would you like still or sparkling?
6 Would you like black or white?
1 – 5   2 – 6   3 – 4

6 Food Test

Name: _____   Total: _____ /40

---

1 Vocabulary – food *6 points*
Complete the table with the words in the box.

| cereals cheese eggs lemon melon mushroom |
| onion pasta pear pepper rice seafood |

fruit	vegetables	proteins	carbohydrates
apple	carrot	meat	bread
banana	beans	fish	potato
1 _____	4 _____	7 _____	10 _____
2 _____	5 _____	8 _____	11 _____
3 _____	6 _____	9 _____	12 _____

2 Pronunciation – vowel sounds *6 points*
Match the foods with the same vowel sound.

1 b<u>ea</u>ns   a) g<u>a</u>rlic
2 p<u>e</u>pper   b) <u>o</u>range
3 tom<u>a</u>to   c) ch<u>ee</u>se
4 c<u>au</u>liflower   d) gr<u>a</u>pes
5 <u>a</u>pple   e) br<u>ea</u>d
6 pot<u>a</u>to   f) c<u>a</u>rrot

3 Vocabulary – containers *8 points*
Complete the sentences with the words in the box.

| beans flowers ice-cream chocolate chocolates |
| milk fruit coffee |

I'd like …

1 a tin of _____ .
2 a carton of _____ .
3 a bar of _____ .
4 a tub of _____ .
5 a box of _____ .
6 a bowl of _____ .
7 a jar of _____ .
8 a vase of _____ .

4 Nouns: countable & uncountable *3 points*
Are the following nouns countable or uncountable? Write *C* or *U*.

1 furniture _____   4 city _____
2 church _____   5 water _____
3 milk _____   6 jewellery _____

5 Quantity: *much, many, a lot & any* *8 points*
Complete the following with *much, many, a lot* or *any*.

A: How (1) _____ DVDs have you got?
B: I haven't got (2) _____ . Just two or three.

*   *   *

C: How (3) _____ money have you got?
D: I haven't got (4) _____ . Not a cent.

*   *   *

E: How (5) _____ countries have you visited?
F: I've visited (6) _____ . More than 20, I think.

*   *   *

G: How (7) _____ wine is there?
H: Not (8) _____ , I'm afraid. Just one glass.

6 *would like* *9 points*
Reorder the words in 1, 2 and 3 to make some requests. Then reorder the words in 4, 5 and 6 to make the responses. Finally, match the requests to the responses.

1 We / please / like / a bottle of water / 'd
_____

2 like / 'd / a coffee / please / I
_____

3 'd / to book a room / I / like
_____

4 Would / like / you / a single or a double ?
_____

5 like / Would / still or sparkling / you ?
_____

6 you / Would / black or white / like ?
_____

7 Work Overview

This unit combines the topics of jobs and personal characteristics. The grammar focus is on the use of *can*, *can't*, *have to* and *don't have to* to talk about possibility and necessity.

The first section introduces students to a variety of words to describe a person's character. They practise saying these with the correct stress patterns, try taking a personality test and then discuss the results.

They then look at how relevant personal characterstics are for particular jobs and read an article about a woman with two very different jobs which require very different characteristics. They discuss whether they would like to have two jobs and, if so, which ones they would choose. This leads into work on talking about possibility and necessity in the context of jobs, and students complete interviews with two filmstars who have very different attitudes to being rich and famous, and the effects it has had on their lives.

In the final section, students have the opportunity to do some extended speaking in an Anecdote about a person they know who has a good job. They then read, correct and complete a job application letter, and then write their own, using this as a model.

Section	Aims	What the students are doing
Introduction page 30	*Lexis*: describing character	Finding adjectives to describe character in a word snake.
		Completing a table with adjectives to describe character. **Pairwork: Student A & B**
		Completing a table according to stress patterns, then listening to check.
		Taking a personality test and discussing the results.
Which job? page 31	*Lexis*: jobs	Matching characteristics with jobs.
		Asking questions to complete a questionnaire about suitability for particular jobs. **Pairwork: Student A & B**
	Reading skills: reading for gist	Looking at vocabulary from a text and categorising it.
		Reading a text and discussing jobs.
Close up page 32	*Grammar: can, can't, have to, don't have to*	Matching jobs with things you *can/can't*, *have to* and *don't have to* do.
		Making true statements about possibility and necessity.
		Completing two interviews with appropriate words.
		Discussing the advantages and disadvantages of being rich and famous.
A good job page 33	*Conversation skills*: fluency work	Anecdote: talking about someone who has a good job.
	Writing: an application letter	Correcting and completing a letter of application for a job.

More information about topics in this unit

Which job?, Reading 2 *www.soulsport.co.uk/charlottedutton*

7 Work Teacher's notes

Books closed. Whole class. Activate student's knowledge of character adjectives by asking each of them to think of an adjective to describe themselves, preferably beginning with the same letter as their first name. Start them off with an example using your own name, eg: *Hello, I'm energetic Eric*. Go round the class, seeing how many adjectives they can think of. If students have little prior knowledge of adjectives, this activity could also be done at the end of the unit to revise the vocabulary they have learned.

Lexis: describing character (p 30)

1 Pairwork. Students look at the word snake and find ten adjectives. Check answers with the class. Draw students' attention to the section on *Words to describe character* on page 110.

> adventurous, ambitious, creative, energetic, hard-working, independent, practical, romantic, serious, sociable

2 41 SB p 121

Ask students to try to complete the table before you play the recording. Encourage them to say the adjectives aloud so that they get a feel for what sounds right. You might like to begin by focusing on the stress patterns at the top of the table and eliciting an example word which follows each pattern (not necessarily an adjective). The number of adjectives which should be put in each column is indicated to help the students.

Play the recording for students to check their answers. Then play it again for them to repeat the words.

> A: practical, serious, sociable
> B: ambitious, creative, hard-working, romantic
> C: adventurous
> D: energetic, independent

> **41**
> A: *practical / serious / sociable*
> B: *ambitious / creative / hard-working / romantic*
> C: *adventurous*
> D: *energetic / independent*

3 **Pairwork: Student A & B** Students turn to their respective pages and follow the instructions. This activity involves pronouncing adjectives with the correct stress and matching them to definitions. Allow plenty of time for this and check answers with the class.

	Words	Definitions
a)	shy	I'm nervous about meeting people.
b)	honest	I always tell the truth. I never lie.
c)	friendly	I'm kind and pleasant to other people.
d)	sensible	I'm never silly. I never do stupid things.
e)	confident	I'm sure about my own ideas and qualities.
f)	easy-going	I'm relaxed. I never worry about anything.
g)	sensitive	I understand other people's feelings.
h)	cheerful	I'm happy and I'm always smiling.
i)	clever	I understand things quickly and easily.
j)	helpful	I like helping people.

4 **Pairwork: Additional material** Establish that a personality test is a test that is supposed to show what kind of person you are. Go through the instructions with the class and then let them choose their pictures and read the results. Encourage them to report back to the class on whether or not they agree with the assessment.

Which job? (p 31)

Books closed. Whole class. Remind students of the work they did on job vocabulary in Unit 2. See how many words for jobs they can remember and perhaps play another game of *What's my job?*

Lexis: jobs (p 31)

1 Pairwork. Students work together to discuss the characteristics listed and to match them to the jobs. Check answers with the class and help students with any difficult vocabulary. Elicit suggestions round the class for further characteristics that would go with each job.

> a) 4 b) 1 c) 6 d) 5 e) 2 f) 3

2 **Pairwork: Student A & B** Students turn to their respective pages and follow the instructions. In this activity, students ask their partners questions about their characteristics and their likes. They use this information to choose an appropriate job for them and discuss their choices. Draw students' attention to the section on *Jobs* on page 110. Go round, offering help and encouragement and have a class feedback session on the results.

Reading (p 31)

1 Pairwork. Focus attention on the title of the article and the two photos of Charlotte Dutton. Elicit from the students what her job is and what type of person they think she is. They then work in pairs to decide which of the words in the box is associated with modeling and which with snowboarding. Do not check answers at this stage.

2 Students read the article and check their answers to Exercise 1. Ask them for their reactions to the text. Would they like to be Charlotte Dutton? Do they think snowboarding is a real job?

Note: Students can find out more about this talented snowboarder and model by logging on to: *www.soulsports.co.uk/charlottedutton*

> Modeling: slim, Paris, designer clothes
> Snowboarding: muscles, freezing, strong, warm baggy clothes, crash helmet

3 Pairwork. Students discuss whether they would like to do two jobs and which jobs they would choose. Encourage them to report back to the class on what they decide.

Close up (p 32)

can, can't, have to, don't have to

You might like to begin by focusing attention on the words in the margin (*can, can't, have to* and *don't have to*) and asking students to find and underline them in the text on page 31. Explain that we use these words to talk about possibility and necessity. Give a few examples of your own, eg: *I can't be late for school. I have to arrive on time every day. I can get up late on Saturdays. I don't have to go to school on Saturdays.* There is more information and help with these structures in the Language reference section at the bottom of the page.

1 Pairwork. Students match the beginnings and endings of the sentences. Check answers with the class.

> a) A snowboarder has to wear a crash helmet.
> b) A DJ doesn't have to get up early in the morning.
> c) A writer can work from home.
> d) A tourist guide has to know a lot of history.
> e) A model can't eat fattening food.
> f) A cook has to have very clean hands.

2 Pairwork. Students discuss the sentences and match them with the correct meanings. They then discuss whether or not the sentences are true for them. Check answers with the class and ask them to report back on their discussions.

> a) 4   b) 2   c) 1   d) 3

3 Pairwork. Students work together to complete the interviews. When they have finished, don't check the answers but ask them to say what the difference is between Cherry and Max's attitudes to being rich and famous. (Cherry hates it because of all the things she can't do; Max loves it because of all the things he can do.)

4 📼 42 SB p 121

Play the recording for students to check their answers to Exercise 3. Then put them in pairs to discuss other advantages and disadvantages of being rich and famous. In a class feedback session find out how many advantages and disadvantages the students could think of.

> Interview A
> 1 have to
> 2 have to
> 3 have to
> 4 have to
> 5 can
> 6 can't
> 7 can't
> 8 can't
> 9 can't
> 10 have to
>
> Interview B
> 1 don't have to
> 2 can
> 3 can
> 4 can
> 5 can
> 6 can

📼 42
Interview A
(I = Interviewer; C = Cherry Tree)

I: Cherry Tree, your new film is a big hit. How do you feel?
C: I feel terrible.
I: Sorry?
C: I feel terrible because I hate being famous. It's boring. I have to go to parties. I have to sign autographs.
I: But you're ...
C: I have to wear make-up all day. I have to kiss Brad Pitt.
I: Oh dear. That's terrible. But you're rich now. You can buy anything you want.
C: Yes, but there are photographers everywhere. I can't walk down the street. I can't go shopping. I can't go clubbing and I can't have a private life.
I: Well, why did you make the film?
C: And I have to answer stupid questions!

> **Interview B**
> (I = Interviewer; M = Max Nova)
>
> I: *Max Nova, can you answer a few questions?*
> M: *Sure, no problem.*
> I: *Your film is a big success. How do you feel?*
> M: *I feel fantastic. I love being rich, and I love being famous!*
> I: *Now that you're rich and famous, is your life very different?*
> M: *Oh yeah, very different. I don't have to worry about money any more. I can buy anything I want. I can buy a new car, I can buy a big house, I can travel first class ... and I can meet some very interesting people.*

A good job (p 33)

Books closed. Whole class. Write the words *A good job* on the board and ask students to brainstorm good jobs. Write up all their suggestions.

Anecdote (p 33)

See the Introduction on page 4 for more ideas on how to set up, monitor and repeat Anecdotes.

1 📼 **43 SB p 121**

Pairwork. Play the recording for students to read and listen to the questions. Then give them time to think about their answers to the questions.

> 📼 **43**
> *Think about someone who has a good job.*
> *What is his or her name?*
> *What does he or she do?*
> *Where does he or she work?*
> *Who does he or she work for?*
> *What time does he or she start and finish work?*
> *How much does he or she earn?*
> *How much does he or she travel?*
> *Would you like this job?*

2 Encourage students to take time to prepare what they are going to say and, if necessary, make some notes, but discourage them from writing out a script.

3 Students take turns to tell each other about the person they have chosen and their job.

Writing (p 33)

1 Give students plenty of time to read the letter and discuss it with a partner. They should decide together which five sentences are not necessary and cross them out. Allow them to compare answers with other pairs before checking with the class.

> Cross out these sentences:
> I don't really want to work, but I need the money.
> Unfortunately I failed some of my exams this year, but I can take them again in the autumn.
> I sometimes get up a bit late, but I'm very nice and friendly.
> I can also count from 1 to 10 in German, Japanese, Arabic, Icelandic and Bulgarian.
> I would prefer the afternoon, if you don't mind.

2 Go through the items with the class and then ask them to match them with the numbered gaps in the letter. Check answers with the class.

> a) 2   b) 1   c) 4   d) 6   e) 5   f) 3   g) 7

3 This writing exercise could be set for homework. Otherwise, allow plenty of time in class. Encourage students to use the letter here as a model, but to add personal details of their own. Display the letters in the classroom and invite students to vote on the best application for each job.

Test

Scoring: one point per correct answer unless otherwise indicated.

1
1. honest
2. shy
3. confident
4. sensible
5. sensitive
6. easy-going
7. helpful
8. cheerful

2
1. friendly
2. practical
3. creative
4. hard-working
5. clever
6. romantic

3
1. nurse
2. tourist guide
3. model
4. cook
5. DJ
6. writer
7. accountant
8. graphic designer

4
1. you <u>can't</u> leave school before you are sixteen.
2. you <u>don't</u> <u>have</u> to carry an ID card.
3. you <u>can</u> <u>drive</u> a car when you are seventeen.
4. you have <u>to</u> be sixteen to buy cigarettes.

5
1. We don't have to wear a suit at work.
2. We have to arrive at work before 9am.
3. We can make private phone calls at work.
4. We can't use mobile phones in our English class.
5. We can use mobile phones at break time.
6. We have to use English in our work.

6
1. ad<u>ven</u>turous
2. am<u>bi</u>tious
3. ener<u>ge</u>tic
4. <u>se</u>rious
5. inde<u>pen</u>dent
6. <u>so</u>ciable
7. <u>sen</u>sible
8. <u>con</u>fident

58   UNIT   7   *Work*   Visit *www.insideout.net*

7 Work Test

Name: _____   Total: _____ /40

1 Vocabulary – describing character (1)   8 points
Match the character adjectives with the definitions.

> cheerful   confident   easy-going   helpful   honest
> sensible   sensitive   shy

1 'I always tell the truth. I never lie.'
2 'I'm nervous about meeting people.'
3 'I'm sure about my own ideas and qualities.'
4 'I'm never silly. I never do stupid things.'
5 'I understand other people's feelings.'
6 'I'm relaxed. I never worry about anything.'
7 'I like helping people.'
8 'I'm happy and I'm always smiling.'

2 Vocabulary – describing character (2)   6 points
Add the missing vowels (a, e, i, o, u) to complete these character adjectives.

1 fr __ __ ndly
2 pr __ ct __ c __ l
3 cr __ __ t __ ve
4 h __ rd-w __ rk __ ng
5 cl __ v __ r
6 r __ m __ nt __ c

3 Vocabulary – jobs   8 points
Write the job. You are given the first letter(s).

1 I work in a hospital. n_____
2 I take visitors around my city.
   t_____ g_____
3 I often visit Paris, Milan and New York and I wear expensive clothes. m_____
4 I prepare meals in a restaurant. c_____
5 I play the music in clubs. D_____
6 I write books. w_____
7 I organise people's money. a_____
8 I design pictures and artwork in magazines.
   g_____ d_____

4 Modals (1) – can, can't, have to, don't have to   4 points
Correct the grammar mistake in each sentence.

In the United Kingdom, ...
1 you don't can leave school before you are sixteen.
2 you haven't to carry an ID card.
3 you can to drive a car when you are seventeen.
4 you have be sixteen to buy cigarettes.

5 Modals (2) – can, can't, have to, don't have to   6 points
Rewrite the sentences so the meaning is the same. Use can, can't, have to or don't have to.

For example: It's not okay to eat food in our office.
              We *can't eat food* in our office.

1 It's not necessary to wear a suit at work.
   We _____ at work.
2 It's necessary to arrive at work before 9am.
   We _____ before 9am.
3 It's okay for us to make private phone calls at work.
   We _____ at work.
4 It's not okay for us to use mobile phones in our English class.
   We _____ in our English class.
5 It's okay for us to use mobile phones at break time.
   We _____ at break time.
6 It's necessary for us to use English in our work.
   We _____ in our work.

6 Pronunciation – word stress   8 points
Underline the most stressed syllable in each word.

1 adventurous   5 independent
2 ambitious   6 sociable
3 energetic   7 sensible
4 serious   8 confident

8 Sea Overview

The topic of this unit, the sea, is dealt with in terms of recreation and holidays connected to the sea. The grammar focus is on the past simple of both regular and irregular verbs. Students also do more work on time expressions and are introduced to time linkers, useful for connecting sentences when telling stories. There are opportunities in the unit for guided and free story writing and extended speaking.

Students start by talking about water sports and listening to three people talking about how often they do particular water sports. This leads into a study of time expressions and some exposure to the past simple.

In the next section, a reading text about the man who invented the wetsuit introduces more past simple verbs, both regular and irregular. The *-ed* endings of regular verbs are looked at and differences in pronunciation noted.

More detailed work on regular and irregular past simple verbs follows and students complete lists of verbs and play bingo with past tense forms.

Next, they read a story about a shark attack. They complete the text with time linkers and then write a guided story about a disastrous trip to a football match in Spain. This leads into a freer piece of story writing and an Anecdote about their last summer holiday.

Section	Aims	What the students are doing
Introduction page 34	*Listening skills*: listening for specific information	Listening to people talking about water sports and completing a table.
		Rewriting questions and asking and answering questions about water sports.
	Lexis: time expressions	Completing a table with time expressions.
		Writing sentences using time expressions.
Surfing USA page 35	*Reading skills*: reading for gist and for specific information	Identifying the meaning of a text title.
		Finding specific information in a text on a wetsuit company.
	Grammar: *-ed* endings	Determining the past simple forms of verbs from the reading text.
Close up page 36	*Grammar*: past simple	Examining the form of the past simple of regular and irregular verbs.
		Writing the past forms of irregular verbs.
		Playing a game of bingo with past forms of verbs.
		Completing questions with past tense forms and interviewing a partner. **Pairwork: Student A & B**
Jaws page 37	*Reading skills*: reading for specific information	Reading a story about a shark attack.
		Identifying true and false statements.
		Completing the story with time linkers.
	Writing: a story	Writing a story with pictures, a framework and suggested sentences as prompts.
		Writing a story about a journey or holiday, using time linkers.
	Conversation skills: fluency work	Anecdote: talking about students' last summer holiday.

More information about topics in this unit

Surfing USA, Reading *www.oneill.com/history/jack*
Jaws, Reading & Writing 2 *www.richard-e-grant.com*

8 Sea Teacher's notes

Books closed. Whole class. Write the words *land* and *sea* in the centre of the board. Write the following words randomly around the board: *tree, boat, town, house, fish, swim, walk, drive, sail, beach,* and ask students to put them into the correct category.

Groupwork. Students look at the photos and discuss the questions. You could appoint a secretary in each group to take notes and report back to the class on the discussion. See how many other water sports the class can name. Draw students' attention to the section on *Water sports* on page 110.

Listening (p 34)

1 44 SB p 121

You might like to start by drawing students' attention to the Language toolbox, which shows the past simple of the verbs *be* and *go*. Then go through the instructions with the class and point out that we talk about doing water sports in the past by using the past simple of *go* and the name of the sport: *went swimming, went sailing,* etc. Play the recording for students to listen and note the correct time expressions. They should then correct the table. Check answers with the class.

	went swimming	went sailing
Pete	in August	–
Shanaz	–	6 weeks ago
Nacho	yesterday	a long time ago

	went windsurfing	went scuba-diving
Pete	last summer	–
Shanaz	–	–
Nacho	–	last year

44

(I = Interviewer; P = Pete; S = Shanaz; N = Nacho)

1 Pete

I: Excuse me. I'm from a new sports shop. Can I ask you some questions about water sports?
P: Sure.
I: Em, what's your name?
P: It's Pete.
I: Okay, Pete, do you ever go swimming?
P: Oh yes, I love swimming.
I: And when was the last time you went swimming?
P: Em, in August. I was on holiday.
I: And do you ever go sailing?
P: No – I'd like to, but I don't know anybody with a boat.
I: Okay, how about other water sports?
P: I sometimes go windsurfing.
I: When was the last time you went windsurfing?
P: Last summer with my friend. We were on holiday.
I: Great. Well, come along to our shop some time. Here's the address.
P: Yeah, thanks.

2 Shanaz

I: Excuse me. I'm from a new sports shop. Can I ask you some questions about water sports?
S: Oh, okay.
I: What's your name?
S: Shanaz.
I: Right, Shanaz, do you ever go swimming?
S: No. I can't swim.
I: Oh, I see. Um, do you ever go sailing?
S: Yeah, I go on my friend's boat.
I: Oh good, and when was the last time you went sailing?
S: About six weeks ago.
I: And do you do other water sports?
S: No, I told you, I can't swim.
I: Oh, right. Thank you.

> **3 Nacho**
>
> I: Excuse me. I'm from a new sports shop. Can I ask you some questions about water sports?
> N: Water sports?
> I: Yes, what's your name?
> N: Nacho Fernandez Almira Olivera.
> I: Okay, em, Nacho, do you ever go swimming?
> N: Yes, yes, a lot.
> I: Oh great. When was the last time you went swimming?
> N: Yesterday.
> I: Right, and do you ever go sailing?
> N: Yes, but not often.
> I: When was the last time you went sailing?
> N: I can't remember. A long time ago.
> I: Do you ever do other water sports?
> N: Yes, I love scuba-diving.
> I: Wow. When was the last time you went scuba-diving?
> N: Last year. In Egypt.
> I: Lovely. Well, our new shop is in the centre of town ...

2 Students work individually to rewrite the two questions in the correct order. Check answers with the class to make sure that everyone has the correct questions. Elicit that the difference between the two questions is that the first is asking about things in general and the second about a specific time in the past. Students then work in pairs to ask and answer the questions.

> a) Do you ever go swimming?
> b) When was the last time you went swimming?

3 Pairwork. Students continue asking and answering the two questions in Exercise 2, but substituting other sports for *swimming*. Go round, checking that they are forming the questions correctly and answering appropriately.

Lexis: time expressions (p 34)

1 Pairwork. Focus attention on the table and establish that the two columns show different ways of saying the same thing. Look at the example with the class. Answers here will depend on when your students complete the table, so make sure that they are appropriate to the day, month, year and time of day that they are doing this activity.

> Answers depend on when the students do this exercise.

2 Students work individually to write one true and one false sentence about themselves. Make sure they use the time expressions in Exercise 1.

3 Pairwork. Students take turns to read out their sentences to their partner, who has to try to identify the false sentence.

Surfing USA (p 35)

Reading

1 You might like to encourage students to skim-read the text quickly just to decide which meaning matches the title. Skim-reading is a useful skill at any level. It gives students confidence to realise that they often do not have to understand every word of a text in order to get the general meaning of it. You could set a time limit of three minutes.

> b) Wetsuits keep you warm in cold water.

2 If your students skim-read the text to answer the question in Exercise 1, then they will need time to read the text more thoroughly before they do this activity. However, don't allow them to search the text for each piece of information. Set a time limit of five minutes for them to read it and then ask them to close their books. Call out each item in turn and ask them to write down their answers. At the end, find out who thinks they have the best memory, but don't confirm or deny any answers at this stage.

3 Students open their books and check how accurately they remembered the text in Exercise 2. They can then discuss the questions in pairs. Encourage them to report back to the class.

Note: You can read more about the Jack O'Neill story by logging on to: *www.oneill.com/history/jack*

> a) In California.
> b) Because the water was cold.
> c) On the carpet of a DC-3 plane.
> d) In 1952.
> e) To show/demonstrate the wetsuits.
> f) Because he lost an eye in a surfing accident.

-ed endings (p 35)

1 You might like to establish the difference between regular verbs and irregular verbs in the past at this stage. If so, ask students to look again at the text about Jack O'Neill and to underline all the verbs in it that are talking about events in the past. When they have done this, ask them to look at the verbs they have underlined. There are two groups: those that end in -ed and those that do not. Explain that we call those that end in *-ed regular* verbs and those that have other forms *irregular* verbs.

This activity focuses on the regular verbs in the article. Draw students' attention to the box of verbs, which shows both the infinitive and the past simple forms. Elicit that these are all regular verbs (because of the *-ed* ending), but demonstrate by reading out the examples that sometimes the addition of the *-ed* ending adds another syllable to the word. Students should decide which verbs belong in which column of the table. Encourage them to read the words aloud so that they get a feel for what sounds right. Do not check answers at this stage.

2 ▭ **45 SB p 122**

Play the recording for students to listen and check their answers. Then play it again for them to repeat the words.

> A Same syllables: work / worked; use / used; stop / stopped; open / opened; love / loved; discover / discovered; ask / asked
>
> B Extra syllable: want / wanted; start / started; point / pointed

> ▭ **45**
>
> A: *Same syllables*
> *work – worked; use – used; stop – stopped;*
> *open – opened; love – loved;*
> *discover – discovered; ask – asked*
>
> B: *Extra syllable*
> *want – wanted; start – started; point – pointed*

Close up (p 36)

Past simple

1 Pairwork. If you introduced the concept of regular and irregular verbs in the previous section, students should have no trouble answering the questions here. There is more information on the form and use of the past simple in the Language reference section at the bottom of this page and in Verb structures on page 114. Check answers with the class.

> a) The verbs in B.
> b) The verbs in A.
> c) 1 Add *d*.
>   2 Cross out *y* and add *ied*.
>   3 Double the consonant and add *ed*.
>   4 Add *ed*.

2 Pairwork. Students work together to complete the past forms of the verbs. Make sure they practise saying them aloud. Draw their attention to the Irregular verbs list on page 117, which they can refer to any time they need reminding of an irregular past form. Do not check answers at this stage.

3 ▭ **46 SB p 122**

Play the recording for students to listen and check their answers to Exercise 2. Then play it again for them to repeat the words.

> a) go / went   do /(did)   send / sent
> b) have /(had)   sell / sold   tell / told
> c) bring / brought   swim /(swam)
>   think / thought
> d) meet / met   let / let   get /(got)
> e) read / read   hear /(heard)   say / said
> f) can /(could)   teach / taught   catch / caught
> g) fly / flew   know / knew   buy /(bought)
> h) see /(saw)   keep / kept   sleep / slept

> ▭ **46**
> a) *went, did, sent*
> b) *had, sold, told*
> c) *brought, swam, thought*
> d) *met, let, got*
> e) *read, heard, said*
> f) *could, taught, caught*
> g) *flew, knew, bought*
> h) *saw, kept, slept*

4 ▭ **47 SB p 122**

Go through the instructions carefully with the class. Ensure that they know that they can choose any nine of the verbs that they like and that they must put the past tense forms on their cards. The winner is the student who calls out *Bingo!* first. Refer them to the tapescript on page 122 to check their answers.

> ▭ **47**
>
> *And here are the words for tonight's bingo.*
>
> *meant, meant   stole, stole   drank, drank*
> *wore, wore   hit, hit   woke, woke   fought, fought*
> *gave, gave   won, won   forgot, forgot   grew, grew*
> *chose, chose   ran, ran   paid, paid   cost, cost*
> *understood, understood   lent, lent   cut, cut*
> *spent, spent   began, began   threw, threw*
> *felt, felt   stood, stood   became, became*
> *learnt, learnt   met, met   built, built   made, made*
> *sang, sang   rang, rang*

Follow-up activity

Students could play bingo again in groups. Each group prepares a list of verbs like in the tapescript for Exercise 4 (with each verb repeated), but in a different order. Each student in the group then prepares their own bingo card. They nominate one person in the group to be the reader. The reader moves to another group and reads out the list for that group to play bingo.

5 Pairwork: Student A & B Students turn to their respective pages and follow the instructions. In this activity, students complete questions with past tense verbs and then interview their partners. Check the questions have been completed correctly before they start interviewing their partners.

Student A
a) went
b) travelled
c) used
d) spoke
e) drove
f) earned
Student B
a) had
b) telephoned
c) made
d) held
e) gave
f) took

Jaws (p 37)

Books closed. Whole class. Find out if anyone has seen the film *Jaws* (or its sequel *Jaws II*). If so, ask them to tell the class as much as possible about the film.

Reading & writing (p 37)

1 Encourage the students to skim-read the text to find out if the sentences are true or false. Set a time limit of five minutes and then check answers with the class.

a)	False.
b)	True.
c)	False.
d)	False.
e)	True.
f)	False.

2 48 SB p 122

Pairwork. Go through the time linkers in the box first and make sure students understand them. They then work together to fit them into the text. When they have finished, play the recording for them to check their answers.

Note: For more information on Richard E Grant and the films he has appeared in log on to: www.richard-e-grant.com

1	One day
2	After a few hours
3	Suddenly
4	At first
5	Eventually
6	Two or three weeks later
7	Many years later

48
Shark attack!

When he was eight, British actor, Richard E Grant went on holiday to Mozambique with his parents and his younger brother. One day, they went fishing in a small motor boat on an enormous lagoon called San Martina. After a few hours, the motor stopped, and they couldn't start it again. They shouted, but nobody heard them. Suddenly, something moved in the water near the boat.

At first, they thought it was a dolphin. But then they realised it was a big, grey shark. It started knocking the boat. The boat rocked from side to side, and they nearly fell into the water. They were terrified. Grant's father tried to push the shark away, and his mother held him and his brother. They thought they were going to die.

Eventually, people in a fishing boat heard them and took them home. Everybody in the town heard about their story and talked about it. Grant's father became a local hero. Two or three weeks later, a local fisherman caught the shark and put it in the main square. Everybody came to see the monster and took pictures of it.

Many years later, when Grant saw the film 'Jaws', he relived the terrible experience.

3 Pairwork: Additional material Ask students to turn to page 95. This activity provides guided writing practice with pictures, a suggested framework and sentences which have to be completed with past simple verbs as prompts.

a)	enjoyed, had, read, slept
b)	went
c)	watched
d)	decided
e)	realised
f)	asked, said
g)	looked, found
h)	travelled, was
i)	arrived, was
1	d) Harry and Joss were Manchester United fans. One day, they decided to travel to Spain to watch Manchester United play against the Spanish team, Deportivo La Coruña.
2	g) The next day, they looked at a map of Spain and found the nearest airport – Santiago.

64 UNIT 8 *Sea*

3 b) Then, they went to the travel agents and booked flights to Santiago.

4 h) Two weeks later, they travelled to Manchester airport. Their flight was on time.

5 a) At first, they enjoyed the flight. They had lunch, read the newspapers and slept for a short time.

6 f) But after a few hours, Joss asked how long the flight to Santiago was. The flight attendant said 'Eleven hours, sir. South America's a long way from Manchester.'

7 e) Suddenly, they realised their mistake.

8 i) Eventually, they arrived in Santiago – but it wasn't Santiago in Spain. It was Santiago in Chile!

9 c) Two days later, they watched the match in a hotel bar.

4 This activity gives an opportunity for students to do a piece of free writing. The guided writing in the previous exercise should help them. This writing could be set for homework. Encourage them to plan their stories by making notes and to use the time linkers to give the stories coherence. If possible, display the students' stories in the classroom and set aside time for everyone to read them. They can then decide on the most interesting/funniest/most scary story.

Optional activity

Write the word JAWS vertically on the board and ask students to write a sentence (or just a phrase) beginning with the letters. The resulting simple 'poem' should be about sharks. For example:
Jagged teeth
A small boat
Wide mouth
Screaming!

Anecdote (p 37)

See the Introduction on page 4 for more ideas on how to set up, monitor and repeat Anecdotes.

1 49 SB p 122

Go through the questions with the class and then play the recording for students to listen and underline the answers that the speaker gives.

a) to the beach
b) in July
c) my sister and a friend
d) by plane and by car
e) in a hotel
f) two weeks
g) went to the beach
h) went out

49
(F = Frank; L = Lottie)

F: I don't know where to go on holiday this year. Where did you go for your last summer holiday?
L: I went to the beach – to Tarifa in the South of Spain.
F: Oh, lovely. When did you go there?
L: Um, in July.
F: Nice. Who did you go with?
L: My sister and a friend.
F: Oh, yes. How did you get there?
L: We flew from London to Malaga, and then we drove from Malaga to Tarifa. There's a really good motorway.
F: Great. Where did you stay?
L: In the Hurricane Hotel. Do you know it?
F: No – what's it like?
L: Fantastic. The rooms are wonderful. And it's near the beach.
F: Mm, you are lucky. How long did you stay?
L: Just two weeks, unfortunately.
F: Oh, well. So what did you do all day?
L: We went to the beach, of course – you can do everything there. I tried kitesurfing – it's amazing.
F: Wow – I suppose you were tired in the evening.
L: Yes, but we went out a lot too – there are some really good tapas bars and clubs in Tarifa.
F: Mm, and did you meet anybody nice?
L: Well, yes, I did actually. He's a windsurfing instructor, and the first time we went out ...

2 Give students time to prepare what they are going to say, using the questions and sentence beginnings in Exercise 1 for inspiration. Allow them to make notes, but discourage them from writing out a script.

3 Pairwork. Students take turns to tell their partners about their last summer holidays.

Test

Scoring: one point per correct answer unless otherwise indicated.

1
1. 11.50am
2. four days
3. one month
4. 2000
5. three hours
6. Friday

2
1. windsurfing
2. canoeing
3. scuba-diving
4. sailing

3 1 – 1 2 – 2 3 – 1 4 – 1 5 – 2 6 – 2
   7 – 1 8 – 1

4
1. enjoyed
2. liked
3. stopped
4. studied
5. tried
6. watched
7. lived
8. travelled

5
1. came
2. did
3. got
4. went
5. had
6. made

6
1. bought
2. forgot
3. sent
4. met
5. saw
6. felt
7. said
8. rang

8 Sea Test

Name: _____   Total: _____ /40

1   Vocabulary – time expressions *6 points*

It is 12pm Thursday 1st January 2004. Complete the gaps.

ten minutes ago → at (1) _____

last Sunday → (2) _____ ago

in December → (3) _____ ago

four years ago → in (4) _____

at 9am → (5) _____ ago

six days ago → on (6) _____

2   Vocabulary – water sports *4 points*

Add the missing vowels (*a, e, i, o, u*) to complete these water sports.

1   w __ nds __ rf __ ng

2   c __ n __ __ __ ng

3   sc __ b __ -d __ v __ ng

4   s __ __ l __ ng

3   Pronunciation – *-ed* endings *8 points*

Do these past simple verbs have one or two syllables? Write *1* or *2*.

For example: *walked* – 1; *acted* – 2.

1   worked _____
2   wanted _____
3   stopped _____
4   asked _____
5   pointed _____
6   started _____
7   loved _____
8   used _____

4   Past simple (1) – regular verbs *8 points*

Write the past simple of the verbs.

1   enjoy _____
2   like _____
3   stop _____
4   study _____
5   try _____
6   watch _____
7   live _____
8   travel _____

5   Past simple (2) – irregular verbs *6 points*

Write the past simple of the verbs.

1   come _____
2   do _____
3   get _____
4   go _____
5   have _____
6   make _____

6   Past simple (3) *8 points*

Complete the sentences by putting the verb into the past simple.

1   Yesterday, I _____ (buy) a new CD.
2   Sorry, I _____ (forget) to phone you last night.
3   I _____ (send) you an email this afternoon.
4   We _____ (meet) at university.
5   I _____ (see) a great film last week.
6   I _____ (feel) really tired this morning.
7   She _____ (say) her name was Silvia.
8   I _____ (ring) you three times yesterday.

9 Solo Overview

The topic of this unit is feelings, particularly with respect to how people feel about being alone. The grammar focus is the past simple.

Students begin by looking at some words to talk about feelings. They match them with photos of facial expressions and then practise making and identifying the meaning of facial expressions with a partner. They then go on to talk about how they feel in particular situations.

In the next section, students read a short text about a woman who started a rowing race across the Atlantic with her husband and finished it alone. They predict what happened to the husband and then read the second part of the text to find out. This leads into a listening on heroes in which the feelings of the lone woman rower are discussed further. Students then discuss the activities they prefer to do alone and those they prefer to do with other people.

Practice in the pronunciation of irregular past simple verb forms leads into a closer study of the past simple. Students take turns to ask a partner about past events and then ask and answer questions about the lives of pop singers.

In the final section, students read about the life of filmstar Greta Garbo, famous for her line *I want to be alone*. They form questions about her life and then read the text to find the answers. This leads into a guided writing activity. First, students put a summary of Garbo's life in order, then they write a summary of the life of someone in their own family.

Section	Aims	What the students are doing
Introduction page 38	*Lexis*: feelings	Listening to words describing feelings and identifying stressed syllables.
		Matching words for feelings with photographs of expressions.
		Taking turns to guess the feelings expressed by a partner.
		Discussing what prompts particular feelings.
Solo voyage pages 39–40	*Reading skills*: reading for gist and for specific information	Reading an article about a rowing race and predicting what happened to one contestant.
	Listening skills: listening for detail	Listening to a radio programme about heroes and matching questions to pictures.
		Completing sentences with prepositions.
		Discussing attitudes to being alone.
	Pronunciation: past simple vowel sounds	Practising the pronunciation of irregular past simple forms.
Close up page 40	*Grammar*: past simple	Completing questions and answers with the past simple.
		Asking questions about past events.
		Asking and answering questions about pop singers.
		Pairwork: Student A & B
The life and times of … page 41	*Reading skills*: reading for specific information	Making comprehension questions for a text about Greta Garbo.
		Reading the text and answering the questions.
		Talking about their favourite Hollywood star.
	Writing: a biography	Putting sentences in order to make a summary of Greta Garbo's life.
		Writing a summary of the life of a relative.

> **More information about topics in this unit**
> Life and times of …, Reading 2 *www.geocities.com/Hollywood/Lot/4117*

9 Solo Teacher's notes

Books closed. Whole class. Tell the students how you are feeling at the moment, eg: *I'm excited because I'm going to a concert tonight. I'm nervous because I'm taking my driving test next week.* Then ask the students to say how they are feeling and why.

Lexis: feelings (p 38)

1 🔊 **50 SB p 38**

Play the recording for students to listen and repeat the words. They should then underline the stressed syllables. Encourage them to say the words aloud as they do this. Then play the recording again for them to check.

Ask them to tick the words they know. Read out the words one by one and ask students to put up their hands if they know the meaning. Students who know the meaning of a word should give examples of situations in which someone might feel this particular emotion, until all the class understand what each word means.

> <u>an</u>gry
> bored
> em<u>ba</u>rrassed
> ex<u>ci</u>ted
> <u>fri</u>ghtened
> <u>ha</u>ppy
> <u>lo</u>nely
> <u>ner</u>vous
> sad
> <u>wor</u>ried

2 Pairwork. Focus attention on the photos. Students try to find a word to describe each of the person's feelings. Allow pairs to compare their results with other pairs and encourage them to use dictionaries if they want to find other words. Check answers with the class.

> a) frightened, worried, nervous
> b) happy, excited
> c) bored
> d) angry
> e) sad, lonely
> f) embarrassed

3 Pairwork. Students take turns to choose a word from Exercise 1 and make an appropriate facial expression for their partner to guess what they are feeling.

4 Pairwork. In the same pairs, students look at the situations in the box and discuss how they feel in these situations.

Solo voyage (p 39)

Books closed. Whole class. Ask students if they know of anyone who has made a difficult journey or done something amazing on their own. Prompt them to think of sports people, explorers, and so on. Tell them that they are going to read about a woman who rowed across the Atlantic Ocean alone.

Reading (p 39)

1 Students read the first part of the report and discuss the questions. Elicit several suggestions about what might have happened to Andrew. If necessary, prompt students with a few questions, eg: *Do you think a shark ate him? Did he fall out of the boat and drown? Did they have an argument? Did he get sick? Did he get bored?* You could get students to vote on the most likely of the suggestions made.

> a) a 3,000-mile rowing race
> b) thirty-four
> c) Students' own answers.

2 **Pairwork: Additional material** Ask students to turn to page 96 and read the second part of the article. Elicit the reason why Andrew left. Ask them what they think of Andrew's actions and what they think about what Debra did next. Do they agree with the comment by the editor of *The Times* that the winner of the race was the girl who came last? Why or why not?

> He left because he was frightened of the ocean.

Listening (p 39)

1 🔊 **51 SB p 122**

Go through the instructions with the class and read the questions. Then play the recording for them to match the questions with the pictures. Check answers with the class and elicit their response to what they have heard. Would they feel the same as Debra if a partner left them to row alone. Would they have gone on with the race?

> a) 4 b) 6 c) 1 d) 5 e) 2 f) 3

🔊 **51**

(I = Interviewer; N = Nelly)

I: Welcome to this week's edition of 'Heroes'. Today we have the popular television presenter, Nelly B, in the studio. Nelly, hello and welcome.

N: Thank you. It's lovely to be here.

I: Nelly, who is your hero and why?

N: My hero is Debra Veal because she spent 113 days alone at sea in a rowing boat.

I: Yes, that is pretty amazing, isn't it? Why did she do it?

N: Well, that's a good question. She started a trans-Atlantic race with her husband, Andrew, but he left after two weeks. He was frightened of the ocean.

I: How did she feel when Andrew left her?

N: I think she was relieved when he left. She just wanted him to be happy and healthy again.

I: What was the main danger of being alone on the boat?

N: It was difficult for her to sleep, because she was frightened of big ships. The tankers are enormous and they can't see a small boat.

I: Did she have any bad experiences?

N: She was frightened of sharks, and one night there was a very big one under the boat – but it wasn't interested in her – it was only interested in eating the fish under the boat.

I: Did she feel lonely?

N: Very lonely. Before the trip, she never spent time alone. She has an identical twin who was with her for the first twenty years of her life, and then she met Andrew.

I: What did she miss most?

N: Well, of course she missed people. But the other thing was fresh food. She missed vegetables and salad. And glasses of red wine.

I: Was Andrew there when she arrived in Barbados?

N: Oh yes, of course. Andrew was there to meet her with a bottle of champagne.

I: And she deserved it! Nelly, thank you so much. Debra Veal is an inspiration. Next week we'll be talking to ...

2 Students work in pairs if necessary to decide on the correct alternatives. You might like to point out that some of the adjective and preposition combinations are in the tapescript on page 122. A good dictionary should also give them information about which prepositions are used with adjectives. Check answers with the class.

a) about
b) about
c) with
d) of
e) in
f) about
g) about
h) about

3 Play the recording again. Students listen and tick the sentences they know to be true. They then discuss with a partner whether they think the others are true or not and report back to the class.

a) Probably true.
b) ✔ True.
c) ✔ True.
d) ✔ True.
e) ✔ True.
f) ✔ True.
g) Probably false.
h) Probably false.

4 Groupwork. Students work in small groups to discuss the questions. Draw their attention to the different ways of saying *alone* in the Language toolbox. You might like to appoint a secretary in each group to take notes of the discussion and report back to the class.

Past simple vowel sounds (p 40)

1 🔊 **52 SB p 122**

Students work individually to write the past simple forms of the verbs in the boxes. Then play the recording for them to check their answers. Play it again for them to listen and repeat the words.

A
think – thought
know – knew
feel – felt
mean – meant
speak – spoke
see – saw

B
fight – fought
wake – woke
spend – spoke
grow – grew
wear – wore
spell – spelt

70 UNIT 9 Solo

> **52**
> A: *think – thought   know – knew   feel – felt*
>   *mean – meant   speak – spoke   see – saw*
> B: *fight – fought   wake – woke   spend – spent*
>   *grow – grew   wear – wore   spell – spelt*

2 **53 SB p 122**

Encourage students to say the words aloud as they match them. Check answers with the class.

> thought – fought
> knew – grew
> felt – spelt
> meant – spent
> spoke – woke
> saw – wore

> **53**
> thought – fought   knew – grew   felt – spelt
> meant – spent   spoke – woke   saw – wore

Close up (p 40)

Past simple

1 Pairwork. Remind students of the work they did on the past simple in the previous unit and draw their attention to the Language reference section at the bottom of the page and Verb structures on page 114. Go through the examples with the class. They then work together to complete the questions and answers. Do not check answers at this stage, but allow them to compare with other pairs.

2 **54 SB p 123**

Play the recording for students to listen and check their answers to Exercise 1. In pairs, they then ask and answer the questions.

> a) Was; Yes, it was. No, it wasn't.
> b) Did; Yes, I did. No, I didn't.
> c) Did; Yes, I did. No, I didn't.
> d) Did; Yes, she did. No, she didn't.
> e) Were; Yes, I was. No, I wasn't.
> f) Did; Yes, they did; No, they didn't.
> g) Did; Yes, I did; No, I didn't.

> **54**
> a)
> 'Was the weather good yesterday?'
> 'Yes, it was.'
> 'No, it wasn't.'
>
> b)
> 'Did you get up early?'
> 'Yes, I did.'
> 'No, I didn't.'
>
> c)
> 'Did you have a bath?'
> 'Yes, I did.'
> 'No, I didn't.'
>
> d)
> 'Did your mother make breakfast for you?'
> 'Yes, she did.'
> 'No, she didn't.'
>
> e)
> 'Were you late for work or school?'
> 'Yes, I was.'
> 'No, I wasn't.'
>
> f)
> 'Did your friends call or text you?'
> 'Yes, they did.'
> 'No, they didn't.'
>
> g)
> 'Did you go out in the evening?'
> 'Yes, I did.'
> 'No, I didn't.'

3 Pairwork. Go through the instructions with the class. Students then take turns to choose an event from box B and ask their partner appropriate questions about it. Go round, checking that the questions have been formed correctly and that students are answering appropriately.

> a) What did you see?
> b) What was it about?
> c) Where did you go?
> d) Who did you go with?
> e) What did you do?
> f) What did you eat or drink?
> g) Where did you stay?
> h) What time did you leave?
> i) How much did you spend?

Follow-up activity

Pairwork. Tell students they are going to play a game. They have to guess six things that their partner did yesterday. Read out the following instructions. They must try to score more points than their partner.

a) Prepare six *Yes/No* questions about your partner's day.
b) Score one point if your partner's answer is *'Yes, I did/was.'*
c) Score no points if your partner's answer is *'No, I didn't/wasn't.'*

4 **Pairwork: Student A & B** Students turn to their respective pages and follow the instructions. Each student has questions to complete about different pop singers and a box with answers to their partner's questions. They complete the questions and then take turns to ask and answer about their pop singers. There are two possible answers in the box for each question (though only one is correct). Students should correct their partners if they choose the incorrect answer to a question. Go round, checking that the questions have been completed correctly. Alternatively, check the questions with the class before students start to ask and answer them.

> Student A
> a) Where was Bob Marley from?
> b) When did Robbie Williams leave *Take That*?
> c) Where was Björk born?
> d) What was George Michael's original name?
> e) When did Kurt Cobain die?
> f) Who did Madonna marry in 2000?
>
> Student B
> a) Where was Jimi Hendrix from?
> b) What was Tina Turner's original name?
> c) Where was Celine Dion born?
> d) When did Sting leave *The Police* to go solo?
> e) When did John Lennon die?
> f) Who did Elvis Presley marry in 1967?

The life and times of ... (p 41)

Books closed. Whole class. Play *Hangman* with the class using the names of famous filmstars. Put a line for each letter of a star's name on the board and invite students to call out possible letters. Write correct letters in the spaces and incorrect letters at the side. For each incorrect guess, draw a portion of a gallows and hanged man. If the drawing is completed before students have guessed the name, you win. If not, the student who guessed the name correctly chooses the next film star. When you have finished, ask students what, if anything, they know about the filmstar Greta Garbo.

Reading (p 41)

1 Pairwork. Go through the instructions with the class. Students then work together to make comprehension questions. Allow them to compare their questions with other pairs. Check answers with the class.

> a) Where was she born?
> b) When did she leave school?
> c) When did she change her name to Greta Garbo?
> d) How many Academy Award nominations did she get?
> e) How was she different from other Hollywood stars?
> f) In which film did she say the famous line, 'I want to be alone'?
> g) When did she retire from cinema?
> h) Where did she spend the rest of her life?

2 Give students plenty of time to read the article and decide on the answers to the questions. Allow them to compare answers with a partner or in small groups before checking with the class. As an alternative, you could give the students a time limit and give a point for each correct answer.

Note: For more information on Greta Garbo, log on to: *www.geocities.com/Hollywood/Lot/4117*

> a) Sweden.
> b) At the age of fourteen.
> c) When she moved to Hollywood.
> d) Four.
> e) She kept her private life very private. She never spoke about her love affairs and she didn't sign autographs or give interviews.
> f) *Grand Hotel*.
> g) At the age of thirty-six.
> h) New York.

3 Pairwork. Students tell each other about their favourite Hollywood stars. Encourage them to give as many details of the person's life as they can and to ask their partners follow-up questions about their favourite stars.

Writing a biography (p 41)

1 Explain that a biography is a description of a person's life. The summary in this exercise is in the wrong order. Students should work individually to decide on the correct order and then compare results with a partner. Check answers with the class.

> 1 f   2 c   3 a   4 e   5 b   6 g   7 j   8 h   9 d   10 i

2 Go through the instructions with the class. Students then work individually to write their summaries. Go round, offering help and encouragement, and answer any queries about difficult vocabulary. This could be set for homework, if you wish.

3 Students compare their summaries with a partner. If possible, display them in the classroom and allow time for students to read them.

Test

Scoring: one point per correct answer unless otherwise indicated.

1
1. nervous *or* worried
2. nervous *or* worried
3. happy *or* excited
4. happy *or* excited
5. sad *or* lonely
6. sad *or* lonely

2
1. angry
2. frightened
3. embarrassed
4. bored

3
1. about
2. about
3. with
4. in
5. of
6. about

4 (½ point per correct answer)
1. fought
2. spoke
3. saw
4. grew
5. went
6. wore
7. thought
8. knew
9. woke
10. spelt
11. spent
12. felt

5
1. Did you <u>study</u> English at school?
2. When <u>did</u> you start to study English?
3. What <u>were</u> your favourite subjects at school?
4. <u>Did you have</u> any homework last night?

6
1. Did, did
2. Were, weren't
3. Was, was
4. Was, wasn't
5. Did, did
6. Did, didn't

7 (2 points per correct answer)
1. Where were you born?
2. Did you live in the USA when you were a child?
3. Did you speak English when you were in the USA?
4. When did you move to Europe?

9 Solo Test

Name: _____   Total: _____ /40

1 Vocabulary – feelings (1) 6 points
Complete the sentences with the correct adjectives.

> happy   excited   sad   nervous   lonely   worried

I've got an exam tomorrow. I'm (1) _____ and (2) _____ .

We go on holiday next week. I'm (3) _____ and (4) _____ .

I've got no friends. I'm (5) _____ and (6) _____ .

2 Vocabulary – feelings (2) 4 points
Add the missing vowels (*a, e, i, o, u*) to complete the adjectives.

1 __ ngry
2 fr __ ght __ n __ d
3 __ mb __ rr __ ss __ d
4 b __ r __ d

3 Vocabulary – adjective + particle 6 points
Add the missing particle: *of*, *with*, *about* or *in*.

1 I'm really excited _____ my new job.
2 I'm worried _____ my mum. She's in hospital.
3 My parents were really angry _____ me.
4 I'm not interested _____ football.
5 I'm frightened _____ spiders.
6 I'm very happy _____ passing my exam.

4 Past simple 6 points
Write the past simple of each verb.

1 fight _____   7 think _____
2 speak _____   8 know _____
3 see _____   9 wake _____
4 grow _____   10 spell _____
5 go _____   11 spend _____
6 wear _____   12 feel _____

5 Past simple questions (1) 4 points
Correct the mistakes in the questions.

1 Did you studied English at school?
2 When you start to study English?
3 What did your favourite subjects at school?
4 Had you any homework last night?

6 Past simple questions (2) 6 points
Complete the questions and answers with the correct form of *was/were* or *did*.

1 '_____ you go to the party last night?'
   'Yes, I _____ .'
2 '_____ Sara and Claudia there?'
   'No, they _____ .'
3 '_____ the music good?'
   'Yes, it _____ .'
4 '_____ there any food there?'
   'No, there _____ .'
5 '_____ you dance?'
   'Yes, I _____ .'
6 '_____ you speak to many people?'
   'No, I _____ .'

7 Past simple questions (3) 8 points
Read the answers. Write the questions.

1 'Where _____ born?'
   'I was born in the USA.'
2 '_____ a child?'
   'Yes, I lived in the USA when I was a child.'
3 '_____ in the USA?'
   'Yes, I spoke English when I was in the USA.'
4 'When _____ to Europe?'
   'We moved to Europe when I was ten.'

10 Review 2 Teacher's notes

Life (p 42)

can, can't, have to, don't have to

1 Pairwork. Remind students of the work they did on possibility and necessity in Unit 7. You might like to elicit a few example sentences to illustrate the use of *can, can't, have to* and *don't have to* before students begin the exercise. Students work together to decide on the correct information and underline the appropriate verbs. Check answers with the class.

> a) don't have to
> b) can
> c) can't
> d) can
> e) have to
> f) can

2 Students make the sentences true for their country. They then write three new sentences and compare them with a partner. In a feedback session, ask students if the situation in their country or countries is the same as in Britain.

Word stress (p 42)

1 Pairwork. Students should take turns to say the words aloud and decide where the correct stress should fall. They underline the stressed syllables and circle words with a different stress pattern from the others in each group. Do not check answers at this stage.

2 **55 SB p 42**

Play the recording for students to check their answers to Exercise 1. Then play it again for them to repeat the words.

> a) sensible   sensitive   (adventurous)
> b) sociable   (independent)   serious
> c) (energetic)   romantic   ambitious
> d) creative   (confident)   hard-working
> e) banana   (margarine)   spaghetti
> f) (cauliflower)   potato   tomato

Quantity (p 42)

1 Pairwork. Remind students of the work they did on talking about quantity in Unit 6. Elicit that we use *much* with uncountable nouns and *many* with countable nouns. They should work together to complete the questions. Allow them to compare their results with another pair, but do not check answers at this stage.

2 **56 SB p 123**

Play the recording for students to check their answers to Exercise 1. They can then ask and answer the questions in pairs.

> a) much
> b) many
> c) many
> d) much
> e) many
> f) much
> g) many

56

> a) How much money did you spend the last time you went out?
> b) How many emails did you receive yesterday?
> c) How many presents did you get on your birthday?
> d) How much time did you spend studying English at the weekend?
> e) How many times did you go skiing last year?
> f) How much fruit did you eat at your last meal?
> g) How many phone calls did you make yesterday?

3 Pairwork. Students ask each other three more questions using *How much* or *How many*. Go round checking that the questions are formed correctly.

Past simple: affirmative (p 43)

1 Pairwork. Remind students that there is a list of irregular verbs on page 117 which shows the past simple forms. Students work in pairs to complete the text with the past simple, then discuss who they think is being described. Allow them to compare with other pairs, but do not confirm or deny answers at this stage.

2 **57 SB p 123**

Play the recording for students to check their answers to Exercise 1. Did they guess the name of the person correctly? In pairs, they discuss any facts they know about the lives of other famous politicians. Encourage them to report back to the class on what they know.

Note: To find more information on Abraham Lincoln, log on to: *www.whitehouse.gov/history/presidents*

1	was born
2	grew up
3	died
4	wanted
5	didn't get
6	started
7	wasn't
8	got engaged
9	died
10	was
11	stayed
12	got married
13	had
14	survived
15	worked
16	lost
17	became
18	shot
19	killed

57
An American life

1809	He was born in Kentucky, USA and grew up in a poor family.
1818	His mother died.
1832	He wanted to study law, but he didn't get a place at college.
1833	He started a business, but it wasn't successful.
1835	He got engaged to be married, but his fiancée died.
1836	He was ill and stayed in bed for six months.
1842	He got married to Mary Todd. They had four children, but only one survived.
1838 –1859	He worked in politics, but he lost eight elections.
1860	He became the 16th President of the United States.
1865	An actor, John Booth, shot and killed him at Ford's Theatre in Washington.

His name? Abraham Lincoln.

Past simple: questions (p 43)

Go through the instructions with the class. You could make this a competition with the first person to find a name for each gap being the winner. Make sure the questions have been correctly formed before students start asking and answering them.

a) Did you go swimming last week?
b) Did you make breakfast this morning?
c) Did you sleep more than eight hours last night?
d) Did you do the washing up yesterday evening?
e) Did you have fish for lunch yesterday?
f) Did you buy a music CD at the weekend?

Anecdote (p 43)

See the Introduction on page 4 for more ideas on how to set up, monitor and repeat Anecdotes.

1 58 SB p 123

Go through the instructions with the class. Let them read the questions through before you play the recording. As you play it, they should underline the answers that the woman gives. Check answers with the class.

a) last weekend
b) my brother's 18th birthday
c) in an Italian restaurant
d) fifteen of us
e) our family
f) my grandmother
g) pizza
h) some wine
i) for nearly three hours

58

We had a delicious meal last weekend – on Friday night. It was my brother's 18th birthday, and the whole family went out. We had the meal in an Italian restaurant. It's called Mario's, and they do fantastic pizzas there – the best in town. There were fifteen of us – me, my brother, our parents, our grandmother, our cousins and my brother's best friends. I sat next to my grandmother, but she fell asleep after two glasses of wine. We all had pizza. Some people drank wine – including me – and the younger ones drank coke. The restaurant made my brother a special birthday cake and we all sang Happy Birthday – I think he was a bit embarrassed. The cake was delicious, and we had some champagne too. I think we stayed in the restaurant for nearly three hours. I didn't get home till 1am. It was a really good evening.

2 Give students plenty of time to think about what they are going to say and how to say it.

3 Pairwork. Students take turns to tell each other about the last time they had a really delicious meal.

Let's talk about ... (p 44)

This is a board game to revise all the main speaking topics from Units 1–9. You will need a dice and counters for each group of about four or five students. Each group will also need a stopwatch or a watch with a second hand.

Go through the instructions carefully with the class and make sure everyone understands how to play the game. As they play, go round monitoring and adjudicating in any disputes.

Test

Scoring: one point per correct answer unless otherwise indicated.

1
1. many
2. many
3. some
4. any
5. a lot
6. much
7. some
8. much

2
1. have to
2. have to
3. can
4. can't
5. have to
6. don't have to

3
1. began
2. bought
3. came
4. did
5. enjoyed
6. got
7. went
8. had
9. made
10. stopped
11. studied
12. thought

4 (1 point for each verb)
1. read, gave
2. broke, fell
3. met, were
4. meant, forgot

5
1. Where did you go on holiday last year?
2. Where did you stay?
3. How long did you go for?
4. Did you enjoy it?

6 1 c 2 a 3 d 4 b

7
1. adventurous
2. ambitious
3. creative
4. energetic
5. practical
6. sociable

8
1. sad
2. happy
3. angry
4. bored

9
1. apple
2. bread
3. carrot
4. cheese
5. chicken
6. grape
7. mushroom
8. pasta

10
1. bar
2. packet
3. jar
4. can
5. tin

11
1. nurse
2. tourist guide
3. accountant
4. model
5. DJ
6. cook

12
1. swimming
2. fishing
3. rowing
4. canoeing
5. kite-surfing

10 Review 2 Test

Name: Total: _____ /80

1 Quantity: much, many, a lot, some & any   8 points
Underline the correct alternative.

A: How (1) **much / many** students are in your class?

B: Not (2) **much / many** – just eight. And (3) **some / any** of them only come to class in the mornings.

*   *   *

C: I haven't got (4) **some / any** homework tonight.

D: Lucky you! I've got (5) **much / a lot**.

*   *   *

E: Was there (6) **much / many** rain last weekend?

F: There was (7) **some / any** rain, but not (8) **much / many**.

2 Modals – can, can't, have to, don't have to   6 points
Read the extract. Then complete the passage below with can, can't, have to or don't have to.

> **Driving in the UK and the USA**
>
> It's necessary to drive on the left in the UK and on the right in the USA. In the USA, it's okay to take your driving test when you are 16, but in the UK, this is not possible until you are 17. In the UK, and in most states in the USA, it's necessary to wear a seatbelt in a car.

In the UK, you (1) _____ drive on the left and in the USA, you (2) _____ drive on the right. In the USA, you (3) _____ take your driving test at 16, but in the UK, you (4) _____ take your driving test until you are 17. You (5) _____ wear a seatbelt in a car in the UK and in most states in the USA. In a few states in the USA, you (6) _____ wear a seatbelt.

3 Past simple (1)   12 points
Write the past simple of the verbs.

1 begin _____   7 go _____
2 buy _____   8 have _____
3 come _____   9 make _____
4 do _____   10 stop _____
5 enjoy _____   11 study _____
6 get _____   12 think _____

4 Past simple (2)   8 points
Complete the sentences with the past tense of the verbs in the box.

| break + fall   mean + forget   meet + be |
| read + give   ~~see + be~~ |

For example: We *saw* a terrible film at the cinema last night. It *was* rubbish!

1 I _____ a great book on holiday last month. Sara _____ it to me for my birthday.

2 Peter _____ his leg last week. He _____ off his motorbike.

3 I first _____ Daniel in 1998. We _____ at university together.

4 I _____ to send you an email yesterday, but I _____ your email address.

5 Past simple (3)   8 points
Read the answers and write the questions.

1 'Where _____?'
   'I went to Thailand on holiday last year.'

2 'Where _____?'
   'I stayed in a great hotel on the island of Phuket.'

3 'How long _____?'
   'I went for three weeks.'

4 '_____?'
   'Yes, I really enjoyed it. It was fantastic.'

6 Vocabulary – adjective + particle 4 points
Match the halves to make complete sentences.

1 I'm frightened   a) about my exam.
2 I'm worried   b) with you.
3 I'm interested   c) of spiders.
4 I'm angry   d) in art.

7 Vocabulary – character 6 points
Add the endings to the character adjectives. Choose from the endings in the box.

-able -al -ic -ious -ive -ous

1 adventur____
2 ambit____
3 creat____
4 energet____
5 practic____
6 soci____

8 Vocabulary – feelings 4 points
Complete the sentences with the adjectives in the box.

happy sad bored angry

1 'Why are you so _____?'
   'My cat died.'
2 I'm so _____ . I passed my exam!
3 She was very _____ with her son when he broke the window.
4 'I'm _____ .'
   'Yes, this video isn't very interesting.'

9 Vocabulary – food 8 points
Add the missing vowels (a, e, i, o, u) to complete the foods.

1 _ ppl _
2 br _ _ d
3 c _ rr _ t
4 ch _ _ s _
5 ch _ ck _ n
6 gr _ p _
7 m _ shr _ _ m
8 p _ st _

10 Vocabulary – containers 5 points
Choose the correct alternative.

1 I bought a **tub** / **bar** of chocolate.
2 I'd like a **packet** / **carton** of biscuits.
3 Did you buy a **can** / **jar** of jam?
4 Can I have a **can** / **bowl** of coke, please?
5 Have we got a **bottle** / **tin** of baked beans?

11 Vocabulary – jobs 6 points
Complete the sentences with the words in the box.

accountant cook DJ model nurse tourist guide

1 A _____ often works in a hospital.
2 A _____ usually knows a place very well.
3 An _____ has to be good at Maths.
4 A _____ usually has to be good-looking.
5 A _____ has to like music.
6 A _____ has to be creative with food.

12 Vocabulary – water sports 5 points
Add the missing vowels (a, e, i, o, u) to complete the water sports.

1 sw _ mm _ ng
2 f _ sh _ ng
3 r _ w _ ng
4 c _ n _ _ _ ng
5 k _ t _ -s _ rf _ ng

11 Looks Overview

This unit is about how people look, in terms of their physical appearance, who they look like and what clothes they wear. The grammar focus is on the present continuous, and vocabulary for describing people's appearance and clothes is introduced.

Students begin by matching descriptions of people to their photographs. They look at the words we use to talk about different aspects of someone's appearance and describe people in photographs and in their own classroom. They then go on to talk about family resemblances and then what clothes people have.

This leads into the next section which has a quiz about what clothes the average man in Britain has and how much he spends on clothes. This provides an opportunity to practise differentiating between some numbers which are often confused. Students also study some common verbs used in connection with clothes.

The topic of describing what someone is wearing is continued in the next section where students listen to descriptions of people arriving for the Oscars ceremony. They identify mistakes in pictures and then do a matching exercise to produce some present continuous sentences.

The final section develops this work on the present continuous, and the unit ends with a fun mime exercise in which students mime actions and make guesses using correct present continuous sentences.

Section	Aims	What the students are doing
Introduction pages 46–47	*Lexis*: description; *look(s) like*; clothes	Matching descriptions to photos of people.
		Categorising words to describe appearance.
		Doing an information gap activity identifying people in pictures. **Pairwork: Student A & B**
		Describing people in the class.
		Using *look(s) like* to talk about people's appearance.
		Identifying clothes items in a photo.
		Studying the plural forms of clothes words.
Mr Average page 48	*Reading skills*: reading for specific information	Doing a magazine quiz.
		Discussing clothing.
	Pronunciation: numbers	Listening to conversations and identifying the correct numbers.
	Lexis: verb collocations	Choosing the correct verbs to talk about clothes.
The Oscars page 49	*Listening skills*: listening for specific details	Listening to a description of people arriving for the Oscars and identifying mistakes in pictures.
		Matching beginnings and endings of present continuous sentences.
Close up page 49	*Grammar*: present continuous	Completing questions and short answers with the present continuous.
		Miming and guessing activities. **Pairwork: Student A & B**

80 UNIT 11 *Looks*   Visit www.insideout.net

11 Looks Teacher's notes

Books closed. Whole class. If students already have some knowledge of words to describe people, play *Who am I?* using famous people. Describe the appearance of someone famous and invite students to guess who it is. A student who gets the answer right can then think of another famous person and describe them. If students do not have enough vocabulary to do this, you could pre-teach some of the words they will encounter in this unit. Bring to class some magazine or newspaper photos of famous people and use them to illustrate vocabulary items such as *curly hair, shaved head, brown eyes, medium-length hair,* etc.

Lexis: description (p 46)

1 Pairwork. Students work together to read the descriptions and match each one with a photo. Allow them to compare results with other pairs before checking answers with the class.

> a) 2   b) 9   c) 6   d) 8   e) 10   f) 5   g) 4   h) 1   i) 7
> j) 3

2 Go through the instructions and the examples in the table with the class. Then allow them a few minutes to put all the words and phrases under the correct headings. Check answers with the class. Make sure students are aware that the *Opinion* column is for things that depend on the point of view of the speaker.

Hair length	Hair style	Hair colour
a shaved head	wavy	brown
short	curly	dark
medium-length	spiky	grey
		fair
		blond
		highlights

Eyes	Other	Opinion
blue	a gold chain	very pretty
dark brown	a moustache	a lovely smile
brown		very sweet

3 Give students a few minutes to add the words in the box to the categories. Allow them to work in pairs if they wish and to discuss which words are usually used for men, which for women and which for both. When checking answers, find out if it is the same in their language(s).

Hair length	Hair style	Hair colour
a shaved head	wavy	brown blond
short	curly	dark highlights
medium-length	spiky	grey red
long	straight	fair black

Eyes	Other	Opinion
blue	a gold chain	very pretty
dark brown	a moustache	a lovely smile
brown	earrings	very sweet
green	glasses	very beautiful
	a beard	very handsome
	a tattoo	He's good looking

> a) All except a moustache, a beard, pretty, beautiful, handsome.
> b) pretty, beautiful
> c) a moustache, a beard, handsome

4 **Pairwork: Student A & B** Students turn to their respective pages and follow the instructions. This is an information gap activity in which students ask each other questions about people's appearance in order to find out their names. Go round making sure that they are using descriptions of the people's appearance to do this and not simply pointing to the pictures or using their relative positions to identify them.

Student A
1 Jane's got long straight black hair. She's got a chain. She's got a bracelet.
2 Emma's got long fair hair. She's got a lovely smile.
3 Mickey is black. He's got short dark hair and he's got a beard and a moustache.
4 Jason is black. He's got short dark hair with blond highlights.
5 Max's got short dark hair. He's got a tattoo on his arm.

Student B
1 Marco's got a shaved head and he's got dark brown eyes.
2 Karen's got medium-length straight brown hair. She's got big earrings.
3 Lily's got curly blonde hair.
4 Paul's got short spiky grey hair and a beard.
5 Susanna's got long wavy blonde hair. She's got glasses. She's got a lovely smile.

5 Pairwork. Students take turns to describe people in the class and guess who is being described. In addition to looking at people in the classroom, students could look at other photos in *Inside Out*.

Lexis: *look(s) like* (p 47)

There is always potential confusion between the use of *looks like* and *looks*. This section deals only with *looks like*. If students ask about the use of *looks*, you may like to point out to students the difference between these two sentences:
He looks like his father.
He looks friendly.
Looks like is used to say that one person resembles another (often a family member). *Looks* is used to describe the way someone looks, eg: happy, sad, friendly, etc.

This could be left for later if you feel it is too confusing to introduce both structures together.

1 Pairwork. Refer students back to the photos on page 46 and tell them that each of the people shown is related to one of the others. Their task is to identify the family relationships. Do not confirm or deny any answers at this stage.

2 Students compare their answers with other pairs. Encourage them to use the language in the box to discuss and justify their choices.

3 59 SB p 123
Play the recording for students to check their answers.

> a) Albert and Jem
> b) Simon and Nancy
> c) Sue and Will
> d) Belen and Carla
> e) Gus and Zainab

> **59**
> Albert is Jem's father. They've got the same smile.
> Simon is Nancy's father. They've got the same mouth.
> Sue is Will's mother. Will looks like Sue.
> Belen is Carla's mother. They've got the same nose.
> Gus and Zainab are brother and sister. They've got the same dark eyes.

4 Students should first work individually to complete the sentences. They then compare with a partner.

Lexis: clothes (p 47)

1 Focus students' attention on the photo and elicit reactions to it. They then identify the items shown in the photo and tick the correct items. Check answers with the class. Point out the use of the word *accessories* to describe things such as belts, hats, etc. and the difference between *formal* and *casual*. You might like to check comprehension by asking students to suggest further items that could go in these three categories. Draw their attention to the section on *Clothes* on page 111.

> In the photo: shoes, shirts, trousers, jackets, suits, ties, belts, rings
> *Not* in the photo: trainers, boots, socks, underpants, coats, tops, T-shirts, tracksuits, jeans, sweaters, hats, sunglasses

2 60 SB p 123
Play the recording for students to listen and identify the correct numbers. Check answers with the class and ensure that everyone can pronounce all the numbers correctly. Elicit their reactions to what they have heard. Does anyone know someone like Stuart who owns a lot of clothes?

> a) 350
> b) 200
> c) 150
> d) 125

> **60**
> (I = Interviewer; S = Stuart)
> I: Stuart, you really like buying clothes, don't you?
> S: Oh yes, I love it.
> I: How many items of clothing have you got?
> S: Well ... I've got 350 shirts. I wear three or four different shirts every day.
> I: Goodness ... Er ... Who does the washing?
> S: My wife does the washing, and I do the ironing. Then I've got 200 suits. I like bright colours – red, blue, green.
> I: Mm, I see.
> S: Then I've got 150 pairs of trousers and 125 pairs of shoes.
> I: Stuart, why have you got so many clothes?
> S: Well, it's my hobby. Some people spend thousands of euros on cars, or holidays. I haven't got a car, and I never go on holiday. I buy clothes.

3 Pairwork. Go through the examples in the table with the class. Students then work together to put the singular and plural forms of all the words in Exercise 1 into the table. Check answers with the class. You may like to point out that the first group (*shoes, trainers*, etc.) are plural nouns. Some of them (such as *trousers, underpants, jeans, sunglasses*) only ever occur in the plural form. The second group are countable nouns.

	Singular	Plural
Plural nouns	a pair of shoes, trainers, boots, socks, underpants, trousers, jeans, sunglasses	2,3,4 pairs of shoes, trainers, boots, socks, underpants, trousers, jeans, sunglasses
Countable nouns	a shirt, jacket, suit, tie, coat, top, T-shirt, tracksuit, sweater, belt, hat, ring	2, 3, 4 shirts, jackets, suits, ties, coats, tops, T-shirts, tracksuits, sweaters, belts, hats, rings

4 Pairwork. Students work together to add clothes to the list in Exercise 1 and note how they are counted. Go round checking that they have chosen suitable items.

Mr Average (p 48)

Books closed. Whole class. Remind students of Stuart, the man in the previous section who had a lot of clothes. Establish the meaning of *average*. Ask students if they think they have a lot of clothes, not many clothes, or if they think they are about average. Ask anyone who admits to having a lot of clothes to tell the class how often they go shopping for clothes and what their favourite items of clothing are.

Reading (p 48)

1 Pairwork. Students discuss the question and report back to the class. In multinational classes, encourage them to say briefly what the magazines are like and what kind of articles they contain.

2 Give students a few minutes to answer the quiz. They should do this individually and then compare their results with a partner.

3 **Pairwork: Additional material** Ask students to turn to page 96 to check their answers to the quiz. Ask them if any of the answers surprise them. They may like to discuss how many items of clothing they think Ms Average has and how much she spends.

> See Student's Book page 96.

4 Pairwork. Students discuss the questions and report back to the class.

Numbers (p 48)

1 61 SB p 48
Play the recording for students to listen to the numbers. Then play it again for them to practise saying them. Ensure that students can differentiate between numbers ending in *-teen* and those ending in *-ty*. Draw students' attention to the section on *Numbers* on page 116.

2 62 SB p 123
Go through the items with students, asking them to pronounce the choices clearly. Then play the recording for them to make their choices. Check answers with the class.

> a) 14   b) 19   c) 15   d) 30

> **62**
> **Conversation a**
> A: *How many hats have you got?*
> B: *Fourteen.*
> A: *Forty?*
> B: *No, fourteen.*
> A: *Oh, fourteen.*
> **Conversation b**
> A: *How many ties have you got?*
> B: *Nineteen.*
> A: *Ninety?*
> B: *No, nineteen.*
> A: *Oh, nineteen.*
> **Conversation c**
> A: *How many rings have you got?*
> B: *Fifteen.*
> A: *Fifty?*
> B: *No, fifteen.*
> A: *Oh, fifteen.*
> **Conversation d**
> A: *How many T-shirts have you got?*
> B: *Thirty.*
> A: *Thirty?*
> B: *Yes, thirty.*
> A: *Oh, right.*

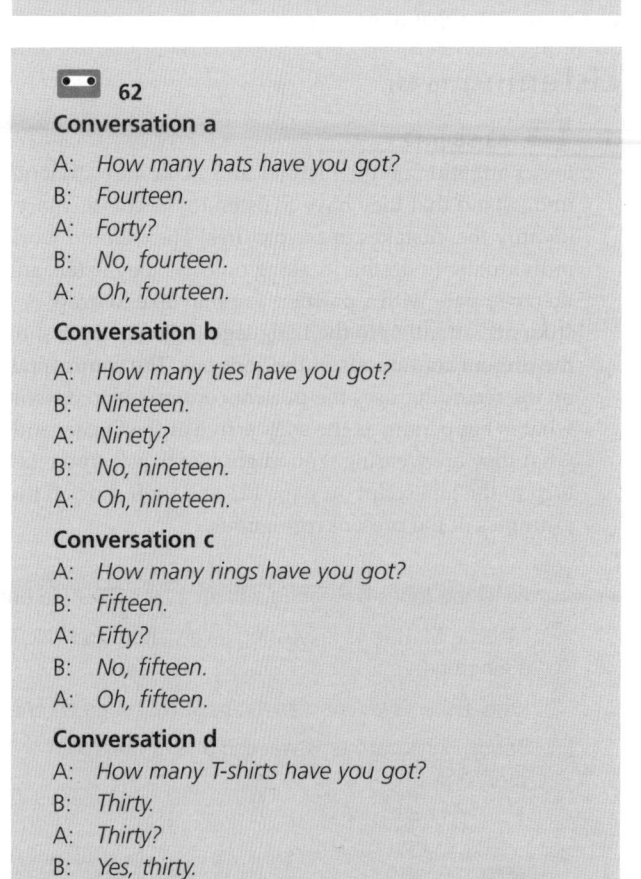

3 Pairwork. Students listen to conversation a) again and practise saying it. They then make similar conversations using different numbers from Exercise 1. Go round, making sure they are pronouncing the numbers correctly.

Lexis (p 48)

1 Pairwork. Students discuss which verb in each sentence is correct and underline their choices. When checking answers, make sure each correct sentence is read out in full to the class so that they hear the correct verb in context and get a feel for what sounds right.

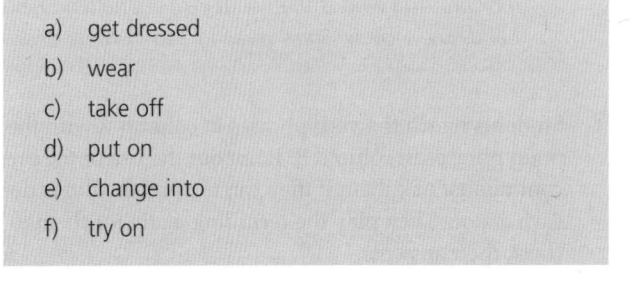

> a) get dressed
> b) wear
> c) take off
> d) put on
> e) change into
> f) try on

2 Students tick the sentences that are true for them and then compare with a partner.

The Oscars (p 49)

Books closed. Whole class. Find out how many students watch the Oscars ceremony on television. What do they think of the clothes that the celebrities wear to this event?

Ask students which actors won the most recent Oscar awards for the best male actor and for the best female actor, and if they can remember what they wore.

Listening (p 49)

1 📼 **63 SB p 123**

Focus attention on the pictures and make sure students understand that they have to listen to the commentary and identify the mistakes in the pictures. They should work individually to do this, making notes as they listen, and then compare with a partner. You may like to draw students' attention to the Language toolbox which shows the present continuous of the verb *talk*. The commentator on the recording uses the present continuous to describe what is happening as the stars arrive at the Oscars and what they are wearing. You might like to ask students to turn to the tapescript on page 123 and underline all the examples of the present continuous.

> Penelope Jones is wearing a blue dress NOT a red one.
>
> Melanie Matthews is wearing a very short dress NOT a long one.
>
> Kerry Fisher is wearing a white suit NOT a green one.
>
> Bobby Finn's partner is wearing a long dress NOT a short one.

> 📼 **63**
>
> Good evening. I'm Ross White and I'm standing outside Hollywood Theatre and I'm waiting for the big stars to arrive for this year's Oscar ceremony.
>
> And here comes Penelope Jones. She's wearing a beautiful blue dress.
>
> Oh, wow – there's Melanie Matthews. She's getting out of her car now – she's wearing a very short dress. Yes, very nice.
>
> Er oh, here's Kerry Fisher. She's wearing a white suit and red boots. What's she doing? Oh, she's waving to her fans. That's nice. Such a big star, but she loves her fans.
>
> Bobby Finn is arriving now. Oh, he's so good-looking. And who is that woman? He's holding her hand. She's lovely. She's wearing a long white dress.

2 Students match the verb phrases in column A with the noun phrases in column B. Point out the use of the present continuous. Ask them if they can remember who is doing each action. Then play the recording again for them to check their answers.

> a) I'm waiting for the big stars. (Ross White)
> b) She's wearing a beautiful blue dress. (Penelope Jones)
> c) She's getting out of her car. (Melanie Matthews)
> d) She's waving to her fans. (Kerry Fisher)
> e) He's holding her hand. (Bobby Finn)

Follow-up activity

In groups of four, students could act out the TV commentary to the arrival of a pair of film stars at the Oscars ceremony, with two students taking the part of the film stars and two the TV commentators describing what they are wearing.

Close up (p 49)

Present continuous

1 Draw students' attention to the Language reference section at the bottom of the page and Verb structures on page 114, where they will find more information about the form and use of the present continuous. Students complete the gaps in the questions and short answers. Do not check answers at this stage.

2 📼 **64 SB p 123**

Play the recording for students to listen, check their answers to Exercise 1 and repeat. They then work in pairs and take turns to ask and answer the questions in Exercise 1.

> a) Are; Yes, I am. No, I'm not.
> b) Are; Yes, I am. No, I'm not.
> c) Is; Yes, he/she is. No, he/she isn't.
> d) Is; Yes, it is. No, it isn't.
> e) Are; Yes, they are. No, they're not.
> f) Are; Yes, I am. No, I'm not.

> 📼 **64**
> a)
> 'Are you wearing jeans?'
> 'Yes, I am.'
> 'No, I'm not.'
> b)
> 'Are you sitting next to a window?'
> 'Yes, I am.'
> 'No, I'm not.'
> c)
> 'Is your teacher standing up?'
> 'Yes, she is.'
> 'No, she isn't.'

d)

'Is the traffic making a noise?'

'Yes, it is.'

'No, it isn't.'

e)

'Are the birds singing outside?'

'Yes, they are.'

'No, they aren't.'

f)

'Are you having a good time?'

'Yes, I am.'

'No, I'm not.'

3 **Pairwork: Student A & B** Students turn to their respective pages and follow the instructions. In this activity, students take turns to mime an action and guess what their partner is miming. Make sure they are using complete sentences with the present continuous, eg: *You are eating an ice-cream*, rather than simply identifying the action.

Test

Scoring: one point per correct answer unless otherwise indicated.

1 1 to 4: curly, spiky, straight, wavy

5 to 7: long, medium-length, short

8 to 10: blond, dark, highlights

2
1 pretty
2 handsome
3 good-looking
4 beautiful

3

R	T	C	S	O	F	W	I	J	E
T	R	A	I	N	E	R	S	Q	L
B	O	V	L	O	H	U	W	A	K
G	U	F	D	V	M	B	E	L	T
D	S	O	C	K	S	L	A	B	S
R	E	N	O	J	C	I	T	U	H
E	R	E	A	X	Y	S	E	R	I
S	S	O	T	Z	W	E	R	V	R
S	U	M	F	H	A	T	Q	O	T

4
1 thir*teen*
2 *thirty*
3 fif*teen*
4 *nine*ty

5
1 take
2 change
3 get
4 wear

6
1 I'm wait*ing* for a taxi at the moment.
2 Peter *is* doing his homework now.
3 Is it rain*ing* at the moment?
4 What *are you* doing?

7
1 Are, am
2 Is, isn't
3 Are, are
4 Is, is
5 Are, 'm not
6 Are, 're not

11 Looks Test

Name: _____   Total: _____ /40

1 Vocabulary – physical description (1) *10 points*
Complete the table with the words in the box.

| blond curly dark highlights long medium-length |
| short spiky straight wavy |

hair style	hair length	hair colour
1 _____	5 _____	8 _____
2 _____	6 _____	9 _____
3 _____	7 _____	10 _____
4 _____		

2 Vocabulary – physical description (2) *4 points*
Add the missing vowels (*a, e, i, o, u*) to complete the adjectives.

1 pr __ tty
2 h __ nds __ m __
3 g __ __ d-l __ __ k __ ng
4 b __ __ __ t __ f __ l

3 Vocabulary – clothes *8 points*
Circle eight more items of clothing in the word square.

R	T	C	S	O	F	W	I	J	E
T	R	A	I	N	E	R	S	Q	L
B	O	V	L	O	H	U	W	A	K
G	U	F	D	V	M	B	E	L	T
D	S	O	C	K	S	L	A	B	S
R	E	N	O	J	C	I	T	U	H
E	R	E	A	X	Y	S	E	R	I
S	S	O	T	Z	W	E	R	V	R
S	U	M	F	H	A	T	Q	O	T

4 Pronunciation – numbers *4 points*
Underline the most stressed syllable in each word.
For example: se<u>ven</u>

1 thirteen   3 fifteen
2 thirty   4 ninety

5 Vocabulary – verbs *4 points*
Complete the sentences with the verbs in the box.

| get wear take change |

When I get home from work I (1) _____ off my shoes and then I (2) _____ into something more casual. At the weekend, I never (3) _____ dressed before ten o'clock and I usually (4) _____ casual clothes like jeans and a T-shirt.

6 Present continuous (1) *4 points*
Correct the mistake in each sentence.

1 I'm wait for a taxi at the moment.
2 Peter doing his homework now.
3 Is it rain at the moment?
4 What you are doing?

7 Present continuous (2) *6 points*
Complete the questions and the answer with the correct auxiliary verbs.

1 '_____ you working today.'
   'Yes, I _____ .'
2 '_____ Greta helping you?'
   'No, she _____ .'
3 '_____ they dancing?'
   'Yes, they _____ .'
4 '_____ Sue going to the shops.'
   'Yes, she _____ .'
5 '_____ you feeling okay?'
   'No, I _____ .'
6 '_____ they phoning for a taxi?'
   'No, they _____ .'

12 Reality Overview

This unit looks at reality in terms of making dreams come true, the recent popularity of reality TV programmes and having hopes and dreams for the future. The grammar focus is on future forms – talking about hopes and wishes for the future and future plans.

Students begin by reading and listening to the story of a woman whose dreams came true when she followed the advice of a speaker at a seminar.

Next they examine the phenomenon of reality TV, discuss their TV likes and dislikes and decide what kind of person the makers of a programme like *Big Brother* are looking for. They complete their own application form for the programme.

The next section looks at ways of talking about things we would like to have or do in the future and ways of talking about our future intentions. Students read and listen to an interview with the winner of a reality TV show and discuss their own good intentions. They also do some work on discriminating between different vowel sounds.

In the final section, students listen to an Abba song, *I Have A Dream*. They use words from the lyrics to make sentences and discuss their feelings about the song and how the lyrics relate to them.

Section	Aims	What the students are doing
Introduction page 50	*Reading skills*: reading for gist	Reading the first part of a story and answering questions.
		Matching items on a list to pictures.
	Listening skills: listening for specific information	Listening to the second part of the story.
		Marking sentences true or false.
		Discussing students' own dream list.
Reality TV page 51	*Lexis*: TV programmes	Listening to extracts from TV programmes and identifying the genre.
		Studying an online application form for a reality TV show.
		Discussing criteria for choosing candidates for a reality TV show.
	Writing: an application form	Completing an application form for a reality TV show.
Close up pages 52–53	*Grammar*: want to, 'd (would) like to, hope to, (be) going to	Reordering sentences.
		Discussing wishes for the future.
		Reading and listening to an interview with the winner of a reality TV show talking about her plans for the future.
		Correcting and discussing good intentions sentences.
		Asking and answering questions about plans for the immediate future. **Pairwork: Student A & B**
	Pronunciation: vowel sounds	Identifying words with different vowel sounds.
I Have A Dream page 53	*Song*: listening for gist and for detail	Listening to the lyrics of an Abba song and completing statements about the song.
		Completing sentences with words from the song.

> **More information about topics in this unit**
>
> **Reality TV, Writing 1** *www.channel4.com/bigbrother*
> **I Have A Dream** *www.abbasite.com*

Reality UNIT 12 87

12 Reality *Teacher's notes*

Books closed. Whole class. Write *I'd like a car* and *I'd like to go to Africa* on the board. Then ask students to write down on three pieces of paper the names of three things that they would like to have or do in the future. Collect in all the pieces of paper, put them in a box and shuffle them. Invite students to take turns to pick three pieces of paper out of the box and read them. If they would like any of the things on their new pieces of paper, they should make sentences like those on the board. If their sentences are correct, wave your magic wand (a ruler, board rubber or the like) and say *Your wish is granted!*

Reading & listening (p 50)

1 Focus attention on the text and the photographs. Go through the questions with the class and then give them time to read the text and find the answers. Check answers with the class.

> a) A dream list – a list of things she wanted in her life.
> b) Pictures of the things she wanted in her life.

2 Give students time to read the story again and to match the photos with Glenna's list. Then check answers with the class.

> 1 d 2 b 3 a 4 c 5 g 6 f 7 e

3 🎧 **65 SB p 124**

Play the recording for students to listen to more of Glenna's story. Elicit from the class whether or not her dreams came true.

> Yes, they did.

> **65**
> *About eight weeks after she made her dream book, Glenna was driving down a California freeway. Suddenly a gorgeous red and white Cadillac passed her. She looked at the car because it was a beautiful car. And the driver looked at her and smiled, and she smiled back. He followed her for the next fifteen miles. He parked, she parked ... and eventually she married him.*
>
> *After their first date, Jim sent Glenna a dozen roses. They dated for two years, and every Monday morning she received a red rose.*
>
> *Then she found out that Jim had a hobby. His hobby was collecting diamonds.*
>
> *They had the traditional wedding Glenna wanted, and Jim chose their honeymoon destination – it was St John's Island in the Caribbean. Then they moved into their beautiful new home.*
>
> *Glenna didn't tell Jim about the dream book for almost a year after they got married.*
>
> *Eight months after she created her dream book, Glenna became vice-president of human resources in the company where she worked – it was her dream job.*
>
> *This sounds like a fairy tale, but it's a true story.*

4 Pairwork. Students listen again and decide if the sentences are true or false. Check answers with the class before asking them to correct the false sentences. Then check answers again.

> a) True.
> b) False. She met him on the freeway (motorway).
> c) False. Every Monday.
> d) True.
> e) True.
> f) False. They went to St John's Island in the Caribbean.
> g) True.
> h) False. One year after.
> i) False. She got her dream job.

5 Give students time to work individually to create their own dream lists. They can then compare with a partner. Encourage them to report back to the class. Does anyone have an unusual item on their dream list?

Reality TV (p 51)

Books closed. Whole class. Reality TV is the fairly recent phenomenon of making TV programmes with ordinary people (and occasionally celebrities). One kind of programme involves people taking part in contests in which they spend long periods of time in a house or some other setting where cameras monitor their every movement day and night. Members of the public then vote every day or every week for one contestant to be removed until only one is left, the winner. These programmes are very cheap to make for the TV companies and have proved very popular, particularly as a source of material for the tabloid press. Find out what reality TV programmes are popular in the students' country or countries, what they think of them and whether they watch them. Would any of them ever consider applying to be a contestant on one of these shows?

Lexis: TV programmes (p 51)

1 🔊 **66 SB p 124**

Go through the list of programmes with the class, then play the recording for them to identify each one. Check answers with the class.

1	A game show
7	A documentary
4	The news
5	A soap opera
3	A sports programme
8	Reality TV
6	A chat show
2	The weather

🔊 **66**

1

A: Next question. On the border of which two South American countries can you find the Iguaçu Falls?
B: Oh. Um. Mm, I know this one. Is it Argentina and Chile? No – Argentina and Brazil.
A: Is that your final answer?
B: Yes.
A: Are you sure?
B: Um, yes.
A: Carol, I asked you where you can find the Iguaçu Falls. Your answer was on the border of Argentina and Brazil. It's the correct answer. You've just won 125,000 euros!!!

2

Plenty of sunshine around today. Temperatures up to 32 degrees. And tomorrow is going to be another beautiful day. There may be some cloud in the north-east, but generally a warm and sunny day.

3

That's it. They've done it. Liverpool have beaten Real Madrid 3–2. A goal by Owen in the dying seconds ... Incredible scenes here ...

4

Police arrested two men after they attempted to rob a bank in the centre of London this morning. The men were armed, but nobody was hurt.

5

A: Oh hello, Mrs Jones. How are you today?
B: Oh, can't complain. Here, have you heard about that Andy Clifford?
A: No, what?
B: Well, I've heard he's going to get married to Rachel Smedley.
A: Rachel Smedley – no!

6

A: Well, Michael, you've had a very successful career in the film business. Did you always want to be a movie star?
B: Not exactly. I grew up on a farm in the Mid-West, and when I was a young boy all I wanted to be was a farmer like my dad.
A: So what made you change your mind?
B: Well, it was ...

7

The shark is the king of the sea. It fills people with fear. But that's not the whole story. Yes, some kinds of shark are dangerous, but most of them are harmless and shy. Take the Spotted Wobbegong – not a beautiful specimen – quite ugly in fact ...

8

A: Anybody want a cup of tea?
B: Yeah, okay.
A: Big Brother: This is Big Brother. Will Lynne please come to the Diary room immediately?
B: Ooh, I wonder what that's all about then?
A: Dunno. Do you want sugar in your tea?

2 Pairwork. Students discuss which types of TV programme they like and hate. Encourage them to give reasons whenever possible.

Writing (p 51)

1 Pairwork. It is unlikely that students will not have heard of *Big Brother* as it is on all over the world, but direct their attention to the information box in the margin if they need more information.

Note: If students are interested, they could log on to the website for the show in Britain: *www.channel4.com/bigbrother*

Students work together to go through the online application form and discuss the questions. Go round, answering any questions on vocabulary. Encourage them to report back to the class.

a) Outgoing, interesting and competitive people.
b) €500,000.

2 Pairwork. Students read the three reasons given by different people. They then discuss who they think the programme makers will choose. In a class feedback session find out how much agreement there is and why students have chosen a particular person.

3 Students work individually to complete the application form for themselves.

4 Allow time for students to read each other's application forms. They can then vote on the best reason for being on the show.

Close up (p 52)

want to, 'd (would) like to, hope to

1 Draw students' attention to the three reasons for appearing on *Big Brother* given by Eric, Sheryl and Lynne in the previous section. Ask students to underline *I hope to, I want to* and *I'd like to* and point out that these verbs are used to express wishes for the future. Go through the example with the class and then ask students to work individually to rewrite the sentences. Check answers with the class. Tell students that they will find more information about future forms in the Language reference section on page 53.

> a) I want to travel around the world.
> b) I don't want to get married.
> c) I'd like to have lots of children.
> d) I wouldn't like to be famous.
> e) I hope to retire before I'm fifty.

2 Students work individually to decide which sentences are true for them and then compare with a partner. You might like to ask them to produce some sentences of their own using *want to, 'd like to* and *hope to*.

3 **Pairwork: Additional material** Divide the class into groups of three and ask them to turn to page 96. In this activity, students choose pictures or draw their own to represent their dreams. They then explain their pictures to their partners. Go round, making sure that students are using *want to, 'd like to* and *hope to* correctly.

(be) going to (p 52)

1 Again, draw students' attention to the Language reference section on page 53 and Verb structures on page 115, where they will find more information about future forms. The Language toolbox on this page also shows how *(be) going to* is used. You may like to point out that *(be) going to* is used for plans that we are quite sure about.

Go through the phrases in the box and elicit that they are used to talk about future plans. Give students time to read the interview and decide where each phrase should go. Do not check answers at this stage.

2 🔊 **67 SB p 124**
Play the recording for students to listen and check their answers. Answer any queries they may have.

> 1 you're going to
> 2 I'm going to
> 3 are you going to
> 4 I'm going to
> 5 I'm going to
> 6 are you going to
> 7 I'm definitely not going to
> 8 are you going to
> 9 we're going to
> 10 I'm going to
> 11 I'm going to

🔊 **67**

(D = Danielle; L = Lynne)

D: Lynne, congratulations. How do you feel?
L: Oh, great. I feel fantastic. I'm so happy.
D: What's the first thing you're going to do when you get out?
L: I'm going to have a big party for all my friends. I missed them so much.
D: Ah. What are you going to do with the money?
L: Well, I'm going to give some of it to charity, and with the rest I'm going to buy a house for my mum.
D: So, which of your Big Brother housemates are you going to see again?
L: There are some people I'd like to see again, and there are two people I'm definitely not going to see again. I think you know who they are.
D: Yes, of course. That was really horrible. But your hair looks okay now.
L: Yeah, well ...
D: Anyway Lynne, the question everyone wants to ask. You and Eddie became really good – er – friends in the House. So are you going to see Eddie again?
L: Well, I don't know. Yes, of course we're going to see one another. But we don't know what's going to happen.
D: What advice would you give to future Big Brother contestants?
L: Don't do it! No, I'm only joking. Be yourself, and be patient. It's very boring in there.
D: Finally, Lynne, what are your future plans?
L: Well, first I'm going to go out and spend some money. Then I want to start my singing career. I'm going to record a CD. Actually, I'd quite like to be a television presenter.
D: Oh – well, good luck.

3 Pairwork. Students look at the sentences and put the words in brackets in the correct position. Allow them to compare with another pair before checking with the class.

> a) I'm going <u>to</u> do more exercise.
> b) <u>I'm</u> going to save money.
> c) I'm <u>going</u> to spend more time with my family.
> d) I'm going <u>to</u> book my holidays earlier.
> e) I'm <u>not</u> going to arrive late for appointments.

4 Pairwork. Students discuss the good intentions in Exercise 3.

5 **Pairwork: Student A & B** Students turn to their respective pages and follow the instructions. In this activity they complete a questionnaire and compare results with a partner.

Vowel sounds (p 53)

1 Encourage students to say the words aloud so that they get a feel for what sounds right. They should circle the word in each group that has a different vowel sound. Do not check answers at this stage.

2 68 SB p 53

Play the recording for students to check their answers to Exercise 1. Then play it again for them to repeat the words.

> a) dream
> b) drink
> c) island
> d) kind
> e) believe
> f) make

3 Again, stress the importance of saying the words aloud as students decide on the correct columns. Check answers with the class.

/iː/	/ɪ/	/aɪ/	/eɪ/
dream	drink	mind	game
people	list	type	wait
reason	think	island	make
believe		kind	
week		advice	
speak		online	

I Have A Dream (p 53)

Books closed. Whole class. Although Abba are a group from the late 1970s, their music is still popular, and there have been revivals, tribute groups and musicals based on their songs. Find out how many Abba songs your students are familiar with and ask why they think the group's popularity has lasted this long. Are there any groups today that they think will still be popular 25 years from now?

Note: Fans of Abba could log on to their official website: *www.abbasite.com* for news, biographies, photos and sound clips.

Song (p 53)

1 69 SB p 53

Play the song as the students read the lyrics. They then work individually to choose the most appropriate words to complete the sentences. They should compare with a partner. If the students like the song, play it again for them to listen for pleasure or sing along.

2 Give students a couple of minutes to complete the sentences, then check with the class.

> a) dream
> b) sing
> c) cope
> d) tale
> e) believe
> f) something

3 Students work individually to decide which sentences in Exercise 2 are true for them. They then compare with a partner.

Test

> Scoring: one point per correct answer unless otherwise indicated.
>
> **1** 1 game show
>   2 chat show
>   3 weather
>   4 sports programme
>   5 documentary
>   6 news
>   7 reality TV
>   8 soap opera
>
> **2** 1 miracles
>   2 tale
>   3 cope
>   4 dream
>
> **3** 1 'm (am)
>   2 to
>   3 'd (would)
>   4 to
>
> **4** (2 points per correct answer)
>   1 One day, I hope to travel around the world.
>   2 Where do you want to go?
>   3 I'd like to visit South America.
>   4 I'm going to learn Spanish.
>   5 Do you want to travel on your own?
>   6 I'm going to go with a friend.
>
> **5** 1 to 3: believe, dream, people
>   4 to 6: drink, list, think
>   7 to 9: advice, kind, type
>   10 to 12: game, make, wait

12 Reality Test

Name: _____   Total: _____ /40

1 Vocabulary – TV programmes *8 points*
Match the TV programme with the extract.

| sports programme   documentary   news   weather |
| game show   soap opera   chat show   reality TV |

1 'And now, question number 15 for £1 million.'
_____

2 'Tonight my guest is Hollywood actor Tim Bond.'
_____

3 'Tomorrow is going to be sunny and hot.'
_____

4 'In ten minutes, Roma versus Real Madrid.'
_____

5 'In tonight's programme: Is there life on Mars?'
_____

6 'Good evening. Here are today's main stories.'
_____

7 'The person who is going to leave the *Big Brother House* today is … Anouska.'
_____

8 'Have you heard? Sandra and her next-door neighbour – they're getting married!'
_____

2 Vocabulary – collocations *4 points*
Complete the sentences with the words in the box.

| dream   cope   tale   miracles |

1 Do you believe in _____ ?
2 When I was a child, my favourite fairy _____ was *Cinderella*.
3 Do you think he can _____ with all this work?
4 I had a bad _____ last night.

3 Future forms (1) *4 points*
Complete the sentences by adding the missing words.

1 I _____ going to go to university after school.
2 I want _____ study English.
3 Then I _____ like to get a job in a foreign country.
4 And I hope _____ live in the USA for a few years.

4 Future forms (2) *12 points*
Reorder the words to make complete sentences.

1 travel around the world / I / One day / to / hope
_____.

2 want / you / go / Where / do / to
_____?

3 I / to / 'd / South America / visit / like
_____.

4 Spanish / to / I / learn / 'm / going
_____.

5 on your own / you / travel / want / Do / to
_____?

6 going / I / with a friend / 'm / go / to
_____.

5 Pronunciation – vowel sounds *12 points*
Put the words into the correct column in the table according to the underlined vowel sound.

| adv<u>i</u>ce   bel<u>ie</u>ve   dr<u>ea</u>m   dr<u>i</u>nk   g<u>a</u>me   k<u>i</u>nd   l<u>i</u>st |
| m<u>a</u>ke   p<u>eo</u>ple   th<u>i</u>nk   t<u>y</u>pe   w<u>ai</u>t |

/iː/ **s<u>ee</u>** | /ɪ/ **k<u>i</u>ss**
1 _____ | 4 _____
2 _____ | 5 _____
3 _____ | 6 _____

/aɪ/ **sk<u>y</u>** | /eɪ/ **d<u>a</u>y**
7 _____ | 10 _____
8 _____ | 11 _____
9 _____ | 12 _____

13 Things Overview

This unit is about material possessions and provides students with the opportunity to talk about shopping. The grammar focus is on comparatives and superlatives.

The unit begins by looking at the personal possessions people are most likely to lose and items they least often lose. Students listen to a conversation in a Lost property office and then write conversations of their own describing lost objects.

The next section turns to the subject of money. They read an article about a woman with financial problems who set up a website to ask people to send her money to help her out. Students practise using vocabulary connected to money and talk about shopping experiences. They also practise the schwa sound (/ə/) in comparative adjectives in preparation for the next section which looks at comparatives and superlatives in more detail. Students write sentences using comparatives and superlatives and do a pairwork activity involving making a questionnaire about their town/city.

Finally, students read about the sale of one of Marilyn Monroe's dresses. They talk about the price they pay for items of clothing and practise saying large numbers.

Section	Aims	What the students are doing
Introduction page 54	*Reading skills*: reading for gist	Matching words and pictures.
		Reading and discussing a short article about losing things.
	Listening skills: listening for specific information	Listening to a phone conversation between a woman and a lost property officer and identifying the lost object.
		Completing questions.
		Writing a conversation.
Shop till you drop pages 55–56	*Reading skills*: reading for gist	Reading and discussing an article about a woman with financial problems.
	Lexis: money	Completing sentences with words connected to money.
	Conversation skills: fluency work	Anecdote: talking about a shopping trip.
	Pronunciation: the schwa /ə/	Practising saying the schwa sound with a series of chants.
Close up page 56	*Grammar*: comparatives and superlatives	Completing a table with comparative forms.
		Using comparatives to make sentences.
		Writing comparative and superlative forms of adjectives.
		Completing and answering a questionnaire on students' own town/city. **Pairwork: Student A & B**
The most valuable things in the world page 57	*Reading skills*: reading for specific details	Predicting answers to questions, then checking with a text on Marilyn Monroe.
		Talking about how much students pay for clothes.
	Lexis: big numbers	Practising saying big numbers and talking about valuable things.

More information about topics in this unit

Shop till you drop, Reading 1 *www.savekaryn.com*
The most valuable thing in the world, Reading 1 *www.marilynmonroe.com*

13 Things Teacher's notes

Books closed. Divide the class into groups and give each group a block of small Post-it notes in a different colour. Tell them that they have five minutes to label as many things in the classroom as they can. Each thing can only be labelled once, but if they think another team has made a spelling mistake or labelled something incorrectly, they can relabel it (without removing the other team's label). When the time is up, the teams get one point for each object they have labelled correctly.

Reading (p 54)

1 Pairwork. Focus attention on the pictures and the words in the box. Give students a few minutes to match them. You could make this a race if you wish, with the first pair to finish putting up their hands and giving the answers.

> a) a wedding ring
> b) an address book
> c) a glove
> d) keys
> e) a TV remote
> f) a handbag
> g) a pet (snake)
> h) money
> i) a mobile phone
> j) glasses

2 **Pairwork: Additional material** Go through the instructions with the class, then give pairs time to discuss the question and make their decision. Discourage them from looking up the answer until they have committed themselves to three objects from the list. Allow them to compare and discuss with other pairs, too. As a follow-up, you could ask them to tell the class whether they have ever lost any of these things and, if so, what happened.

> See Student's Book page 96.

3 Pairwork. Students discuss which things they think people are least likely to lose. Note that this question is not confined to the objects listed in Exercise 1. Students can add their own ideas. When they have made a decision, they read the article to check. Check answers with the class and elicit reactions to the text. Ask how students feel when they lose something and what they do.

> British people are least likely to lose their car, their passport or their laptop computer.

4 Groupwork. Students work together and discuss the questions. You could appoint a secretary in each group to make notes and report back to the class.

Listening (p 54)

1 🎧 70 SB p 124

Elicit or explain that a Lost property office is a place (eg: in a station or large public building) where people who have lost things can go to get them back. Go through the instructions with the class and focus attention on the pictures of the three bags. Play the recording and ask students to say which bag Judy lost.

> Bag b.

🎧 70
(LPO = Lost property officer; J = Judy)

LPO: *Lost property. How can I help?*

J: *Oh, um, hello ... I'm ringing because I lost my bag yesterday.*

LPO: *I see. Well, we received thirty-eight bags yesterday. What colour is it and what's it made of?*

J: *Oh yes, er ... It's black and it's made of leather.*

LPO: *Hm ... black ... leather ... I've got twenty-four black leather bags here. Can you give me some more information?*

J: *Oh dear. Yes. Um, it's got a zip on the front and a long strap.*

LPO: *Has it got any pockets on the front?*

J: *No, but there's a pocket on the side for a mobile phone.*

LPO: *Okay, how big is it?*

J: *It's quite big – I wear it over my shoulder.*

LPO: *So what kind of bag is it? A shoulder bag?*

J: *Yes, a shoulder bag. That's right.*

LPO: *Is there anything in it?*

J: *Yes, there's an address book, and some keys. Oh, and Hissy.*

LPO: *Hissy?*

J: *Yes, Hissy the snake.*

LPO: *There's a snake ... in your bag?*

J: *Yes, but don't worry, it's made of plastic. It belongs to my five-year-old son.*

LPO: *Right, well, I think we have your bag here. The office is open from nine in the morning ...*

2 Students should try to complete the questions from memory. Allow them to compare with a partner before playing the recording again for them to check their answers.

> a) What
> b) What's
> c) Can
> d) How
> e) Is there
> f) What kind

Follow-up activity

One of the Lost property officer's questions is *What's it made of?* You could take this opportunity to teach some words for materials using objects in the classroom. Useful words for materials include *plastic, leather, wood, paper, glass, metal, wool, china, cloth*. Put students into groups and give them one minute to write down as many objects as they can which are made of plastic, then leather, etc. Award one point for each object.

3 **Pairwork: Additional material** Students turn to page 97 and follow the instructions. In this activity, students match descriptions to pictures of bags and then use the descriptions and the questions in Exercise 2 to play a guessing game.

> *Possible answers*
> a) 4 b) 6, 9 c) 1, 2, 5 d) 3 e) 1 f) 6, 9
> g) 3, 6, 9 h) 8 i) 2, 5, 7, 8 j) 2, 5 k) 7 l) 5

4 Pairwork. Students can use the language from the previous two exercises and the tapescript from Exercise 1 on page 124 to write their conversations. Allow time for the conversations to be performed to the class.

Shop till you drop (p 55)

Books closed. Whole class. Ask students whether they usually give money to people who ask for it in the street.

Reading (p 55)

1 Give students a few minutes to read the article, then ask for the answer to the question. Elicit students' reactions to the article. Would they consider giving money to Karyn? Are they surprised that so many people did?

Note: Students may be interested to know that Karyn has continued developing her website and they can find the latest news about her on: *www.savekaryn.com*

> To try to get money to pay off her credit card debt.

2 Pairwork. Students discuss the questions. Encourage them to report back to the class.

Lexis: money (p 55)

1 Ensure that students realise that the words they need to complete the sentences are all in the article about Karyn. Give them a few minutes to find the words and complete the sentences. Check answers with the class.

> a) save
> b) spent
> c) credit
> d) bill
> e) afford

2 Students work individually to decide which of the sentences are true for them. They make changes to the others to make them true. They then compare in pairs.

Anecdote (p 55)

See the Introduction on page 4 for more ideas on how to set up, monitor and repeat Anecdotes.

1 71 SB p 124

Pairwork. Give students plenty of time to decide what they want to talk about and to read and listen to the questions.

> 71
> *Think about the last time you went shopping.*
> *Where and when did you go shopping?*
> *What did you want to buy?*
> *How long did you spend shopping?*
> *Did you get what you wanted?*
> *How much money did you spend and how did you pay?*
> *Did you enjoy your shopping trip?*

2 Give students time to prepare what they are going to say. They can use the sentence beginnings to help them, but discourage them from writing down whole sentences and simply reading them out.

3 Students should maintain eye contact with their partners as much as possible as they talk about their shopping trip so that they are not tempted to read from a script.

The schwa /ə/ (p 56)

1 72 SB p 56

Play the recording for students to listen and repeat. If it helps them to maintain the rhythm, you could ask them to tap gently on the desk in time with the speaker. Elicit what the vowel sounds have in common.

> They are all the same sound (the schwa).

2 Students work individually to decide if any of the lines are true for them and to make their own chants. Go round, offering help and encouragement, and allow them to compare with a partner before they perform their chants to the class.

Close up (p 56)

Comparatives

1 Pairwork. Draw students' attention to the *-er* form of the adjectives in the last exercise. Establish that these are all comparative forms, comparing one thing with another. You might also like to point out the negative comparison *not as ... as* at this stage. Focus attention on the table and let students work together to try to complete it. Check answers with the class and remind them that they will find more information about comparatives in the Language reference section on page 57 and the section on *Adjectives* on page 115.

Note: For adjectives with two or more syllables, the Language reference section illustrates comparative and superlative forms using *more* and *the most*. The Close up exercises practice these forms. You might also like to point out to students that *less* and *the least* can also combine with such adjectives to give the opposite meaning: i.e. *more interesting than – less interesting than, the most expensive – the least expensive*.

> a) rich, richer
> b) slim, slimmer
> c) friendly, friendlier
> d) good, better
> e) interesting, more interesting

2 Pairwork. Draw attention to the list in the margin, then give students time, working individually, to put together their own combinations of nouns and comparative adjectives to produce two true sentences and one false one. They then exchange sentences and guess which of their partner's sentences is false.

3 Pairwork. Students work together to complete the sentences. Check answers with the class.

> a) taller, tall
> b) older, old
> c) more relaxed, relaxed
> d) bigger, big
> e) further, far
> f) more expensive, expensive

4 Students can continue to work in pairs to do this. Make sure they formulate questions correctly when checking their information. Allow plenty of time for this.

Superlatives (p 56)

Establish that whilst comparatives compare two things, superlatives are used for comparisons involving more than two. Remind them that the Language reference section on page 57 and the section on *Adjectives* on page 115 will help them with the form of superlatives. You might like to point out that *the most* + adjective can be replaced by *the least* + adjective to give the opposite meaning (eg: *the most interesting – the least interesting*).

1 Pairwork. Students write both the comparative and the superlative forms of the adjectives. Check answers with the class.

> bad – worse than – the worst
> beautiful – more beautiful than – the most beautiful
> busy – busier than – the busiest
> cheap – cheaper than – the cheapest
> famous – more famous than – the most famous
> far – further than – the furthest
> good – better than – the best
> modern – more modern than – the most modern
> popular – more popular than – the most popular
> ugly – uglier than – the ugliest

2 **Pairwork: Student A & B** Students turn to their respective pages and follow the instructions. Check that they have completed their questions correctly before they interview their partners.

> Student A
> a) ugliest
> b) most famous
> c) oldest
> d) most expensive
> e) biggest
> f) most popular
>
> Student B
> a) most interesting
> b) most beautiful
> c) most modern
> d) busiest
> e) cheapest
> f) quietest

The most valuable things in the world (p 57)

Books closed. Whole class. Write the title of this section *The most valuable things in the world* on the board and ask students for suggestions as to what these might be.

96 UNIT 13 Things

Reading (p 57)

1 Pairwork. Focus attention on the photograph of Marilyn Monroe and ask students if they like the dress she is wearing. Tell them to read the questions and try to guess the answers, but not to read the article at this stage. When they have decided on their guesses (they can compare with other pairs if they wish), they read the article to check. Go through the answers with the class and elicit students' reaction to the text. Do they understand why some people will pay huge sums of money for the clothes of famous people? Is there any celebrity whose clothes they would be prepared to pay lots of money for?

Note: For more information on Marilyn Monroe, log on to the official website: *www.marilynmonroe.com*

> 1 b   2 a   3 b   4 c   5 c

2 Students work individually to come up with figures for each of the items. They then compare with a partner. Be sensitive in classes where there is disparity of income as some students who cannot afford expensive clothes may feel embarrassed if they are compared with richer students.

Lexis: big numbers (p 57)

1 **73 SB p 125**

Allow students to work in pairs to decide on the correct pronunciation of the numbers. Encourage them to say them aloud to get a feel for what sounds right. Then play the recording for them to listen, check and repeat the numbers. Point out the use of commas to divide off thousands. Many languages use commas in decimals. English uses full points. Remind students about the section on *Numbers* on page 116.

> **73**
> a) *Sixty-six thousand, one hundred <u>and</u> twelve.*
> b) *One hundred <u>and</u> ninety-four thousand, four hundred <u>and</u> fifty-nine.*
> c) *Twenty-five thousand.*
> d) *One hundred <u>and</u> fifty-seven thousand, nine hundred <u>and</u> forty-seven.*
> e) *One million, nine hundred <u>and</u> eighteen thousand, three hundred <u>and</u> eighty-seven.*
> f) *Three hundred <u>and</u> twenty-four thousand, one hundred <u>and</u> eighty-eight.*

2 **74 SB p 125**

Before you play the recording, go through the instructions with the class and ask them to try to predict which price goes with each item of clothing. Then play the recording for them to listen and match. Check answers with the class.

> a) some pop star clothing
> b) a bikini
> c) a pair of jeans
> d) a boxing robe
> e) a watch
> f) a film costume

> **74**
> 1 *The most valuable bikini was valued at $194,459. The hand-made, diamond-encrusted bikini was made for Windsor fashion week in 2000.*
> 2 *The most valuable watch was in 18-carat gold made by Patek Phillippe in 1922. A Middle Eastern collector bought it for $1,918,387 in 1999.*
> 3 *Levi Strauss and Co. bought a 100-year-old pair of Levi 501s from a private collector for $25,000 in 1997.*
> 4 *The dress that Judy Garland wore in the 1939 production of 'The Wizard of Oz' was auctioned for $324,188 in 1999.*
> 5 *The owner of the Las Vegas Hard Rock Hotel bought Geri Halliwell's Union Jack dress for $66,112 in 1998. She wore it for a Spice Girls' performance at the 1997 Brit Awards.*
> 6 *The boxing robe Mohammed Ali wore before his so-called 'Rumble in the Jungle' fight with George Foreman in 1974 was sold for $157,947 in a 1997 Beverly Hills sale.*

3 Pairwork. Students discuss their most valuable possessions. You might like to widen this to include items whose value is not monetary, but sentimental.

Test

Scoring: one point per correct answer unless otherwise indicated.

1
1. book
2. remote
3. ring
4. phone

2 1 c 2 a 3 d 4 b

3
1. spend
2. save
3. pay
4. afford

4
1. I'm tall<u>er</u> th<u>an</u> my brot<u>her</u>.
2. I'm not <u>as</u> lucky <u>as</u> you.
3. My sis<u>ter</u> is two years old<u>er</u> th<u>an</u> me.

5
1. Five thousand, six hundred and fifty
2. Forty-five thousand, five hundred and sixty
3. Two hundred and fifty thousand, six hundred
4. One million, seven hundred and sixty-eight thousand, four hundred and thirty

6
1. bigger
2. the happiest
3. the most interesting
4. better
5. the worst
6. further

7
1. The UK is ~~more~~ smaller than the USA.
2. Paris is <u>more</u> beautiful than London.
3. Russia is the ~~most~~ biggest country in the world.
4. Thailand is not as expensive <u>as</u> Japan.
5. Spain is bigger <u>than</u> Portugal.
6. Ukraine is <u>the</u> biggest country in Europe.

8
1. smaller
2. lighter
3. more expensive
4. the best

13 Things Test

Name: _____ Total: _____ /40

1 Vocabulary – collocations *4 points*
Complete the sentences with the words in the box.

> remote   ring   book   phone

1 Can you see my address _____ anywhere?
2 Where is the TV _____ ?
3 Can I see your wedding _____ , please?
4 Have you got your mobile _____ on you?

2 Vocabulary – describing things *4 points*
Match the beginnings with the correct endings.

1 How   a) colour is it?
2 What   b) mobile phone is it?
3 What's   c) big is it?
4 What kind of   d) it made of?

3 Vocabulary – money *4 points*
Complete the sentences with the words in the box.

> afford   pay   save   spend

I (1) _____ all the money I earn and I can never
(2) _____ anything. The problem is that I always
(3) _____ by credit card and I never remember how much I spend. And now I need a new computer, but I can't
(4) _____ one.

4 Pronunciation – schwa /ə/ *8 points*
Underline all the schwas /ə/ in the sentences. There are eight in total.

1 I'm taller than my brother.
2 I'm not as lucky as you.
3 My sister is two years older than me.

5 Vocabulary – big numbers *4 points*
Write the numbers in words.

1 5,650 _____
_____
2 45,560 _____
_____
3 250,600 _____
_____
4 1,768,430 _____
_____

6 Comparison (1) *6 points*
Complete the table.

adjective	comparative	superlative
big	(1) _____	the biggest
happy	happier	(2) _____
interesting	more interesting	(3) _____
good	(4) _____	the best
bad	worse	(5) _____
far	(6) _____	the furthest

7 Comparison (2) *6 points*
Correct the grammar mistakes in the sentences. Add, remove or change a word.

1 The UK is more smaller than the USA.
2 Paris is beautiful than London.
3 Russia is the most biggest country in the world.
4 Thailand is not as expensive Japan.
5 Spain is bigger as Portugal.
6 Ukraine is biggest country in Europe.

8 Comparison (3) *4 points*
Put the adjective into the correct form: comparative or superlative.

My new mobile phone is a lot (1) _____
(small) and (2) _____ (light) than my old
one. It's (3) _____ (expensive) than my old
one, but it's (4) _____ (good) mobile you
can buy at the moment.

14 Energy Overview

This unit is about physical energy. It begins with an exploration of the life of a professional dancer, looks at how often we do things, the way our actions affect how people see us and the excuses often given for avoiding doing things such as exercise. The grammar focus is on the use of *to, enough* and *should*.

Students begin by reading about dancer Joaquín Cortés and completing sentences about his lifestyle and routines. They then go on to discuss their favourite dance styles.

In the next section, the work on how often we do things is continued and names for body parts are introduced. Students then learn some common collocations involving parts of the body.

Next, they look at a magazine questionnaire which assesses how our body language affects other people's perceptions of us. They discuss the results and then consider whether they have a family member or friend who fits any of the descriptions given by the questionnaire.

Students then go on to study excuses which can be given for avoiding doing things such as exercise. They listen to a conversation and make up one of their own. This leads into an examination of the use of *too* and *(not) enough* as well as *should/shouldn't* to describe problems and give advice.

Section	Aims	What the students are doing
Introduction page 58	*Reading skills*: reading for gist	Reading an article about Joaquín Cortés and completing headings.
		Matching beginnings and endings of sentences.
		Talking about dance styles.
	Pronunciation: /ʌ/ sound	Identifying words with different sounds.
Once or twice? page 59	*Lexis*: frequency expressions	Putting expressions of frequency in order.
		Asking and answering questions about how often the students do things.
		Completing and answering a questionnaire on good and bad habits. **Pairwork: Student A & B**
	Lexis: parts of the body	Identifying and classifying parts of the body.
		Finding out how physically flexible the students are.
	Lexis: collocations	Identifying correct collocations with body parts.
		Performing actions using body part collocations.
Image page 60	*Reading skills*: reading for detail	Identifying stressed syllables in adjectives.
		Completing a questionnaire about how other people see you.
		Talking about a relative or friend in connection with the descriptions in the questionnaire.
I'm too tired page 61	*Listening skills*: listening for specific details	Matching excuses with pictures.
		Listening to a conversation about taking exercise.
		Making up conversations giving excuses for not doing things.
Close up page 61	*Grammar*: *too* and *enough*; *should/shouldn't*	Completing sentences with *too* and *enough*.
		Ordering words to make sentences and discussing them.

More information about topics in this unit

Introduction, Reading 1 www.flamenco-world.com/magazine/cortes

14 Energy *Teacher's notes*

Books closed. Whole class. Are you a night person who can stay up late at parties, but is often tired in the morning, or are you a morning person who likes to get up early and is full of energy in the morning, but finds it difficult to stay awake late at night? Ask students to decide whether they are a night or morning person and to suggest some advantages for each. If you have a fairly even distribution of night and morning people in the class, you might like to use this distinction to organise pair and groupwork activities throughout this unit.

Reading (p 58)

1. Focus attention on the photo of Joaquín Cortés and ask students if they have heard about him or seen him and if they know anything about him. Has anyone ever been to a flamenco performance? If so, ask them to tell the class about it. Then ask students to read the article and to complete the headings. Allow them to compare in pairs before checking with the class.

   Note: For more information about Joaquín Cortés and the Joaquín Cortés Flamenco Ballet log on to:
   www.flamenco-world.com/magazine/cortes

1	Ancestry
2	Sleep
3	Practice
4	Family
5	Eating
6	Travel
7	Shoes

2. Students should match up the beginnings and endings of the sentences according to the information in the article. Check answers with the class.

   a) He sleeps for five or six hours a night.
   b) He practises for more than five hours a day.
   c) He sees his family as often as possible.
   d) He eats three times a day.
   e) He travels all the time.
   f) He buys new shoes every month.

3. Pairwork. Students try to name five other dance styles and discuss their favourites.

   Possible answers
   ballet, modern dance, tap, salsa, tango, ballroom, jazz dance, jive, rock 'n' roll, cerok, folk, Middle Eastern dance

Follow-up activity

Ask students to discuss with a partner what dances are typical in their country. If possible, get them to explain or show their partners how to do them. Alternatively, you could ask students if they actually go to a dance class themselves. If so, they could talk about it and demonstrate a dance they have learnt.

/ʌ/ sound (p 58)

1. Encourage students to say the words aloud so that they get a feel for what sounds right. They circle the word in each group that has a different vowel sound. The sound focused on here is the vowel sound /ʌ/, commonly found in words spelled with a *u*, such as *cup*. Draw students' attention to the other spellings that this sound can have.

2. 🎧 75 SB p 58
   Play the recording for students to check their answers, then play it again for them to repeat the words.

   a) home
   b) score
   c) morning
   d) open
   e) shoulder
   f) shouldn't

Once or twice (p 59)

Books closed. Whole class. Pre-teach some of the frequency expressions used in this section by finding out how often students go dancing, go to the cinema, eat in a restaurant, etc.

Lexis: frequency expressions (p 59)

1. Focus attention on the timeline and make sure everyone understands the word *frequent*. Students then decide on the correct order of the expressions in the box. Allow them to compare their results with a partner before checking with the class.

   Not very frequent ←——————→ **Very frequent**
   B D F H A E I J G C

2. Pairwork. Students work together to identify and name the parts of the body listed. They then work individually to write their answers to the questions. They then ask and answer the questions and compare answers.

3 *Pairwork: Student A & B* Students turn to their respective pages and follow the instructions. This activity involves completing questionnaires about good and bad habits and comparing answers.

Lexis: parts of the body (p 59)

1 Pairwork. Students work together to categorise the parts of the body according to how many they possess. They can use dictionaries to find out the meaning of words they don't know. Check answers with the class. Then draw students' attention to the section on *Parts of the body* on page 112.

> I've only got one: back, chin, head, neck, nose, stomach, waist.
>
> But I've got two: arms, ears, feet, hands, hips, knees, legs, lips, shoulders, thumbs.
>
> And I've got: eight fingers, ten toes, thirty-two teeth.

2 Encourage students to try out as many different combinations and unusual combinations as possible. This will get them out of their seats and add a welcome active phase to the lesson.

3 Pairwork. Students try to do the things their partners have written down.

Lexis: collocations (p 59)

1 Remind students that collocations are words that frequently go together. Ask them to decide which is the correct collocation for each of the actions and to underline it. Allow them to compare in pairs, but do not check answers at this stage.

2 🎧 76 SB p 125

Play the recording for students to check their answers to Exercise 1. Then play it again and ask them to do the actions. They then work in pairs to give each other instructions about which actions to do.

> a) knees
> b) legs
> c) arms
> d) head
> e) hands
> f) feet
> g) fingers
> h) shoulders

🎧 76
a) *Bend your knees.*
b) *Cross your legs.*
c) *Fold your arms.*
d) *Nod your head.*
e) *Clap your hands.*
f) *Stamp your feet.*
g) *Click your fingers.*
h) *Shrug your shoulders.*

Image (p 60)

Books closed. Whole class. Write the words *Body language* on the board and ask students if they know what the expression means (the clues as to our mood, character and reactions which are revealed by expressions, movements of the parts of the body, the way we stand, etc.) Elicit suggestions of body language and what it might mean, eg: sitting with your legs crossed away from the person you are talking to can mean that you are not interested in getting to know them more closely; nodding your head when you are listening to someone shows that you are interested in what they are saying, etc.

Reading (p 60)

1 🎧 77 SB p 60

Play the recording for students to repeat the words and then ask them to underline the stressed syllables. Encourage them to say the words aloud as they do this so that they get a feel for what sounds right. Elicit that these are all adjectives which can be used to describe people's personalities. Ask them to choose three words to describe themselves and to compare their choices with a partner.

> ad<u>ven</u>turous, <u>char</u>ming, <u>con</u>fident, <u>dom</u>inant, ener<u>get</u>ic, ex<u>cit</u>ing, im<u>pul</u>sive, <u>in</u>teresting, <u>loy</u>al, <u>qui</u>et, <u>sel</u>fish, <u>ser</u>ious, shy, un<u>frien</u>dly, un<u>so</u>ciable

2 Students work individually to do the questionnaire and look up the results. They then compare the results with the three words they chose to describe themselves in Exercise 1. They compare with a partner and discuss whether they think the questionnaire results are accurate or not.

3 Students work individually to think of a relative or friend who fits each of the descriptions in the *What your score means* part of the questionnaire. They then tell a partner about them.

I'm too tired (p 61)

Books closed. Whole class. Ask students if they ever go to a gym or do any other kind of exercise. How often do they go? What sports do they play and how often do they play them? Encourage them to use the expressions of frequency that they have already studied to talk about how often they exercise.

Listening (p 61)

1 Establish that the excuses are reasons someone might give for not doing exercise. Ask if they have ever used any of these excuses. Then give them a few minutes to match the excuses with the pictures.

> 1 c   2 j   3 a   4 e   5 h   6 g   7 i   8 d   9 f   10 b

2 🎧 **78 SB p 125**
Focus attention on the photograph of Danny and Louise and explain that Danny is trying to persuade Louise to do certain things, including do some exercise, and she is giving excuses for not doing any of them. Play the recording and ask students to tick the excuses in Exercise 1 that Louise uses.

> 1 I'm too tired.
> 3 I've got too much work.
> 4 I've got a bad back.
> 6 The swimming pool is too crowded.
> 7 I've got a cold.
> 9 I haven't got enough money.
> 10 I've got a bad foot.

🎧 **78**
(D = Danny; L = Louise)

D: Do you want to come to the gym later?
L: Oh, no thanks. I can't. I'm too tired.
D: Well, you should do some exercise. Exercise gives you more energy.
L: It's not just that – I've got too much work. And I've got a bad back.
D: That's because you sit at your computer all day. You should go swimming – swimming is really good for your back.
L: I hate swimming – the swimming pool is too crowded – and anyway, I've got a cold.
D: A cold? Oh dear. Maybe you should go away for a few days.
L: Yes, I know, but I haven't got enough money to go away.
D: Look, you seem really fed up. Do you want to go out tomorrow night? We can go clubbing.
L: No, I can't go dancing. I've got a bad foot.
D: Too tired? A bad back? A cold? And a bad foot! Oh dear! I think you need a new body.

3 **Pairwork: Additional material** Students write their own conversations giving excuses for not doing things. Encourage them to use their favourite excuses, whether these are amongst the ones listed in Exercise 1 or not.

Close up (p 61)

Problems & advice

1 Focus attention on the use of *too* and *enough* in the excuses in Exercise 1 in the previous section. You could ask students to underline them. Elicit that *too* is used for an excess of something, and *not enough* when there is a lack of something. There is more information on the use of *too* and *enough* in the Language reference section at the bottom of the page. Give students a few minutes to work individually to complete the sentences with *too* and *enough*. Then check answers with the class.

> a) too
> b) too
> c) too
> d) enough
> e) enough
> f) enough

2 Pairwork. Students discuss whether any of the sentences in Exercise 1 are true for them.

3 Students work individually to reorder the words to make sentences. Check answers with the class. Draw students' attention to the use of *should/shouldn't*, which is used to give advice (see the Language reference section at the bottom of the page and Verb structures on page 115).

> a) He should eat more fruit.
> b) She should buy a new one.
> c) He should change his job.
> d) She shouldn't stay up so late.
> e) He should drink more water.

4 Pairwork. Students change the names in Exercise 3 to make true sentences about people they know, and then compare them with a partner.

Test

Scoring: one point per correct answer unless otherwise indicated.

1

A	N	T	I	C	G
T	O	O	T	H	R
U	S	E	L	I	P
N	E	C	K	N	U

(circled: ANT, TOOTH, USE, LIP, NECK, EYE)

2
1. shoulder
2. back
3. stomach
4. waist
5. hip
6. knee

3 1 b 2 d 3 a 4 f 5 c 6 e

4
1. charming
2. confident
3. dominant
4. loyal
5. selfish
6. serious

5 (2 points per correct answer)
1. How often do you go to the hairdresser's?
2. How often does she go on holiday?

6
1. once a month
2. two or three times a year
3. every one or two weeks
4. many times a day

7
1. 'I haven't got <u>enough</u> money.'
2. 'You <u>shouldn't</u> spend it all on computer games.'
3. 'I've got <u>too much</u> homework tonight.'
4. 'Because you didn't work hard <u>enough</u> at school.'
5. 'The sea is <u>too</u> cold.'
6. 'You <u>should</u> go to the swimming pool.'
7. 'This coffee isn't hot <u>enough</u>.'
8. 'You <u>should</u> ask for another one.'

UNIT 14 *Energy*

14 Energy Test

Name: _____   Total: _____ /40

1 Vocabulary – parts of the body (1) 6 points
Circle six parts of the body in the word square.

A	N	T	I	C	G
T	O	O	T	H	R
U	S	E	L	I	P
N	E	C	K	N	U

2 Vocabulary – parts of the body (2) 6 points
Put the parts of the body in order from head to foot.

hip   knee   shoulder   neck   stomach   waist

head → 1 _____ → 2 _____ → 3 _____
→ 4 _____ → 5 _____ → 6 _____ → foot

3 Vocabulary – parts of the body (3) 6 points
Match expressions on the left with words on the right to make collocations.

1 fold your   a) head
2 shrug your   b) arms
3 nod your   c) feet
4 clap your   d) shoulders
5 stamp your   e) fingers
6 click your   f) hands

4 Vocabulary – describing character 6 points
Add the missing vowels (a, e, i, o, u) to complete the character adjectives.

1 ch __ rm __ ng   4 l __ y __ l
2 c __ nf __ d __ nt   5 s __ lf __ sh
3 d __ m __ n __ nt   6 s __ r __ __ __ s

5 How often 4 points
Reorder the questions.

1 do / go / How often / to the hairdresser's / you ?
   _____ ?
2 she / does / on holiday / How often / go ?
   _____ ?

6 Vocabulary – frequency expressions 4 points
Rewrite the frequency expressions.

1 I go to the hairdresser's   a / month / once.
   _____
2 We go on holiday   year / times / a / two or three.
   _____
3 I go to a restaurant   one or two / weeks / every.
   _____
4 I send an email   a / times / many / day.
   _____

7 Problems & advice 8 points
Rewrite the sentences with the words in brackets.

1 'I haven't got money.' (enough)
   _____
2 'You spend it all on computer games.' (shouldn't)
   _____

           *   *   *

3 'I've got homework tonight.' (too much)
   _____
4 'That's because you didn't work hard at school.' (enough)
   _____

           *   *   *

5 'The sea is cold.' (too)
   _____
6 'You go to the swimming pool.' (should)
   _____

           *   *   *

7 'This coffee isn't hot.' (enough)
   _____
8 'You ask for another one.' (should)
   _____

15 Review 3 Teacher's notes

Looking good (p 62)

Frequency expressions: How often ...?

1 Pairwork. Remind students of the work they did on frequency expressions in the previous unit. Ask them to work together to put the expressions in order. Check answers with the class.

Not very frequent					Very frequent
every year	every nine days	at least once a week	twice a week	almost every day	twice a day

2 Focus attention on the photo and ask if anyone has heard of the British long-distance runner Paula Radcliffe. (She won the London Marathon in a record time in 2003.) Go through the instructions with the class and ask them to write the questions relating to the underlined answers. Note that they should write the questions (as in the example) as if they are the interviewer, ie they should use *you* rather than *she*. They will then have suitable questions to ask a partner in the next exercise.

Note: For more information on Paula Radcliffe, log on to: www.ukathletics.net and click on *Athletes*.

> Almost every day. – How often do you eat chocolate?
> Twice a day. – How often do you run?
> Every nine days. – How often do you have a day off?
> Twice a week. – How often do you do a workout at the gym?
> At least once a week. – How often do you have a sports massage?
> Every year. – How often do you go on holiday?

3 Pairwork. Students ask and answer the questions they wrote in Exercise 2.

Word stress (p 62)

1 Encourage students to say the words aloud as they decide which column they belong in. They then underline the stressed syllables. Don't check answers at this stage.

2 79 SB p 125

Play the recording for students to listen and check their answers. Then play it a second time for them to repeat the words.

A ■ ▪	B ■ ▪ ▪	C ▪ ■ ▪
<u>ca</u>mera	al<u>co</u>hol	ap<u>point</u>ments
<u>cur</u>ly	<u>do</u>minant	col<u>lec</u>tor
<u>is</u>land	<u>ex</u>ercise	con<u>tes</u>tant
<u>love</u>ly	<u>fa</u>vourite	im<u>pul</u>sive
<u>neigh</u>bour	<u>gen</u>erous	per<u>for</u>mance
<u>sel</u>fish	<u>jew</u>ellery	suc<u>cess</u>ful
<u>sto</u>mach		

79
A: *camera, curly, island, lovely, neighbour, selfish, stomach*
B: *alcohol, dominant, exercise, favourite, generous, jewellery*
C: *appointments, collector, contestant, impulsive, performance, successful*

Future forms (p 63)

1 Pairwork. Establish that the word *to* is missing from each sentence. They have to work together to decide where *to* should go in each sentence. Check answers with the class.

> a) I want <u>to</u> stay in and watch TV this evening.
> b) I'm going <u>to</u> buy some new clothes next weekend.
> c) I want <u>to</u> get a better mobile phone – mine is very old.
> d) I'd like <u>to</u> join a gym and do more exercise.
> e) One day, I hope <u>to</u> study at a British university.
> f) I'd like <u>to</u> learn another foreign language.

2 Students work individually to decide which sentences are true for them and to tick them. They then compare with a partner.

3 Students work individually to copy and complete the sentences. They then explain them to a partner. Encourage students to ask their partner follow-up questions to find out more details.

Comparatives & superlatives (p 63)

1 Groupwork. In groups of three, students write down the comparative and superlative forms of the adjectives. Remind them of the work they did on this in Unit 13. Check answers with the class.

> big, bigger, the biggest
> long, longer, the longest
> good, better, the best
> interesting, more interesting, the most interesting
> far, further, the furthest
> expensive, more expensive, the most expensive
> old, older, the oldest
> bad, worse, the worst
> noisy, noisier, the noisiest
> safe, safer, the safest

2 In the same groups of three, students work individually to write their sentences, getting the necessary information from their partners as they work. They can then compare sentences with each other.

3 Groupwork. Give students time to discuss each question and come to a decision. They should write their final choices down.

4 Encourage each group to defend its choices against the suggestions of the other groups, using comparatives and superlatives, eg: *We think football is much more exciting than volleyball or golf.*

Optional activity

Put the following list on the board and ask students to choose three of them. They should then make notes comparing the two things in each one and talk about these two things to a partner.
a) You now / You ten years ago
   For example: *I'm taller now, my hair is longer and I've got less free time.*
b) Your language / English
c) Your character / Your best friend's character
d) Your mother's side of the family / Your father's side of the family
e) Your primary school / Your secondary school
f) The place you were born / The place you live now

Anecdote (p 63)

See the Introduction on page 4 for more ideas on how to set up, monitor and repeat Anecdotes.

1 🔊 **80 SB p 125**
Pairwork. Give students plenty of time to decide who they are going to talk about and to read and listen to the questions. Play the recording more than once if necessary.

> 🔊 **80**
> *Think about someone you think is good-looking. It can be someone you know or a famous person.*
> *What's his or her name?*
> *What does he or she do?*
> *How old is he or she?*
> *What colour hair has he or she got?*
> *What style is it?*

> *What colour eyes has he or she got?*
> *What other features has he or she got?*
> *What sort of clothes does he or she wear?*
> *What do you think he or she is doing now?*

2 Give students time to prepare what they are going to say. They can use the sentence beginnings to help them and make notes, but discourage them from writing down whole sentences and simply reading them out.

3 Students should maintain eye contact with their partners as much as possible as they talk about their good-looking person so that they are not tempted to read from a script.

Clothes (p 64)

1 Pairwork. Students work together to identify the items of clothing in the picture. Check answers with the class.

> You can see fourteen items of clothing.
> You can't see: belt, suit, sunglasses, sweater, tie, trousers (unless you count *jeans* as *trousers*).

2 Pairwork. Students work together to categorise the items from Exercise 1 according to whether we talk about them as single items or as pairs. Check answers with the class.

> I've got a: belt, coat, dress, jacket, ring, shirt, skirt, suit, sweater, tie, T-shirt.
>
> I've got a pair of: boots, earrings, jeans, shoes, socks, sunglasses, tights, trainers, trousers.

3 Pairwork. Students discuss what they wear in all the different situations. Encourage them to report back to the class.

4 Pairwork. Go through the instructions to establish who the characters are in the sketch, and focus attention on the picture in Exercise 1. Ask what students can deduce from the characters' body language (eg: *Richard looks unhappy*). Students then work together to predict who says each of the sentences. Allow them to compare their results with another pair, but do not check answers at this stage.

5 🔊 **81 SB p 65**
Play the recording and allow students to read the sketch at the same time. They should check their answers to Exercise 4 and decide why Richard says *OH NOOOOO!* at the end. Elicit students, reactions to the sketch. Are they keen on shopping or, like Richard, do they have to accompany a keen shopper and sit around waiting for them to try on hundreds of items of clothing?

> a) E b) R c) A d) E e) E f) A g) E h) A
> Because he's bored and tired and he wants to go home (to watch a football match).

6 Groupwork. Students work together and follow the instructions. If they are keen on drama, you might want to allow them to bring costumes and props to a subsequent lesson to use when they perform their sketches. Remind them of the importance of body language and intonation in showing how you feel about something. Allow plenty of time for the groups to perform for the class.

Test

Scoring: one point per correct answer unless otherwise indicated.

1
1. 'm cooking
2. are watching
3. is playing
4. 're listening to

2
1. **I'm** going to start my own business next year.
2. **I** want to be a millionaire before I am 30.
3. I hope **to** retire when I am 40.
4. **I'd** like to live by the sea when I retire.
5. I **don't** want to live in the city.
6. Would **you** like to be rich one day?

3
1. 'How often do you go to the cinema?' 'Once or twice a month.'
2. 'How often do you have an English lesson?' 'Three times a week.'

4
1. smaller
2. longer
3. bigger
4. more expensive
5. hot
6. more attractive

5
1. the tallest
2. the heaviest
3. The most poisonous
4. The worst

6
1. What
2. How
3. What
4. What
5. How
6. How

7 1 to 4: beautiful, good-looking, handsome, pretty
5 to 8: confident, quiet, serious, shy

8
1. shirt
2. trainers
3. jacket
4. trousers
5. socks
6. jeans
7. boots
8. tracksuit

9 1 b 2 d 3 a 4 c

10 1 and 2: chin, lip
3 and 4: knee, toe
5 and 6: finger, thumb

11
1. head
2. fingers
3. arms
4. legs

12
1. two hundred **and** fifty
2. twenty-five thousand, seven hundred **and** ninety-five
3. six hundred **and** fifty thousand, two hundred **and** thirty
4. one million, four hundred **and** fifty thousand, two hundred **and** eighty

13
1. I'm too busy.
2. I've got too much work.
3. I haven't got enough money.
4. I should stay at home.

14 1 and 2: sister, taller
3 and 4: come, enough
5 and 6: believe, key
7 and 8: sit, win
9 and 10: advice, fly
11 and 12: take, play

15 Review 3 Test

Name: _____   Total: _____ /80

---

1 Present continuous *4 points*

Complete the sentences with the correct verb in the present continuous.

> cook   listen to   play   watch

At the moment ...

1 I _____ dinner.
2 My parents _____ television.
3 My brother _____ a computer game.
4 You _____ your new CD.

2 Future forms *6 points*

Correct the grammar mistakes in the sentences.

1 I going to start my own business next year.
2 I'm want to be a millionaire before I am 30.
3 I hope retire when I am 40.
4 I like to live by the sea when I retire.
5 I want not to live in the city.
6 Would like you to be rich one day?

3 *How often* & frequency expressions *4 points*

Reorder the questions and the answers.

1 'How often / go to the cinema / do / you ?'
   '_____?'
   'month / a / Once or twice.'
   '_____.'

2 'How often / have / do / an English lesson / you?'
   '_____?'
   'times / a / Three / week.'
   '_____.'

4 Comparison – comparatives *6 points*

Complete the sentences with the correct form of the adjective.

1 The United Kingdom is _____ than France. (small)
2 The Nile is _____ than the Amazon. (long)
3 The Pacific Ocean is _____ than the Atlantic. (big)
4 London is _____ than Bangkok. (expensive)
5 China is not as _____ as India. (hot)
6 Paris is _____ than London. (attractive)

5 Comparison – superlatives *4 points*

Complete the sentences with the superlative form of the adjective.

1 Robert Wadlow is _____ person ever. He was 2.74 metres when he died in 1940. (tall)
2 Jon Brower Minnoch is _____ person ever. He was 635 kg. (heavy)
3 _____ animal in the world is a frog. One gram of its poison can kill 100,000 people. (poisonous)
4 _____ natural disaster ever was an earthquake in China in 1556. It killed 830,000 people. (bad)

6 Vocabulary – describing objects *6 points*

Complete the questions with the correct question word, *What* or *How*.

1 _____ kind of car is it?
2 _____ much did it cost?
3 _____ does it look like?
4 _____ colour is it?
5 _____ old is it?
6 _____ fast can it go?

7 Vocabulary – describing people *8 points*

Put the words in the box into the correct categories.

> beautiful confident good-looking handsome
> pretty quiet serious shy

Physical description	Character
1 _____	5 _____
2 _____	6 _____
3 _____	7 _____
4 _____	8 _____

8 Vocabulary – clothes *8 points*

Add the missing vowels (*a, e, i, o, u*) to the clothes.

1 sh __ rt
2 tr __ __ n __ rs
3 j __ ck __ t
4 tr __ __ s __ rs
5 s __ cks
6 j __ __ ns
7 b __ __ ts
8 tr __ ck s __ __ t

9 Vocabulary – money *4 points*

Match words from each column to make expressions.

1 I usually pay by   a) too much last night.
2 I can't afford   b) credit card.
3 I spent   c) cash.
4 I paid in   d) a new computer.

10 Vocabulary – parts of the body (1) *6 points*

Put the parts of the body into the correct category.

> chin finger knee lip thumb toe

head	legs/feet	hands
1 _____	3 _____	5 _____
2 _____	4 _____	6 _____

11 Vocabulary – parts of the body (2) *4 points*

Choose the correct alternative.

1 He is nodding his **head** / **arms**.
2 She clicked her **feet** / **fingers**.
3 I folded my **arms** / **legs**.
4 He crossed his **feet** / **legs**.

12 Vocabulary – numbers *4 points*

Write the numbers as words.

1 250 _____
   _____ .

2 25,795 _____
   _____ .

3 650,230 _____
   _____ .

4 1,450,280 _____
   _____ .

13 Problems & advice *4 points*

Reorder the endings to the sentence.

I want to go on holiday, but …

1 busy / too / I'm.
   _____ .

2 too / I've got / work / much.
   _____ .

3 money / I haven't got / enough.
   _____ .

4 at home / should / I / stay.
   _____ .

14 Pronunciation – vowel sounds *12 points*

Put the words in the correct column according to the underlined sound.

> adv<u>i</u>ce bel<u>ie</u>ve c<u>o</u>me en<u>ou</u>gh fl<u>y</u> k<u>ey</u> t<u>a</u>ke pl<u>ay</u>
> s<u>i</u>ster s<u>i</u>t t<u>a</u>ller w<u>i</u>n

/ə/ oth<u>er</u>	/ɪ/ k<u>i</u>ss
1 _____	7 _____
2 _____	8 _____

/ʌ/ c<u>u</u>p	/aɪ/ sk<u>y</u>
3 _____	9 _____
4 _____	10 _____

/iː/ s<u>ee</u>	/eɪ/ d<u>ay</u>
5 _____	11 _____
6 _____	12 _____

16 *dotcom* Overview

The topic of this unit is computers and useful websites. The grammar focus is on the present perfect and past participles.

It begins with work on how we use modern technology and which websites students use. They then listen to a conversation between a mother and her son. The mother needs her son's help to send an email. Several useful computer terms are introduced and practised.

Students then read about a successful website which reunites old school friends. They discuss this website and how many of their old school friends they keep in touch with. This leads on to some work on phrasal verbs, and students then do an information gap exercise, reading texts about two friends who got back in touch with each other through the Friends Reunited website.

The focus then turns to past participles and the form and use of the present perfect. Students read a conversation between the two school friends they read about in the previous section. The two friends talk about things on a list that they have and haven't done. Students complete questions and answers using the present perfect and look at how it is used to refer to completed actions in 'time up to now'.

Finally, in an Anecdote, students have an opportunity for some extended speaking practice in which they talk about an old school friend they would like to get in touch with.

Section	Aims	What the students are doing
Introduction page 66	*Lexis: to*-infinitives	Matching website addresses with reasons for using them.
		Talking about websites the students use.
		Talking about what the students use different gadgets for.
	Lexis: computer terms	Listening to a conversation and identifying what a mother wants to do with her computer.
		Deciding which computer terms the mother understands and which she doesn't.
		Matching computer terms and definitions.
		Making lists of computer terms.
dotcom success page 67	*Reading skills*: reading for specific information	Reading an article about a successful website which reunites old school friends.
		Marking sentences true and false.
		Talking about old school friends.
	Lexis: phrasal verbs	Completing phrasal verbs with the correct particles.
		Matching phrasal verbs with their meanings.
	Reading skills: reading for specific information	Doing an information gap activity involving two texts about school friends. **Pairwork: Student A & B**
Close up pages 68–69	*Grammar*: past participles; present perfect	Completing a table with infinitive, past simple and past participle forms.
		Completing a conversation with past participles.
		Talking about a *10 things to do before we're 30* list.
		Completing questions and answers using the present perfect.
		Studying the form of the present perfect.
		Completing and answering questions about past experiences. **Pairwork: Student A & B**
	Conversation skills: fluency work	Anecdote: talking about an old school friend.

More information about topics in this unit
dotcom success, Reading 3 *www.friendsreunited.co.uk*

16 dotcom Teacher's notes

Books closed. Whole class. Ask students to make a list of things that they use a computer for. You might like to start them off with some suggestions, eg: checking the spelling of words, paying bills, sending letters to friends, booking flights, etc. This could be a group activity with groups competing to come up with the longest list.

Lexis: *to*-infinitives (p 66)

1 Pairwork. Students match websites and reasons for using them. Check answers with the class.

> a) 3 b) 6 c) 4 d) 2 e) 1 f) 5

2 Pairwork. Draw students' attention to the example and point out the use of the *to*-infinitive. Students discuss which websites they know or use frequently. Make sure they are making complete sentences using the *I use X to do Y* structure.

3 Students work individually to complete their two sentences in as many ways as they can. They then compare with a partner.

Lexis: computer terms (p 66)

1 **82 SB p 125**

Go through the instructions with the class, play the recording and elicit the answer to the question. You might like to ask them if they think this is a typical conversation between a mother and a son. Are their own parents as knowledgeable about computers as they are, or do they sometimes have to help them do relatively simple things?

> She wants to send an email to Carol.

82
(T = Tom; M = Mum)

T: Hello.
M: Hello, Tom.
T: Oh hi, Mum. Are you okay?
M: Fine, thanks. But I need some help with my new computer.
T: Ah – do you want to surf the net?
M: No, I just want to send an email to Carol.
T: Okay. That's no problem. First, find the email icon.
M: Icon? What's an icon?
T: It's a little picture, like a symbol.
M: Where is it?
T: It's on your desktop.
M: Well, there's nothing on my desk.
T: No – Mum – your desktop is on your computer screen.
M: Oh. Well, I can see lots of little pictures there.
T: Right. You need to click on the email icon.
M: Click?
T: Press the button on your mouse.
M: Mouse?
T: THE THING IN YOUR HAND.
M: Oh, yes. Okay, I've done that.
T: Now, click on the new message icon and type Carol's email address in the box which says 'to'.
M: Okay.
T: Then type your message in the box and phone me back.
M: Okay. Bye.

2 Play the recording again. Students tick the terms Tom's mum understands and put a cross by those she doesn't. Check answers with the class.

> a) ✔ b) ✔ c) ✘ d) ✘ e) ✘ f) ✘

3 **83 SB p 125**

Go through the items in column A with the class before you play the recording. Students then listen and underline the terms Tom uses.

> c) to go online
> f) a screen
> h) a toolbar

83
(T = Tom/Thomas; M = Mum)

T: Yes, hello, Mum.
M: I'm ready to send that email.
T: Okay. To send the message, you need to go online.
M: Online?
T: Yes, you need to connect to the internet.
M: Ah yes. I knew that.

> T: *Now at the top of your screen there's a toolbar. Click on the 'Send and receive' icon, and this will connect you to the net through your modem.*
> M: *Oh, Thomas, speak English! I don't understand computer language.*
> T: *Oh, I don't believe this. Okay, what can you see at the top of your screen?*
> M: *Well, there are lots of little pictures and ...*

4 Pairwork. Students work together to match the computer terms with their definitions. Allow them to compare with other pairs before checking answers with the class. Ask them how many of these terms they already knew.

> a) 8   b) 2   c) 7   d) 9   e) 1   f) 3   g) 6   h) 5   i) 4

5 Groupwork. Students work together in small groups to make lists of English computer terms that are used in their language(s). Find out which group has the longest list.

dotcom success (p 67)

Books closed. Whole class. Ask if any members of the class have their own websites or are thinking of setting one up. What kind of information do they (or are they going to) put on their website?

Reading (p 67)

1 Go through the questions with the class, then give students a few minutes to scan the text to find the answers. Allow them to compare answers in pairs before checking with the class.

> a) You can find out what friends are doing now.
> b) Everyone wants to know what old classmates are doing.
> c) Students' own answers.

2 Students read the article more carefully and decide whether the sentences are true or false. They should correct the false sentences. Allow them to compare answers in pairs before checking with the class.

> a) True.
> b) False. She was a software engineer.
> c) False. The website is advertised by word of mouth.
> d) True.
> e) False. The offices are in somebody's house.
> f) False. The company employs twelve people.

3 Give students a few minutes to think about the questions, then encourage them to discuss their answers in pairs or small groups.

Note: *www.friendsreunited.co.uk* is currently in the top ten most visited websites in the UK. The site puts old school and college friends back in touch with each other. In October 2000, husband and wife team Julie and Steve Pankhurst set up the site. It was Julie's idea – she wanted to contact some old school friends.

Although they have spent nothing on advertising, they had 7.52 million registered members by 1st September 2002. The site gets an average of five to eight million hits a day.

Lexis: phrasal verbs (p 67)

1 Establish that phrasal verbs are verbs which are made up of more than one element, usually a main verb and one or more particles. Examples they may be familiar with include *wake up, take off, try on,* etc. The answers here are all in the text. Give students a few minutes to find them and complete the sentences. Check answers with the class.

> a) on
> b) out
> c) up
> d) up
> e) on
> f) after

2 Students look at the phrasal verbs in context and decide on the meanings. Check answers with the class.

> a) log on – access
> b) find out – discover
> c) give up – stop
> d) set up – create
> e) take on – employ
> f) look after – be responsible for

3 Students work individually to decide if the statements are true for them and then compare with a partner.

Reading (p 67)

Pairwork: Student A & B Please note that although this is a pairwork activity, it is not an optional exercise in that it prepares for much of the work on page 68.

Students turn to their respective pages and follow the instructions. This activity has several stages and each student has the answers to their partner's tasks. Students first complete the gaps in their emails and check answers with their partner. They then complete the summary of what happened using their own ideas before checking again with their partner.

Close up (p 68)

Past participles

1 Remind students that there is information on irregular verbs on page 117. Past participles are one of the elements needed to construct the present perfect, which students will be studying next (there is more information in the Language reference section on page 69). You might like to direct their attention back to the article on page 67 where they will find the past participles of *spend* (*The company has spent*), *take* (*The couple and their business partner have taken*) and *have* (*The site has had many success stories*).

Infinitive	Past simple	Past participle
change	changed	changed
do	did	done
go	went	been
hear	heard	heard
make	made	made
meet	met	met
record	recorded	recorded
spend	spent	spent
travel	travelled	travelled
visit	visited	visited

Irregulars are: *do*, *go*, *hear*, *make*, *meet* and *spend*.

2 ▭ 84 SB p 125

Go through the instructions with the class. Then give students a few minutes to complete the conversation. Play the recording for them to check their answers, then check again with the class.

1	changed
2	heard
3	done
4	visited
5	recorded
6	travelled
7	been
8	made
9	spent
10	met

▭ 84
(D = Darren; G = Geoff)

D: Geoff?
G: Darren! Wow, you haven't changed at all.
D: And you look exactly the same – good to see you.
G: Wow, I can't believe it – after fifteen years.
D: Yeah. Have you heard from any other old classmates?
G: Yes, a couple of people – that Friends Reunited website is brilliant.
D: Hey, have you got that list?
G: Yes, here it is.
D: Oh yes, I remember. '10 things to do before we're 30.' Well, we're 29 – how many things have you done?
G: Not many – three I think. I've been snowboarding, and I've done a bungee jump, and I've visited John Lennon's grave in New York. And that's it really. What about you?
D: Let's see – I haven't recorded a CD – I stopped playing music when I left school.
G: Yeah, me too.
D: And I've been to a U2 concert but I haven't met them.
G: Have you travelled much?
D: Well, I've been to South America three times.
G: Wow!
D: But I haven't been to the Himalayas yet, or Egypt.
G: Have you ever been snowboarding?
D: Yes, I've done that. But I haven't done a bungee jump. I haven't made a lot of money either – I'm a teacher!
G: Well, I've made a lot of money, but I've spent it. Anyway, have you met the love of your life?
D: No, I haven't met anyone special yet. How about you?
G: Yes, I forgot to tell you. I'm married to Pamela.
D: Pamela?
G: Yes, you know, the gorgeous singer in our band.

3 Pairwork. Students look at the list and discuss the questions. Find out who in the class has done the most things on the list.

a) Geoff has been snowboarding, done a bungee jump, visited John Lennon's grave, made a lot of money, met the love of his life.
b) Darren has been to South America, been snowboarding.

Present perfect (p 69)

1 Pairwork. Students work together to complete the questions and answers. Do not check answers at this stage.

2 ▭ 85 SB p 126

Play the recording for students to listen, check and repeat. They then work in pairs to ask and answer the questions in Exercise 1. Encourage them to ask each other follow-up

114 UNIT 16 *dotcom* Visit www.insideout.net

questions to find out more details and then to report back to the class.

> a) Have; Yes, I have. No, I haven't.
> b) Has; Yes, it has. No, it hasn't.
> c) Have; Yes, I have. No, I haven't.
> d) Have; Yes, I have. No, I haven't.
> e) Have; Yes, they have. No, they haven't.
> f) Have; Yes, I have. No, I haven't.

> **85**
> a)
> 'Have you ever visited the website for your old school?'
> 'Yes, I have.'
> 'No, I haven't.'
> b)
> 'Has your school ever tried to get in touch with you?'
> 'Yes, it has.'
> 'No, it hasn't.'
> c)
> 'Have you ever been to a reunion at your school?'
> 'Yes, I have.'
> 'No, I haven't.'
> d)
> 'Have you ever received an email from an old friend?'
> 'Yes, I have.'
> 'No, I haven't.'
> e)
> 'Have your parents ever sent you an email?'
> 'Yes, they have.'
> 'No, they haven't.'
> f)
> 'Have you ever met somebody new on the internet?'
> 'Yes, I have.'
> 'No, I haven't.'

3 Go through the questions with the class and elicit the answers. Refer them to the Language reference section on this page for more information. The timeline may help them to see how 'time up to now' works.

> The present perfect tense. *Have* + past participle.

4 **Pairwork: Student A & B** Students turn to their respective pages and follow the instructions. This activity gives more practice in using the present perfect to talk about experience up to now.

Anecdote (p 69)

See the Introduction on page 4 for more ideas on how to set up, monitor and repeat Anecdotes.

1 **86 SB p 126**

Pairwork. Give students plenty of time to decide who they are going to talk about and to read and listen to the questions. Play the recording several times if necessary.

> **86**
> Think about an old school friend you would like to get in touch with.
> What's his or her name?
> Where did you first meet?
> How old were you?
> Why did you become friends?
> What sort of things did you talk about?
> What sort of things did you do together?
> What is your best memory of him or her?
> When was the last time you saw him or her?
> What do you think he or she is doing now?
> Why would you like to get in touch with him or her?

2 Give students time to prepare what they are going to say. They can use the sentence beginnings to help them, and they can make notes, but discourage them from writing down whole sentences and simply reading them out.

3 Students should maintain eye contact with their partners as much as possible as they talk about their old school friends so that they are not tempted to read from a script.

Test

Scoring: one point per correct answer unless otherwise indicated.

1
1. to send
2. to get
3. to buy
4. to have

2
1. to delete
2. to save
3. to download
4. to go online
5. to log on
6. to search

3
1. desktop
2. icon
3. file
4. toolbar
5. screen
6. mouse

4
1. out
2. up
3. after
4. up

5
1. been
2. done
3. gone
4. heard
5. made
6. met
7. spoken
8. tried

6
1. has travelled
2. have (never) met
3. have (you ever) tried
4. have(n't) been

7
1. Have, have
2. Has, hasn't
3. Have, haven't
4. Has, has

16 dotcom Test

Name: Total: _____ /40

1 Vocabulary – *to*-infinitive *4 points*
Complete the sentences using the *to*-infinitive of the verbs.

> buy   get   have   send

1 I use my computer _____ emails.
2 I use the bus _____ to work.
3 I went to the shops _____ some bread.
4 I'm going on holiday _____ a rest.

2 Vocabulary – computer terms (1) *6 points*
Match the words with their definitions.

> to delete   to download   to go online   to log on
> to save   to search

1 to remove something from a computer
   = _____

2 to make a computer retain information
   = _____

3 to move information from the internet to a computer
   = _____

4 to connect to the internet = _____

5 to access a website, for example by typing a password
   = _____

6 to look for information on the internet
   = _____

3 Vocabulary – computer terms (2) *6 points*
Add the missing letters to complete the words. All the words are connected with computers.

1 d __ skt __ p
2 ic __ n
3 f __ le
4 t __ __ lbar
5 scr __ __ n
6 m __ __ se

4 Vocabulary – phrasal verbs *4 points*
Underline the correct particle.

1 I need to find **out** / **up** the times of trains to London.
2 You really should give **in** / **up** smoking.
3 Can you look **after** / **on** my cat when I'm on holiday?
4 I set **out** / **up** my website last year.

5 Past participles *8 points*
Here are the infinitive and past simple forms of some verbs. Add the past participle.

1 be – was/were – _____
2 do – did – _____
3 go – went – _____
4 hear – heard – _____
5 make – made – _____
6 meet – met – _____
7 speak – spoke – _____
8 try – tried – _____

6 Present perfect (1) *4 points*
Complete the sentences by putting the verb into the present perfect.

1 Sam _____ (travel) around the world.
2 I _____ never _____ (meet) a famous person.
3 _____ you ever _____ (try) Indian food?
4 I _____ n't _____ (be) to Australia.

7 Present perfect (2) *8 points*
Complete the questions and the responses with the correct form of *have*.

1 '_____ you ever been to Russia?'
   'Yes, I _____ .'

2 '_____ Pierre ever been to London?'
   'No, he _____ .'

3 '_____ you heard from Helen recently?'
   'No, I _____ .'

4 '_____ Gregor got married?'
   'Yes, he _____ .'

17 Drive Overview

This unit is about road travel, specifically driving to work or school and attitudes to road use. The grammar focus is on question forms with *How* + adverb/adjective and *What* + noun. Prepositions of movement are focused on and opportunities are given for students to give directions.

Students begin by reading an article about two very different drives to work. They match sentences with the articles on the best and worst drive.

In the next section, students look closely at the formation of questions with *How* + adverb/adjective and *What* + noun. They complete questions about the article in the previous section and then answer them. A pairwork activity then gives them further practice in forming and answering questions of this type. Prepositions of movement are introduced next and students choose the correct alternatives in sentences. They then practise describing their route to work or school, using these prepositions.

Then, students listen to six people talking about what drives them mad on the roads. Students match the people to pictures and identify some of the specific language used. They then practise using ordinal numbers. This leads into practice of giving and following directions on a map.

The final section of the unit takes the form of a board game. As students play this, they have opportunities to practise forming questions and doing some extended speaking on given topics connected to journeys.

Section	Aims	What the students are doing
Introduction page 70	*Reading skills*: reading for gist	Categorising sentences according to which part of an article on best and worst drives they refer to. Talking about journeys to work or school.
Close up page 71	*Grammar*: questions with *How* + adverb/adjective and *What* + noun	Completing comprehension questions about the article in the previous section. Answering the questions. Forming and answering questions about journeys and discussing the questions. **Pairwork: Student A & B**
	Lexis: prepositions of movement	Choosing correct alternatives to complete sentences. Writing a description of the students' way to work or school.
It drives me mad! page 72	*Listening skills*: listening for specific details	Listening to people talking about what irritates them on the road and matching the people to pictures. Talking about situations on the road that make the students angry.
	Pronunciation: ordinal numbers	Completing a table with ordinal numbers. Listening to sets of directions and matching starting and finishing points on a map. Giving directions to each other.
On the way home page 73	*Conversation skills*: fluency practice	Playing a board game involving asking questions and speaking on a given topic for 30 seconds.

> **More information about topics in this unit**
>
> **Introduction, Reading 2** www.lighthouse.net   www.greatoceanrd.org.au
> www.bangkoksite.com.com

17 Drive Teacher's notes

Books closed. Whole class. Ask students if they can remember any long car journeys from their childhood. Where were they driving to and why? How long did it take? Did they enjoy the journey? Did they play any games in the car to occupy themselves on the journey? If they come up with any suggestions, see if they can play these games in English.

Reading (p 70)

1 Pairwork. Before students begin, you might like to brainstorm some ideas with the class about what might make a drive to work 'the best' or 'the worst'. Students then work together to decide which drive each of the six sentences refers to. Encourage them to do this without looking up the answers in the text – you might ask them to cover the text as they do the task. Allow them to compare results with another pair, but do not check answers at this stage.

2 Students work individually to read the article and check their answers to Exercise 1. They then discuss which (if any) of the drives described is similar to their drive to work or school. Encourage them to report back to the class.

Note: If students would like to know more about the Cape Otway lighthouse, log on to: *www.lighthouse.net*
For information on the Great Ocean Road, log on to: *www.greatoceanrd.org.au*
For more information about Bangkok log on to: *www.bangkoksite.com*

a) B   b) W   c) B   d) W   e) W   f) B

Close up (p 71)

Questions with *How* + adverb/adjective & *What* + noun

1 Pairwork. Students work together to complete the questions. Remind them that the Language reference section on this page is there to help them with information about the formation and use of these question types.

a) far
b) many
c) often
d) long
e) sort
f) far
g) long
h) time
i) fast

2 You could see how many of the questions the students can answer from memory without looking back at the article, before they read it again and check.

a) About 200 kilometres.
b) Hundreds of thousands.
c) Every day.
d) About forty minutes.
e) dramatic rock formations, a rainforest, spectacular waterfalls, the national park ...
f) Seven kilometres.
g) Two hours.
h) 5am.
i) Half a kilometre an hour.

3 **Pairwork: Student A & B** Students turn to their respective pages and follow the instructions. They practise forming and asking and answering questions about daily travelling.

Student A
a) How often do you travel by train?
b) What time do you get up in the morning?
c) How fast is your car?
d) How much money do you spend on travelling every week?
e) How far do you live from the school? OR How far is it from your house to the school?
f) How long does it take you to get to work/school?

Student B
a) How often do you travel by bus?
b) What time do you start work?
c) How old is your car?
d) How many people can you get in your car?
e) How far do you live from the city centre? OR How far is it from your house to the city centre?
f) How long do you take to get ready in the morning? OR How long does it take you to get ready in the morning?

Lexis: prepositions of movement (p 71)

1 Pairwork. Draw students' attention to the Language toolbox where the various prepositions of movement are illustrated. They then work together to choose the correct alternative in each sentence. Check answers with the class.

You could then draw students' attention to the section on *Prepositions of movement* on page 112.

a) down
b) out of
c) across
d) along
e) past
f) up
g) through
h) over
i) into

2 Give students a couple of minutes to consider the question, then ask them to compare answers with a partner.

3 Students work individually to write their descriptions. Go round, offering help and encouragement. Emphasise that they should include as many of the prepositions of movement as they can. They then compare with a partner.

It drives me mad! (p 72)

Listening

1 87 SB p 126
Go through the instructions with the class and give them a couple of minutes to look at the illustrations before you play the recording. You may need to explain that *mad* here means angry rather than mentally ill; *crazy* is often used in a similar way. Allow them to compare answers in pairs before checking with the class.

1 b   2 e   3 a   4 d   5 f   6 c

87
(P = Presenter; M1, 2, 3 = Men; W1, 2, 3 = Women)

P: This is City Radio. My name is Andy Cowle. Earlier, we asked people in the street, 'What drives you mad on the road?' Here are some of their answers.

1
M1: I can't stand it when people drive very slowly. They usually go out at the weekend, and drive very slowly on country roads where it's impossible to overtake them.

2
W1: I hate it when people park their cars on the pavement. The road is for cars – the pavement is for pedestrians!

3
M2: I hate it when drivers indicate to turn left ... and turn right! ... or go straight on! It's so dangerous!

4
W2: Well, I don't like getting stuck in traffic jams. In my city, the rush hour in the morning, and in the evening, is awful. I try to work at home as much as possible.

5
M3: Road works drive me mad, especially on the motorway. You go on the motorway to save time, and then you get stuck in a traffic jam because of the road works.

6
W3: It drives me mad when people use their mobile phones in the car. I nearly had an accident last week because this woman was talking on her phone and she didn't see the traffic lights turn red. She nearly killed me.

2 Pairwork. Go through the instructions with the class to make sure everyone knows what they have to do. Students then work together to match the words in the box with the illustrations and think of three situations of their own to tell their partner about.

a – indicate, turn left, turn right, go straight on
b – impossible to overtake
c – have an accident, the traffic lights
d – get stuck in traffic jams, rush hour
e – park on the pavement, pedestrians
f – road works, go on the motorway

Optional activity

You might like to direct students' attention to the tapescript on page 126 and ask them to underline all the expressions that mean the speaker doesn't like something
(*I can't stand it when ..., I hate it, I don't like ..., It drives me mad when ...*). Do the students know any others (eg: *It drives me crazy when ..., It makes me angry when ..., I get cross when ...*)?

Ordinal numbers (p 72)

1 88 SB p 126
Pairwork. Draw students' attention to the table and ask them for examples of when we might use words like *first, fifth, eighth* and *tenth*, eg: *My first car was a Renault. Today is my cousin's tenth birthday*, etc. Point out that numbers like these (ordinal numbers) are very useful when we give directions. Remind students about the section on *Ordinal numbers* on page 112. Students work together to complete the table. When they have finished, play the recording for them to listen, check and repeat.

1st	2nd	3rd	4th	5th
first	second	third	fourth	fifth
6th	7th	8th	9th	10th
sixth	seventh	eighth	ninth	tenth

> **88**
>
> first second third fourth fifth sixth
> seventh eighth ninth tenth

2 **89 SB p 126**

Focus attention on the street plan. Go through the instructions with the class to make sure everyone knows what they have to do. Then play the recording. You may like to pause after each element to give students time to think and mark in the routes. Check answers with the class and play the recording again as a final check.

> 1 B3   2 B2   3 B1

> **89**
>
> 1 Your starting point is A1. Go straight on, take the third right, the second left, and go straight on. Where are you?
>
> 2 Your starting point is A2. Take the first left, the first right, the fifth right, and the first left. Where are you?
>
> 3 Your starting point is A3. Go straight on, take the fourth left, the second right, and go straight on. Where are you?

3 Pairwork. Students take turns to give each other directions using the map. Go round offering help and encouragement and making sure that they are using ordinal numbers correctly. They then think about their immediate surroundings and take turns to give similar directions to places nearby.

On the way home (p 73)

This board game gives students further practice in making questions and talking about different aspects of journeys. Students work in small groups. Ensure that you have sufficient dice and counters (one dice for each group and one counter for each student). Go through the instructions with the class to make sure that everyone knows how to play. As they play, go round offering help and encouragement and adjudicating in any disputes.

If you feel that square 23 (*Talk about the first time you travelled abroad.*) and square 26 (*Talk about the last time you went on a plane.*) are inappropriate for your students, change square 23 to *Talk about the first time you travelled to your capital city*, and square 26 to *Talk about the last time you went on a bus.*

Test

Scoring: one point per correct answer unless otherwise indicated.

1
1 far: c
2 long: f
3 many: a
4 much: d
5 fast: e
6 often: b

2 (2 points per correct answer)
1 What sort of car have you got?
2 What time do you set off for work?

3
1 out of
2 down
3 past
4 over
5 along
6 into

4
1 turn
2 indicate
3 straight
4 overtake
5 left
6 park

5
1 traffic lights
2 road works
3 pavement
4 pedestrian
5 accident
6 traffic jam

6
1 1st
2 second
3 3rd
4 fourth
5 5th
6 sixth

17 Drive Test

Name: _____   Total: _____ /40

1 Questions (1)   *12 points*
First complete the questions with the words in the box. Then match the questions to the answers.

fast far long many much often

1 How _____ is it from Paris to London?
2 How _____ does it take to get from Paris to London by train?
3 How _____ trains are there each day?
4 How _____ does the train cost?
5 How _____ is the train?
6 How _____ do you visit London?

a) 25 a day
b) once a month
c) 600 km
d) 300 kmh
e) €150
f) 35 minutes

2 Questions (2)   *4 points*
Reorder the words the make questions.

1 car / sort of / What / got / you / have
   _____ ?
2 you / set off / time / What / do / for work
   _____ ?

3 Vocabulary – prepositions of movement   *6 points*
Complete the directions with the prepositions in the box.

along down into out of over past

To get to my house from school, you drive (1) _____ the school car park and go (2) _____ the hill. At the bottom of the hill, turn left. Go (3) _____ the shops and (4) _____ the bridge. Turn right and drive (5) _____ the river. After a kilometre, turn (6) _____ Old Avenue. My house is number 42.

4 Vocabulary – traffic situations (1)   *6 points*
Complete the driving instructor's instructions with the words in the box.

indicate left overtake park straight turn

'Okay, please (1) _____ right here. Remember to (2) _____ . Good. Now go (3) _____ on. You can (4) _____ the red car. Now turn (5) _____ . Very good. Please (6) _____ next to the bank. Well done!'

5 Vocabulary – traffic situations (2)   *6 points*
Add the missing vowels (*a, e, i, o, u*) to complete these words about traffic situations.

1 tr _ ff _ c l _ ghts
2 r _ _ d w _ rks
3 p _ v _ m _ nt
4 p _ d _ str _ _ n
5 _ cc _ d _ nt
6 tr _ ff _ c j _ m

6 Vocabulary – ordinal numbers   *6 points*
Add the missing figures or words.

For example: *10th = tenth*

1 _____ = first
2 2nd = _____
3 _____ = third
4 4th = _____
5 _____ = fifth
6 6th = _____

18 Justice Overview

This unit is called *Justice*, but it is not so much about crime and punishment as the ways people get their own back on those who have hurt or offended them in some way. It provides an opportunity for storytelling and focuses on the use of time adverbials and the past continuous.

The unit begins with two stories of people who got their revenge on their partners in unusual ways. Students choose their own endings for the stories. They then do some work on time adverbials and their use in storytelling and look at the way adverbs are formed from adjectives. They then practise punctuating a story and do a dictation exercise in which each student dictates a different line of a story (including punctuation) to a partner. The section ends with another tale of revenge.

Next students look at the form and use of the past continuous tense, again something very useful in storytelling. They complete questions and answers and practise these with a partner.

The final section has a modern fairy tale shown in pictures. Students predict the story and then work in groups to write their own versions of it. They listen to the original version on the recording and compare it with their own. They then discuss the various stories and decide which ending they like best.

Section	Aims	What the students are doing
Introduction pages 74–76	*Reading skills*: reading for specific information	Completing expressions from two stories and matching each to the appropriate story.
		Choosing an ending for each story and listening to the completed stories.
		Discussing the students' reactions to the stories.
	Lexis: time adverbials	Putting time adverbials in the order they appear in the stories.
		Retelling the stories using time adverbials.
	Lexis: adverbs of manner	Completing a table with adverbs and adjectives.
		Studying adverb formation.
		Reordering sentences.
		Rewriting sentences to make them true.
	Punctuation	Punctuating a story.
		Dictating alternate lines of a story to a partner. **Pairwork: Student A & B**
Close up pages 76–77	*Grammar*: past continuous	Studying how tenses are used in a story.
		Completing questions and answers using the past continuous.
		Asking and answering the questions.
Once upon a time page 77	*Writing*: a story	Matching words to pictures and predicting the content of a story.
		Using pictures as cues to write a modern fairy tale in groups.
		Listening to the original tale for comparison with the students' own versions.

18 Justice Teacher's notes

Books closed. Whole class. Write the expression *get your own back* on the board and explain that it means to get revenge on someone who has done something wrong to you. Ask students how they feel when someone does something to hurt or offend them. Do they find it easy to forgive, or do they want to do something back to that person? What examples can they give of ways to get your own back.

You may want to start them thinking by giving them the example of a woman who found out that her husband was seeing another woman. She moved out of their house, but before she left, she unscrewed the ends of the curtain poles, filled them with raw prawns, then put them back together again. It took the husband months to find out where the disgusting smell was coming from.

Reading (p 74)

1   Focus attention on the pictures and the words in the box. Ask students to complete the labels. Check answers with the class.

> a) paint   d) wine
> b) party   e) bag
> c) club   f) scissors

2   Give students plenty of time to read the stories and match the items in Exercise 1 to the appropriate story. They then compare with a partner and discuss the importance in the story of each item.

> *Revenge is sweet*: a, d, f
> She took the pot of paint to pour over his new car.
> She took all his bottles of fine wine and gave them away.
> She used the pair of scissors to destroy his suits.
>
> *Dinner by post*: b, c, e
> He invited her to a dinner party on his birthday.
> She went to a night club instead.
> He sent her the dinner by post in a plastic bag.

3   **90 SB p 74**

Pairwork. Students discuss and decide on the best ending for each story. When they have made their choices, play the recording for them to listen and check their answers. Were their endings the same as the original stories?

> 'Revenge is sweet': e
> 'Dinner by post': b

4   Pairwork. Students discuss the stories and decide which one they like best. You might like to ask the class who they think came off best in 'Dinner by post' – the man who posted the dinner or the woman who made a critical comment about the amount of salt in it.

Lexis: time adverbials (p 75)

1   Give students time to read the stories again and decide on the correct order for the time adverbials. Check answers with the class.

> *Revenge is sweet*
> a) One day
> b) Then
> c) Next
> d) That night
> e) Finally
>
> *Dinner by post*
> 1 Last year
> 2 At first
> 3 At the end of August
> 4 That evening
> 5 The next morning
> 6 A week later

2   Pairwork. Students take turns to retell one of the stories using the time adverbials they have just looked at. Encourage them each to choose a different story and to do this without looking back at the texts on page 74. They could be allowed to refer to the lists of adverbials in Exercise 1.

Lexis: adverbs of manner (p 75)

1   Pairwork. Students work together to complete the tables with adverbs and adjectives. Allow them to look for the appropriate words in the stories on page 74 if they need to. Elicit that we use adverbs to describe how someone does something.

> a) unhappily
> b) bad
> c) angry
> d) quickly
> e) beautiful
> f) carefully
> g) quietly

> 1 different
> 2 early
> 3 late
> 4 tidy
> 5 attractive
> 6 good
> 7 loudly

2 Pairwork. Students discuss the questions, referring to the tables in Exercise 1 for help. Check answers with the class.

> a) By adding *ly*.
> b) Replace *y* with *ily*.
> c) well, early, late

3 You may want to do the first one with the class as a further example before asking them to rewrite the other sentences. Check answers with the class.

> a) I eat my food very slowly.
> b) I drive my car very quickly.
> c) I plan my days very carefully.
> d) I play the guitar very badly.
> e) I spend my money very intelligently.
> f) I arrive for appointments very early.
> g) I talk on the phone very quietly.
> h) I speak English very well.

4 Give students a few minutes to work individually to decide which sentences are true for them and to rewrite those that are not. They then compare sentences with a partner.

Punctuation (p 76)

1 Pairwork. Draw students' attention to the Language toolbox in the margin. They will need to know and be able to pronounce the words for the various punctuation marks when they come to do Exercise 2. Students look at the story of the shoplifter and work together to rewrite it using the correct punctuation and capital letters. Encourage them to use the words in the Language toolbox as they do this so that they become familiar with them. Check answers with the class. You may like to point out that in much printed material these days, including many English language coursebooks, single speech marks (quotation marks) are often used for speech. Double speech marks are more common in American English texts.

> **A** shoplifter was trying to steal a watch from an exclusive jewellery shop when the manager caught him.
> **"P**lease don't call the police! I'll buy the watch**,"** said the shoplifter**.**
> **T**he manager thought about it for a moment and then said**, "W**ell okay – that's 500 dollars**."**
> **"O**h dear**,"** said the shoplifter**, "T**hat's more than I planned to spend. **C**an you show me something less expensive**?"**

2 **Pairwork: Student A & B** Go through the instructions with the class and make sure they have done the first two tasks before they turn to their respective pages. To make the dictation task more challenging, ask students to sit back to back. When they have finished, they can check their answers by comparing the lines of text on their two pages.

> *Usher's revenge*
> A: A man arrived at the theatre
> B: to see a mystery play,
> A: but his seat was too far
> B: from the stage.
> A: So he said to the usher,
> B: "Find me a better seat
> A: and I'll give you a generous tip."
> B: The usher moved him into the front row
> A: and the man gave him 25 cents.
> B: The usher looked at his tip for a moment
> A: and then he bent down and whispered to the man,
> B: "The wife did it!"

Close up (p 76)

Past continuous

1 Pairwork. Read the example sentence with the class and then ask them to work in pairs to discuss the questions. Check answers with the class. Remind them that the Language reference section on page 77 and the Verb structures on page 114 are there to give them further help. You might like to elicit further examples of sentences which describe something that was in progress when another event happened.

> a) saw; was driving
> b) Past continuous.
> c) Past simple.

2 Pairwork. Students work together to complete the questions and answers. Allow them to compare with other pairs, but do not check answers at this stage.

3 91 SB p 126
Play the recording for students to listen and check their answers. Then play it again for them to repeat. They then work in pairs and take turns to ask and answer the questions in Exercise 2.

a) Were; Yes, I was. No, I wasn't.
b) Were; Yes, they were. No, they weren't.
c) Were; Yes, I was. No, I wasn't.
d) Was; Yes, it was. No, it wasn't.
e) Were; Yes, I was. No, I wasn't.
f) Were; Yes, I was. No, I wasn't.

91

a)
'Were you living in the same house this time last year?'
'Yes, I was.'
'No, I wasn't.'

b)
'Were your parents watching TV at 11.30 last night?'
'Yes, they were.'
'No, they weren't.'

c)
'Were you having an English lesson this time yesterday?'
'Yes, I was.'
'No, I wasn't.'

d)
'Was it raining when you woke up this morning?'
'Yes, it was.'
'No, it wasn't.'

e)
'Were you wearing a hat when you went out this morning?'
'Yes, I was.'
'No, I wasn't.'

f)
'Were you speaking English when the lesson started?'
'Yes, I was.'
'No, I wasn't.'

Optional activity

Tell students that they are going to play a game called *Alibi*. Give them these instructions.

Yesterday something disappeared from the classroom.
- Decide what disappeared, when it disappeared and where it was exactly.
- Choose two suspects from the class. The two suspects prepare their alibi (or story explaining where they were, what they were doing, etc. when the disappearance occured).
- The class interview the suspects individually and note down the answers.
- The class decides if the suspects are guilty or not guilty.

Once upon a time (p 77)

Writing a story

1 Pairwork. Focus attention on the pictures and ask students to work together to match the words in the box to the appropriate pictures. Check answers with the class and then elicit several suggestions as to what the story is about.

a) a castle, a beautiful princess, a pond
b) a beautiful princess, a frog, a handsome prince, an evil witch
c) a frog, a beautiful princess, a kiss
d) a frog, a handsome prince, a beautiful princess, clothes, children

2 Groupwork. Put the students into groups to work on their stories. Encourage them to spend plenty of time discussing the questions in column A and possible endings to the sentences in column B. They then write up their story and give it a title. If possible, arrange for the stories to be displayed in the classroom and for all the students in the class to have a chance to read the other groups' stories.

3 92 SB p 126

Groupwork. Play the recording for students to listen to the original story. Ask them to discuss in their groups how it compares with theirs. (Emphasise that their versions are just as valid as the original; they have not failed if their stories are completely different.)

92
The princess and the frog

Have you ever heard the story of the princess and the frog?
   Well, once upon a time, there was a princess. She was beautiful, confident and independent.
   She lived in a castle in a country far away.
   One day, she was sitting near a pond in the grounds of her castle. She was thinking about her life.
   There she met a frog.
   The frog said to her, 'Beautiful princess, I was once a handsome prince. But then an evil witch changed me into a frog. Kiss me and I will turn back into a handsome, young prince. Then, my darling, we can get married and live in your castle with my mother. You can prepare my meals, wash my clothes and look after my children.'
   Later, as the princess was enjoying a meal of frog's legs in a delicious cream sauce, she smiled and thought to herself, 'Thanks, my prince ... but no, thanks.'

4 Play the recording again and ask students (in pairs or their groups) to answer the questions in column A in Exercise 2. Check answers with the class.

a) She was beautiful, confident and independent.
b) She lived in a castle in a country far away.
c) She was sitting near a pond.
d) She was thinking about her life.
e) She met a frog.
f) He said he was once a handsome prince, but then an evil witch changed him into a frog.
g) The princess ate the frog.

5 Whole class. Make sure that all students have a chance to read the other stories. They compare them and discuss which ending they like best.

Optional activity

Ask students to write a modern ending for another old story or fairy tale (eg: *Romeo and Juliet*, *Little Red Riding Hood*, etc.)

Test

Scoring: one point per correct answer unless otherwise indicated.

1 1 c   2 b   3 d   4 a

2
1. angrily
2. badly
3. carefully
4. early
5. well
6. late
7. loudly
8. quickly

3
1. I can run very quickly.
2. My friend sings beautifully.
3. Your sister speaks English well.
4. Our boss arrived late today.

4
1. ,
2. .
3. '
4. ?
5. " "
6. !

5
1. year
2. first
3. day
4. later
5. end

6
1. was watching
2. was raining
3. were studying
4. were (you) doing
5. was wearing

7
1. Were, was
2. Were, weren't
3. Was, wasn't
4. Was, was

18 Justice Test

Name: Total: _____ /40

1 Vocabulary – collocations *4 points*
Match the halves to complete the expressions.

1   a dinner   a) wine
2   a plastic   b) bag
3   a night   c) party
4   a bottle of   d) club

2 Vocabulary – adverbs (1) *8 points*
Complete the table.

adjective	adverb
angry	1 _____
bad	2 _____
careful	3 _____
early	4 _____
good	5 _____
late	6 _____
loud	7 _____
quick	8 _____

3 Vocabulary – adverbs (2) *4 points*
Reorder the words to make sentences.

1   I / quickly / very / run / can
    _____

2   beautifully / My friend / sings
    _____

3   speaks / Your sister / well / English
    _____

4   today / Our boss / late / arrived
    _____

4 Punctuation *6 points*
Write these punctuation marks.

1   comma _____   4   question mark _____
2   full stop _____   5   speech marks _____
3   apostrophe _____   6   exclamation mark _____

5 Vocabulary – time adverbials *5 points*
Complete the sentences with the words in the box.

day   end   first   later   year

1   I met Andre last _____ .
2   At _____ , I didn't like him.
3   But one _____ , we fell in love.
4   A week _____ , we decided to get married.
5   The wedding is at the _____ of May.

6 Past continuous (1) *5 points*
Complete the sentences with the verbs in the past continuous tense.

do   rain   study   watch   wear

1   I _____ football on TV when you phoned.
2   It _____ when I woke up this morning.
3   We _____ at university when we first met.
4   _____ you _____ your homework at seven o'clock?
5   Sue _____ her new dress when I saw her.

7 Past continuous (2) *8 points*
Complete the questions and answers with *was / wasn't* or *were / weren't*.

1   '_____ you going shopping when I saw you?'
    'Yes, I _____ .'

2   '_____ your friends having an argument a few minutes ago?'
    'No, they _____ .'

3   '_____ it snowing this morning?'
    'No, it _____ .'

4   '_____ your neighbour having a party last night?'
    'Yes, he _____ .'

19 Extreme Overview

The topic of this unit is extremes, particularly extremes of weather. The grammar focus is on the passive. There is also a lexical treatment of *will* and *might*.

Students begin by reading and listening to a poem about geography. They match word lists from the poem to pictures and practise saying the poem with the correct word and sentence stress.

The next section has a text about a very unusual hotel in Sweden. It is made entirely of ice and it melts every spring and is rebuilt every winter. Students discuss the Ice Hotel and then talk about other buildings that they know well.

Students then look closely at the formation of the passive and compare and contrast passive and active sentences.

Finally, they look at various words used to describe the weather and this leads into practice of the use of *will* and *might* in predictions. Students finish by talking to a partner about their favourite time of year.

Section	Aims	What the students are doing
Introduction page 78	*Reading skills*: reading for gist	Matching word lists and pictures.
		Reading and listening to a poem and predicting the title.
		Talking about geographical features.
	Pronunciation: word and sentence stress	Underlining the stressed syllables in a poem.
		Listening and repeating the poem with the correct rhythm.
Extreme hotels page 79	*Reading skills*: reading for gist	Matching statistics with their meanings and checking in an article about the Ice Hotel.
		Answering questions about the text.
		Talking about a building the students know well.
Close up page 80	*Grammar*: passives	Comparing active and passive sentences.
		Studying the construction of active and passive sentences.
		Completing a table with questions and answers using the passive.
What's the weather like? page 81	*Lexis*: the weather; *will* and *might*	Completing a chart with weather words.
		Reading a text about the weather at the North Pole.
		Writing a weather forecast for London in winter.
		Completing predictions about the weather using *will* and *might*.
	Conversation skills: fluency work	Anecdote: talking about the students' favourite time of the year.

> **More information about topics in this unit**
> **Extreme hotels, Reading 2** *www.icehotel.com/english*

19 Extreme Teacher's notes

Books closed. Whole class. Much of the vocabulary in this unit is to do with natural features and weather and some may already be familiar to your students. To review the vocabulary they already know, divide the class into two teams and ask two members from the same team to sit facing each other at the front of the class. One of them should have their back to the board, the other should be facing it. Write a word from this unit that the students should already know on the board. (You could ask the teams to go through the unit finding words they already know the meanings of to give the other team, but don't tell them why you want them or they may deliberately choose words the other team will not know!) The student facing the board gives one-word clues to their partner to help them guess what the word is. If the word is guessed correctly after one clue, the team is awarded ten points, the number of points goes down by one for each clue that has to be given. The other team then takes a turn.

Reading (p 78)

1 Focus attention on the photographs and elicit students' reactions to them. Which one do they like best? Would they like to visit any of these places? Then ask them to read the word lists and match each one with a picture. They should use dictionaries to check the meaning of any words they don't know. Allow them to compare their results in pairs and then check answers with the class.

> A 3   B 1   C 4   D 2

2 🎧 93 SB p 78
Go through the titles with the class before you play the recording. Then ask them to listen, read the poem and decide which is the most appropriate title. Then elicit their opinions on geography – do they love it or hate it? Encourage them to give their reasons. Point out that *farther* in the last line of the poem is an alternative spelling for *further*.

> b) I love Geography

3 Pairwork. Students discuss the geographical features in the photographs. If possible, have students from different countries working together so there is more to talk about.

Word & sentence stress (p 78)

1 Read the first two lines of the poem to the class, emphasising the stress on the underlined words. Then ask them to go through the rest of the poem deciding which words should be stressed. Encourage them to say the lines of the poem aloud as they do this so that they get a feeling for what sounds right. Check answers with the class.

> I love Geography by John Kitching
> Other people, other places,
> Different customs, different faces,
> Drought and desert, field and plain,
> Snow and ice and monsoon rain,
> Volcanoes, glaciers,
> Bubbling springs,
> Clouds and rainbows,
> Countless things.
> Stars and planets, distant space,
> Whatever's ugly, full of grace.
> Seas and rivers,
> Cliffs and caves,
> The wondrous ways this world behaves.
> So much to learn; so much to know;
> And so much farther still to go.

2 🎧 94 SB p 78
Play the recording. Students read the poem aloud at the same time, trying to match the rhythm, stress and speed of the speaker. There is a metronome on the recording to help them with the beat, but you may also like to encourage them to tap lightly on their desks as they speak to help them keep in time.

3 🎧 95 SB p 78
Play the recording for students to listen and say the poem in time with the beat of the metronome.

Extreme hotels (p 79)

Reading

Books closed. Whole class. Ask students to talk about the most unusual hotel they have ever stayed in. If they don't have any experiences to talk about, ask for suggestions as to what hotels are made of (brick, concrete, wood, possibly canvas). Ask them if they can imagine a hotel made of ice and to suggest what the advantages and disadvantages of such a building might be.

1 Pairwork. Encourage students to work together to match the figures with their meanings without looking up the answers in the text. When they have finished, they can read the article and check their answers.

> 40,000 = Tons of ice and snow used to build the hotel.
> 1990 = Year the first hotel was constructed.
> 64 = Number of rooms in the hotel.

> 14,000 = Number of hotel guests last year.
> −30 = Temperature in Celsius outside the hotel.
> −5 = Temperature in Celsius inside the hotel.

2 Pairwork. Students work together to answer the questions. When you have checked their answers, elicit their personal reactions to the article. Would they like to visit this hotel?

Note: There is more information and pictures of the Ice Hotel, Sweden, on: *www.icehotel.com/english*

> a) On the shores of the Torne River in the old village of Jukkasjarvi, Sweden.
> b) Ice and snow.
> c) Ice.
> d) Reindeer skins.
> e) Different artists from all over the world.
> f) 'absolutely stunning', 'one of the most beautiful places I've ever seen', 'unique'

3 Pairwork. Give students a couple of minutes to decide which building they are going to talk about and to think about their answers to the questions in Exercise 2. Then ask them to talk about their buildings in pairs.

Close up (p 80)

Passives

1 Pairwork. Draw students' attention to the box and the headings *Active* and *Passive*. Read out the example sentences under each heading. Then ask them to work together to examine the sentences and answer the questions. Check answers with the class and point out that the Language reference section at the bottom of the page and the Verb structures on page 115 have more information about the formation and use of the passive. Elicit some more passive sentences from the class. You might also ask them to look back at the text about the Ice Hotel on page 79 and underline all the passive sentences.

> a) (2) after the verb
> b) (1) before the verb
> c) True.
> d) (1) *be*
> e) (3) the past participle
> f) True.
> g) *Somebody* appears in the active sentences.
> h) We don't know who *somebody* is.
> i) True.

2 Pairwork. Students complete the questions and answers. Allow them to compare with another pair but don't check answers at this stage.

3 96 SB p 127

Play the recording for students to listen and check their answers. They then work in pairs to ask and answer the questions in Exercise 2. Encourage them to ask follow-up questions to obtain further details about each answer.

> a) Was; was; wasn't
> b) Were; were; weren't
> c) Is; it is. it isn't.
> d) Were; Yes, I was. No, I wasn't.
> e) Is; Yes, it is. No, it isn't.
> f) Was; Yes, it was. No, it wasn't.

> **96**
> **a)**
> 'Was your house built before 1980?'
> 'Yes, it was.'
> 'No, it wasn't.'
> **b)**
> 'Were your shoes designed in Italy?'
> 'Yes, they were.'
> 'No, they weren't.'
> **c)**
> 'Is your salary paid by cheque?'
> 'Yes, it is.'
> 'No, it isn't.'
> **d)**
> 'Were you invited to any parties last week?'
> 'Yes, I was.'
> 'No, I wasn't.'
> **e)**
> 'Is your name spelt the same way in English?'
> 'Yes, it is.'
> 'No, it isn't.'
> **f)**
> 'Was your mobile phone made in Japan?'
> 'Yes, it was.'
> 'No, it wasn't.'

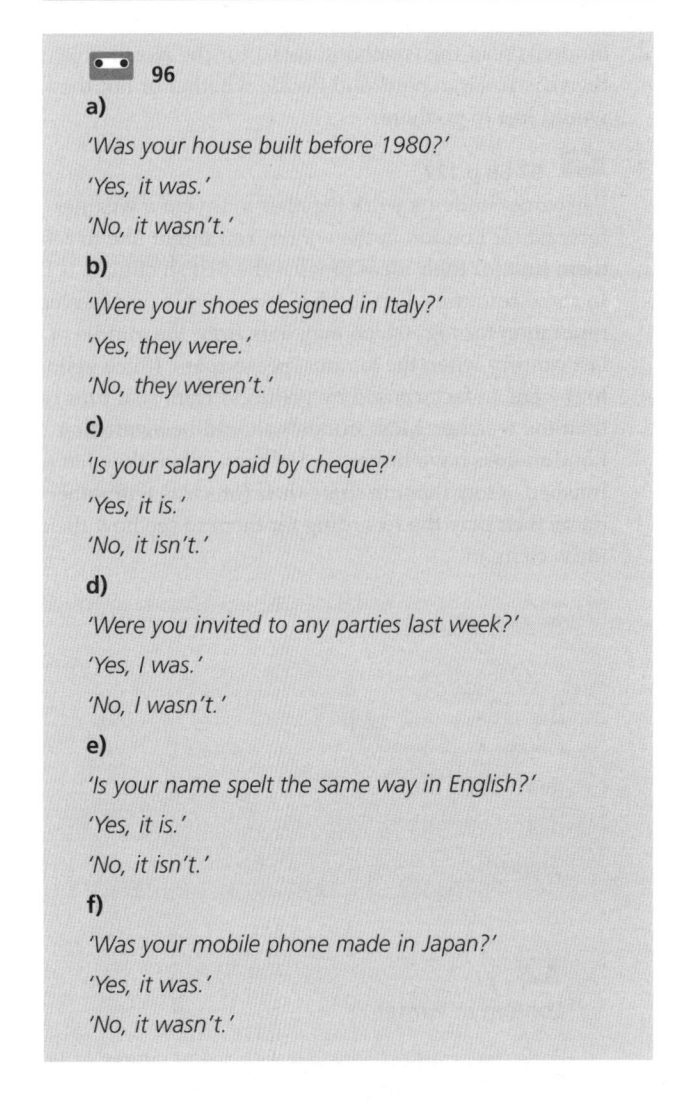

What's the weather like? (p 81)

Books closed. Whole class. Ask students to say what the weather is like today. Encourage them to talk about whether the sun is shining or it is raining, what the temperature is, etc.

Lexis: the weather (p 81)

1 Students complete the chart. Allow them to compare results with a partner before checking with the class. Go through any vocabulary items they don't understand, then elicit what kind of weather they like and whether they would prefer to be very hot or very cold. Draw students' attention to the section on *Weather* on page 113.

> 1 sun
> 2 cloudy
> 3 rain
> 4 foggy
> 5 wind
> 6 snowy
> 7 storm

2 Students read the weather forecast for the North Pole. They then discuss it in pairs and decide whether or not they would like to go there.

3 🔲 **97 SB p 127**
Pairwork. Students work together to invent a weather forecast for London in the winter. You might like to ask them first for their ideas of what the British climate is like. In some countries, London has a somewhat undeserved reputation for fog, which may date from the middle of the last century when the famous 'peasoupers' (thick yellowish fog) were, in fact, caused by pollution from coal fires rather than the weather. Most students should be aware that London does have rather a lot of rain! When they have finished, allow them to share their forecasts with other pairs, then play the recording for them to see how their ideas compare.

> *Possible answers*
> very wet
> 9 or 10
> cloudy
> rain
> dull
> sunnier

> 🔲 **97**
> **London in winter**
> *Today will start off very wet with temperatures of 9 or 10 degrees Celsius.*
> *It will be cloudy in the afternoon, and there will probably be rain later on. It will be dull all day.*
> *Tomorrow will be the same, and the next day, and the day after.*
> *Summer might be a bit sunnier, but not much.*

Lexis: *will & might* (p 81)

1 Draw students' attention to the subheading of this section and elicit or explain that *will* and *might* are used to make predictions. *Will* is used for those predictions where we are pretty certain what will happen, *might* for those we are less sure about. Refer students to the Verb structures on page 115 for information on the formation of *will* and *might*. Go through the example with the class, then ask them to complete the remaining predictions. Check answers with the class. Point out that the predictions in the first two sentences are more likely to happen than the sentences *c*, *d* and *e*.

> a) The south will have better weather than the north.
> b) Tomorrow will probably be warmer than today.
> c) I think we will have a lot of snow next winter.
> d) There might be a storm before the weekend.
> e) It might rain later today.
> f) It won't be sunny tomorrow.

2 Students work individually to rewrite the sentences for where they live. They then compare with a partner.

Optional activity

Ask students to write a weather forecast for tomorrow. You might offer a small prize for the one which turns out to be most accurate.

Anecdote (p 81)

See the Introduction on page 4 for more ideas on how to set up, monitor and repeat Anecdotes.

1 🔲 **98 SB p 127**
Play the recording and ask students to underline the woman's answers as they listen. Then check answers with the class.

> a) October
> b) autumn
> c) warm but not hot
> d) colourful
> e) light clothes
> f) for walks in the hills
> g) it's beautiful

> 🔲 **98**
> *I like October. It's autumn in Japan. Yes, autumn is my favourite time of year. In Kyoto the weather is beautiful in October. It's warm, but not hot. In summer it's too hot – I hate it – but in October, the temperature is perfect.*
> *Also, the countryside is very colourful at that time of year. The trees are red and orange. We have a*

name for this in Japan – it's called 'koyo' – it means the changing colour of the trees in autumn. I usually wear light clothes – T-shirts and dresses. You don't need a coat when you go out. It's lovely.

Of course October is not holiday time, but at the weekend we go for walks in the hills and we have picnics. We enjoy looking at the countryside at that time of year.

I like that time of year because it's beautiful. Yes, I think Kyoto is the best place in the world at that time of year.

2 Pairwork. Give students plenty of time to decide what they are going to talk about and to prepare what they are going to say. They should read the question and sentence beginnings again and they can make notes, but discourage them from writing down whole sentences and simply reading them out.

3 Pairwork. Students take turns to tell each other about their favourite time of year. Encourage them to report back to the class on what they hear. Draw students' attention to the section on *Seasons* on page 113.

Test

Scoring: one point per correct answer unless otherwise indicated.

1
1. rainbow
2. volcano
3. river
4. clouds
5. cliffs
6. desert
7. cave
8. glacier

2
1. It's sunny.
2. It's cloudy.
3. It's rainy/raining.
4. It's foggy.
5. It's windy.
6. It's snowy/snowing.

3
1. It was raining this morning.
2. The rainbow is beautiful.
3. Some people are climbing the mountain.
4. The monsoon is in July in Thailand.

4
1. I think I will go out with my friends tonight.
2. We might go for a meal.
3. I think we might go to an Indian restaurant.
4. I hope it won't be too expensive.

5 (2 points per correct answer)
1. was first played
2. is watched
3. was invented
4. is used
5. was sent
6. are sent

19 Extreme Test

Name: Total: _____ /40

1 Vocabulary – geographical features *8 points*

Add the missing vowels (*a, e, i, o, u*) to complete these words about geographical features.

1. r _ _ nb _ w
2. v _ lc _ n _
3. r _ v _ r
4. cl _ _ ds
5. cl _ ffs
6. d _ s _ rt
7. c _ v _
8. gl _ c _ _ r

2 Vocabulary – weather *6 points*

For each symbol write a phrase to describe the weather.

For example, ⛈ *It's stormy.*

1. ☀ _____
2. ☁☁☁ _____
3. 🌧🌧 _____
4. 〰〰〰 _____
5. 〰➤ _____
6. ❄❄❄ _____

3 Pronunciation – word & sentence stress *10 points*

Underline the stressed syllables in each sentence. The number in (brackets) shows the number of stressed syllables.

1. It was raining this morning. (2)
2. The rainbow is beautiful. (2)
3. Some people are climbing the mountain. (3)
4. The monsoon is in July in Thailand. (3)

4 Vocabulary – *will* & *might* *4 points*

Put the word in (brackets) into the correct place in the sentence.

1. I think I go out with my friends tonight. (will)
   _____
2. We go for a meal. (might)
   _____
3. I think we go to an Indian restaurant. (might)
   _____
4. I hope it be too expensive. (won't)
   _____

5 Passives *12 points*

Complete the second sentence with the verb in the passive. The meaning should be the same as the first sentence.

1. People first played football over 2,000 years ago.
   Football _____ over 2,000 years ago.
2. In Spain, a million people watch football each week.
   In Spain, football _____ by a million people each week.
3. The US army invented the internet in the 1960s.
   The internet _____ by the US army in the 1960s.
4. In the USA, 60 million people use the internet each day.
   In the USA, the internet _____ by 60 million people each day.
5. Somebody sent the first text message in 1995.
   The first text message _____ in 1995.
6. In the UK, people send a million texts every hour.
   In the UK, a million texts _____ every hour.

20 Review 4 Teacher's notes

Experiences (p 82)

Present perfect

Pairwork. Remind students of the work they did on the present perfect in Unit 16 and elicit that this tense is used to talk about experience up till the present. Look at the example with the class and remind them that they need the past participle of each verb to complete the question. Students work individually to complete the questions and guess the answers for their partners. Check answers before they go on to the next stage to make sure that everyone is using the structure correctly. They then take turns asking the questions to find out if they guessed correctly. Encourage them to ask follow-up questions to obtain more details.

Computer experiences
a) bought
b) downloaded
c) been
d) deleted
e) set up
f) taken part

Driving experiences
g) been
h) driven
i) had
j) driven
k) lent
l) lost

Word stress (p 82)

1 Pairwork. Encourage students to say the words aloud as they decide which are the stressed syllables. They should then circle the word in each group which has a different stress pattern or a different number of syllables. Allow them to compare their answers with other pairs but don't check answers at this stage.

2 99 SB p 82
Play the recording for students to listen and check their answers to Exercise 1. Then play it again for them to repeat the words.

a) scenery (volcano) dangerous
b) (pronounced) surface happened
c) (pollution) evening business
d) desert (delete) concert
e) angrily tidily (regularly)
f) conversation (expression) preposition

Past participles (p 82)

100 SB p 127
Remind students that they have played bingo before (on page 36) and that they have to complete the card with the past participles of nine verbs of their choice as instructed. Play the recording for them to listen and mark their cards every time they hear one of their verbs. When one student shouts *Bingo!*, stop the recording and check with the tapescript that the student has marked their card correctly.

100
And here are the words for tonight's bingo.

meant, meant   caught, caught   slept, slept
worn, worn   made, made   woken, woken
done, done   brought, brought   shot, shot
had, had   spent, spent   paid, paid   kept, kept
felt, felt   broken, broken   fallen, fallen
thought, thought   found, found   lent, lent
spoken, spoken   eaten, eaten   written, written
sat, sat   met, met   taught, taught   read, read
heard, heard   driven, driven   sold, sold   built, built

Past simple & past continuous (p 83)

1 Pairwork. Draw students' attention to the pictures and ask them to predict what the story they are going to read is about. Then let them work together to complete it with the words in the box. Give them plenty of time to discuss how they think the story ends. Elicit several ideas from pairs around the class, but don't confirm or deny anything at this stage.

1 was filming
2 went
3 was talking
4 gave
5 continued
6 didn't come
7 was planning
8 went
9 found
10 shook

'Don't know. Radio broken.'

2 🎧 **101 SB p 127**

Play the recording for students to check their answers to Exercise 1 and to see if they predicted the end of the story correctly.

> 🎧 **101**
>
> A Hollywood director was filming an important film in the desert when an old Native American man came up to him and said, 'Tomorrow rain.'
>
> The next day it rained.
>
> A few days later, the director was talking to the cameraman about the next day's filming. The Native American went up to him and said, 'Tomorrow storm.'
>
> He was right again, and he saved the director thousands of dollars.
>
> The director was very impressed and gave the old man a job.
>
> The old man continued to predict the weather correctly, but then he didn't come for three weeks.
>
> The director was planning to film an important scene and he needed good weather. So he went to look for the Native American.
>
> When he found the old man, he said, 'Listen, I have to film an important scene tomorrow. What will the weather be like?'
>
> The old man shook his head and said, 'Don't know. Radio broken.'

Anecdote (p 83)

See the Introduction on page 4 for more ideas on how to set up, monitor and repeat Anecdotes.

1 Students work individually to complete the questions. Remind them of the work they did on questions forms in Unit 17. Check answers with the class.

1	Where
2	How
3	How
4	What
5	How
6	What
7	What
8	Who
9	What
10	When

2 🎧 **102 SB p 127**

Go through the instructions with the class and play the recording for them to read and listen to the questions. Give them plenty of time to think about their answers.

> 🎧 **102**
>
> Think about a journey that you did many times when you were younger.
> Where did your journey start and finish?
> How far was it?
> How did you travel?
> What time did you usually set off?
> How long did it take you?
> What sort of countryside did you go through?
> What sort of buildings did you go past?
> Who did you usually travel with?
> What did you usually do on your journey?
> When was the last time you did this journey?

3 Give students plenty of time to prepare what they are going to say. They can use the sentence beginnings to help them, and can make notes if they wish, but discourage them from writing down whole sentences and simply reading them out.

4 Pairwork. Students should maintain eye contact with their partners as much as possible as they talk about their journeys so that they are not tempted to read from a script.

The Revision Game (p 84)

This board game revises all the main structures found in *Inside Out* Elementary. Divide the class into groups of three, four or five. Appoint a Checker in each group. This person doesn't play the game so it would be a good idea to organise several sessions so that students can take turns being the Checker. You will need a coin for each group and a counter for each player.

Go through the instructions with the class and demonstrate how to toss a coin and determine if it lands *heads* or *tails*. If you are using coins without a head pictured on them, you will have to decide in advance which side is *heads* and which *tails*.

As the students play the game, go round making sure they are following the rules correctly and assist the Checkers with any difficult decisions.

> **Player 1 (Red)**
> 1 ✔
> 2 Are you retired?
> 3 (Speaking task)
> 4 ✔
> 5 How much rice is there?
> 6 Did you have a good day yesterday?
> 7 (Speaking task)
> 8 ✔
> 9 I went to Paris three years ago.
> 10 How long does it take you to get to work?

Player 2 (Blue)

1 ✔
2 Has your sister got a job?
3 (Speaking task)
4 There's a lot of pasta.
5 ✔
6 What did you watch on TV last night?
7 (Speaking task)
8 Are the birds singing?
9 He met the love of his life in 1996.
10 ✔

Player 3 (Orange)

1 ✔
2 She's sometimes late for the lesson.
3 (Speaking task)
4 You can smoke.
5 Was the weather good yesterday?
6 ✔
7 (Speaking task)
8 I'm not as tall as my father.
9 It's not big enough.
10 ✔

Player 4 (Green)

1 ✔
2 I hardly ever get up after 11am.
3 (Speaking task)
4 She hates doing the housework.
5 ✔
6 Where were you born?
7 (Speaking task)
8 I'm going to have a big party.
9 ✔
10 What time do you get up?

Test

Scoring: one point per correct answer unless otherwise indicated.

1 1 f   2 e   3 a   4 c   5 d   6 b

2 (2 points per correct answer)
  1 Have (you ever) been
  2 's been
  3 Have (you) met
  4 've seen
  5 Has (Frank) phoned
  6 haven't been

3 (2 points per correct answer)
  1 were (you) living
  2 were (you) doing
  3 Were (you) working
  4 was studying

4 (2 points per correct answer)
  1 was built
  2 was sold
  3 were invented
  4 are sold

5 1 To visit
  2 To buy
  3 To check
  4 To save

6 1 We think we <u>might</u> go to Spain this year.
  2 When <u>will</u> you go?
  3 Possibly April. It <u>won't</u> be too hot then.
  4 Okay, but you <u>might</u> get some rain in April.

7 1 I speak English <u>well</u>.
  2 I always do my homework <u>carefully</u>.
  3 I never arrive <u>late</u> at school.
  4 My teacher speaks <u>clearly</u> in class.

8 1 up   2 on   3 out   4 after

9 1 c   2 d   3 a   4 f   5 e   6 b

10 1 over   2 through   3 up   4 down   5 out of   6 into

11 1 on   2 Turn   3 traffic   4 hour

12 1 to 4: clouds, planet, rainbow, stars
  5 to 8: cliffs, desert, field, volcano

13 1 sunny
  2 windy
  3 rainy
  4 cloudy
  5 freezing
  6 foggy

20 Review 4 Test

Name: _____   Total: _____ /80

1 Questions *6 points*

Match the beginnings and endings of the questions about a holiday to Bali.

1 How long   a) did the hotel room cost?
2 What sort of   b) did you go to the beach?
3 How much   c) was the hotel from the beach?
4 How far   d) did you get up in the mornings?
5 What time   e) hotel did you stay in?
6 How often   f) was the flight to Bali?

2 Present perfect *12 points*

Complete the sentences by putting verbs into the present perfect.

A: (1) _____ you ever _____ (be) to the USA?
B: No, but my brother (2) _____ (be) there.

              *   *   *

C: (3) _____ you _____ (meet) Tom's new girlfriend?
D: No, but I (4) _____ (see) a photo of her.

              *   *   *

E: (5) _____ Frank _____ (phone) you today?
F: I don't know. I (6) _____ (not go) to the office today.

3 Past continuous *8 points*

Complete the sentences by putting the verbs in the past continuous tense.

A: Where (1) _____ you _____ (live) in 2002?
B: I was in Paris, actually.
A: Nice! What (2) _____ you _____ (do) there?
    (3) _____ you _____ (work)?
B: No, I (4) _____ (study) French for a year.

4 Passives *8 points*

Complete the sentences with the verbs in the passive.

1 The first piano _____ (build) in 1698.
2 The first electric guitar _____ (sell) in 1930.
3 CDs _____ (invent) in the 1970s.
4 Four billion CDs _____ (sell) every year.

5 Vocabulary – *to*-infinitive *4 points*

Complete the answers using the infinitive of the verbs.

| buy   check   save   visit |

1 'Why did you go to Australia?'
   '_____ my brother.'
2 'Why are you going to the shop?'
   '_____ some milk.'
3 'Why do you need the computer?'
   '_____ my emails.'
4 'Why are you staying in tonight?'
   '_____ money.'

6 *will* & *might* *4 points*

Put the word in (brackets) into the correct place in the sentence.

1 'We think we go to Spain this year.' (might)
   _____

2 'When you go?' (will)
   _____

3 'Possibly April. It be too hot then.' (won't)
   _____

4 'Okay, but you get some rain in April.' (might)
   _____

138

7 Vocabulary – adverbs *4 points*

First change the adjective in (brackets) into an adverb and then put it in the correct place in the sentence.

1   I speak English. (good)
   _____

2   I always do my homework. (careful)
   _____

3   I never arrive at school. (late)
   _____

4   My teacher speaks in class. (clear)
   _____

8 Vocabulary – phrasal verbs *4 points*

Complete the sentences with the correct particle: *after*, *on*, *out* or *up*. Use each particle once.

1   I'm going to give _____ my job and travel round the world.
2   I'm just going to log _____ to the internet.
3   I need to find _____ about flights.
4   Will you look _____ my cat when I'm away?

9 Vocabulary – computer terms *6 points*

Match the halves to make expressions.

1   go   a) the net
2   search   b) to a website
3   surf   c) online
4   send   d) for something on the net
5   download   e) something from the net
6   log on   f) an email to someone

10 Vocabulary – prepositions of movement *6 points*

Write the correct preposition by each picture.

| into   out of   over   up   down   through |

1   _____
2   _____
3   _____
4   _____
5   _____
6   _____

11 Vocabulary – traffic situations *4 points*

Add the missing words to complete the sentences.

1   At the traffic lights, go straight _____ .
2   _____ left after the supermarket.
3   Sorry I'm late. I was stuck in a _____ jam.
4   It's quicker to walk during the rush _____ .

12 Vocabulary – geographical features *8 points*

Put the words in the box into the correct category.

| cliffs   clouds   desert   field   planet   rainbow   stars   volcano |

sky	land
1 _____	5 _____
2 _____	6 _____
3 _____	7 _____
4 _____	8 _____

13 Vocabulary – weather *6 points*

Add the missing vowels (*a, e, i, o, u*) to complete the weather report.

'Today, the weather will be warm , (1) s __ nny and dry in the south of the country for most of the day. In the north, it will start off (2) w __ ndy, (3) r __ __ ny and (4) cl __ __ dy. The rain will stop this afternoon, but temperatures will be near (5) fr __ __ zing, and it will be very (6) f __ ggy this evening. Have a nice day.'

The Magic Touch

1. Read the story of Harry Potter. There are sixteen lines. Twelve of them contain one extra word. Find the extra words and write them in the column on the right. The first two lines have been done as examples.

1	Only five years ago, J.K. Rowling was just another single mother struggling to make a	✓
2	living. Now she's a superstar. She is the author of the popular Harry Potter books (for the	the
3	children of all ages). In the last five years, more than 100 million of copies of the books	_____
4	have been sold worldwide, and only the Bible has been translated into more than languages.	_____
5	Now, the first one book in the series, *The Philosopher's Stone*, has been made into a film	_____
6	which is sure to break all box office records.	_____
7	The film follows on the exact details of the book. The story starts with Harry Potter,	_____
8	whose parents died when he was a baby, is living with his mother's sister, Aunt Petunia.	_____
9	She and her husband, Uncle Vernon, and son, Dudley, are very cruel to Harry and have force	_____
10	him to sleep in a cupboard under the stairs. Then he does receives a letter from Hogwarts	_____
11	School of Witchcraft and Wizardry, which tells him off he is actually a wizard. The letter	_____
12	offers him a place at the school. He leaves the normal humans (who magic people call	_____
13	*muggles*) and starts to studying to be a wizard. He meets a friendly giant, a three-headed dog,	_____
14	a very smart owls, unicorns, baby dragons and some other mysterious creatures and he learns	_____
15	how to play a game called *Quidditch* (a sort of cross between hockey and football, played	_____
16	high in the air on top a broomstick).	_____

2. Complete the rest of the story. Put a word from the box into each space. Some words are used several times. The first two lines have been done as examples.

| from | up | of | to | as | in | by | with | on | for |

The film is two and a half hours long and cost an estimated £125 million to make. However, the makers 1) _of_ the film, Warner Brothers, are confident that they will make a huge profit 2) _on_ the book, film and merchandising rights. Coca-Cola have already paid £103 million just to have their name associated 3) _____ the film, even though not one 4) _____ their drinks ever passes Harry Potter's lips.

American director Steven Spielberg registered interest 5) _____ directing the film. He was keen to move the story 6) _____ England 7) _____ America and use the young American actor Haley Joel Osment, star 8) _____ *The Sixth Sense*, 9) _____ the title role. But the English author, J.K. Rowling, was understood to be unhappy about this idea. 10) _____ the end, the director's job went to fellow American Chris Columbus, whose other films include *Mrs Doubtfire* and *Home Alone*. He agreed that the film should be set 11) _____ England and the role 12) _____ Harry Potter should be taken 13) _____ an English boy. Almost 16,000 boys were auditioned 14) _____ the role until, finally, 11-year-old Daniel Radcliffe was chosen 15) _____ 'the perfect Harry'.

The film goes 16) _____ general release 17) _____ November 16th, and with Rowling's magic touch 18) _____ to now, it just can't fail!

Inside Out

e-lesson

1. The Magic Touch

There's something in the air! Halloween's over and Christmas is just around the corner. What better time to bring a little sprinkling of magic into our lives? The blockbuster film *Harry Potter and the Philosopher's Stone* brings us a touch of well-needed escapism and this week's worksheet takes a look at the Harry Potter phenomenon.

Level
Intermediate and above

How to use the lesson

1. Give each of your students a copy of the worksheet and ask them to fold their piece of paper in half so that only the first exercise is visible.

2. Divide the class into pairs and ask your students to work together to find the extra word (where appropriate) in each line.

3. Check answers in open class.

4. Tell your students they have three minutes to complete the rest of the story (the bottom half of their piece of paper). If they need more time, give them an extra minute, or this stage could even be done as homework.

5. When the time limit is up stop your students and ask them to check their answers with the person sitting next to them.

6. Check answers in open class.

Answers to 1
1. ✓   2. the   3. of (after million)   4. than   5. one   6. ✓   7. on   8. is
9. have   10. does   11. off   12. ✓   13. to   14. a   15. ✓   16. top

Answers to 2
1. of   2. on   3. with   4. of   5. in   6. from   7. to   8. of   9. in
10. In   11. in   12. of   13. by   14. for   15. as   16. on   17. on   18. up

2. Related Websites
Send your students to these websites, or just take a look yourself.

http://www.kidsreads.com/harrypotter/jkrowling.html
Interview with the author, games, links who's who and much more
http://www.harrypotterfans.net/
The unofficial Harry Potter fan club, with FAQs and chat room
http://www.harrypotterrealm.com/
Welcome to Harry Potter's Realm of Wizardry
http://www.comingsoon.net/potter/
Preview of the Harry Potter movie

This page has been downloaded from www.insideout.net.
It is photocopiable, but all copies must be complete pages. Copyright © Macmillan Publishers Limited 2003.

Inside Out

US Quiz

Decide if the following statements about the United States are true or false.
Then bet a minimum of **10** points up to a maximum of **100** on your choice.

		T/F	Points bet	Points lost	Points won
1	The US has a population of nearly 300 million people.	___	___	___	___
2	The tallest building is the Sears Tower in Chicago, Illinois.	___	___	___	___
3	George W. Bush is the 53rd president of the United States.	___	___	___	___
4	Washington and Georgia are the only states named after US presidents.	___	___	___	___
5	America was named after the Italian explorer Amerigo Vespucci.	___	___	___	___
6	The largest state in the US is Texas.	___	___	___	___
7	Washington DC is the capital of Washington state and of the USA.	___	___	___	___
8	The smallest state in the US is New York.	___	___	___	___
9	Although Hawaii is a US state, its flag features the British Union Jack.	___	___	___	___
10	The bald eagle is the symbol of the USA.	___	___	___	___
11	The largest lake in North America is Lake Superior.	___	___	___	___
12	From its source in Minnesota, flowing through 31 states to its exit point in the Gulf of Mexico, the Mississippi is longer than the Nile.	___	___	___	___
13	There are 51 states.	___	___	___	___
14	John F. Kennedy's most famous speech started "I have a dream…"	___	___	___	___
15	Four presidents have been assassinated in the history of the US.	___	___	___	___
16	*DC* in Washington DC stands for Department Capital.	___	___	___	___

Total points (subtract first column from second column) _____ _____

Total points won _____

This page has been downloaded from www.insideout.net.
It is photocopiable, but all copies must be complete pages.
Copyright © Macmillan Publishers Limited 2003.

Inside Out

e-lesson

1. US Quiz

Formerly known as the President's Palace, the White House was given its present name by President Theodore Roosevelt on October 12th, 1901. If you knew that, you are sure to do well in this week's worksheet, *US Quiz*, which contains a number of statements about the United States, some which are true and some which are false.

Level
Lower intermediate upwards

How to use the lesson
1. Tell your students they are going to look at some statements about the USA and decide if they are true or false. They are then going to bet anything from 10 to 100 points (depending on how confident they feel) on their guess.

2. Divide the class into pairs or small groups and give each student a copy of the quiz.

3. Ask your students to discuss each statement and decide if they think it's true or false. In the first column they should write T or F. In the second column they have to write in the number of points they are willing to bet on their guess (10 points only if they don't feel very confident going up to 100 if they are very sure of their answer). They can't bet 0 points.

4. After giving enough time for students to discuss their answers, it's time to score. Each pair/group calls out their answer and how many points they have bet. If they have answered correctly, students enter their points in the final column (points won). If they have answered incorrectly, they should enter their points in the third column (points lost). At the end of the quiz, students add up their entries in the third and fourth columns and then subtract the total of the third column from the total of the fourth column to give the total number of points they have won. The pair/group with the most points is the winner.

Follow up
This quiz could constitute part of a project on the United States. With help from the websites below, your students could find out much more about the US and make a presentation and class display.

Answers
1 **True**.
2 **True**. Standing at 442m high, this is the tallest building in the United States.
3 **False**. Since George Washington took office in 1789, there have been 43 presidents.
4 **False**. Georgia is named after George II, King of England.
5 **True**. Although Columbus had officially 'discovered' the Americas, he had believed them to be part of Asia.
6 **False**. Alaska is the largest state. It is about 2.5 times larger than Texas.
7 **False**. Olympia is the capital of Washington state. Washington DC is the capital of the United States.
8 **False**. The smallest state is Rhode Island. It covers an area of 4,000 sq km.
9, 10, 11 **True**.
12 **False**. The Mississippi is 3,780 km long, while the Nile is 6,648 km long.
13 **False**. There are 50 states. Some people count Washington DC as a state, but it isn't.
14 **False**. Martin Luther King Jr. was responsible for the famous *'I have a dream…'* speech.
15 **True**. The four unfortunates were Lincoln, Garfield, McKinley and John F. Kennedy.
16 **False**. It stands for *District of Columbia*.

2. Related Websites
Send your students to these websites, or just take a look yourself.

http://www.ipl.org/div/kidspace/stateknow/
Check out the States
http://www.dc.gov/
Learn about the capital city
http://www.whitehouse.gov/history/presidents/
All you need to know about the presidents of the US

This page has been downloaded from www.insideout.net.
It is photocopiable, but all copies must be complete pages. Copyright © Macmillan Publishers Limited 2003.

The Teacher Development Series

- Helps teachers develop their own personal and effective style of teaching
- Highlights recent developments in methodology
- Combines learning theory and practical experience

'Teacher development is the process of becoming the best teacher that you can be. It means becoming a student of learning, [examining] how the relationship between students and teachers influences learning.'

Adrian Underhill
Series Editor

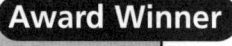

Learning Teaching
Jim Scrivener

Widely used and recommended on training courses for teachers of EFL, *Learning Teaching* can help you learn to teach in more effective ways.

It provides a user-friendly guide on everything you need to know to get into the classroom and start teaching.

0 435 24089 7

Uncovering Grammar
Scott Thornbury

Challenges the traditional view of grammar as a 'thing' to be learnt, suggesting that it is a 'process' that emerges. This award-winning book looks at what grammar adds that words alone can't do; where does grammar come from and how is grammar best acquired?

0 333 95282 0

Sound Foundations
Adrian Underhill

'Bringing phonology alive'

This detailed book on phonology is divided into two sections: the first shows the reader how sounds are physically made, the second section shows how to teach students these sounds.

0 435 24091 9

Sound Foundations Chart and Guide

The *Guide* provides an introduction to using the *Sound Foundations Chart*.

0 435 24094 3

Visit **www.teacherdevelopment.net** for more information on the *Teacher Development Series* and its authors